Learning Ext JS

Build dynamic, desktop-style user interfaces for your data-driven web applications

Shea Frederick

Colin Ramsay

Steve 'Cutter' Blades

PUBLISHING

BIRMINGHAM - MUMBAI

Learning Ext JS

First published: November 2008

Production Reference: 1201108

Published by Packt Publishing Ltd.
32 Lincoln Road
Olton
Birmingham, B27 6PA, UK.

ISBN 978-1-847195-14-2

www.packtpub.com

Cover Image by Michelle O'Kane (michelle@kofe.ie)

Credits

Authors

Shea Frederick

Colin Ramsay

Steve 'Cutter' Blades

Reviewer

James Kennard

Senior Acquisition Editor

David Barnes

Development Editor

Swapna V. Verlekar

Technical Editor

Gagandeep Singh

Copy Editor

Sumathi Sridhar

Editorial Team Leader

Akshara Aware

Project Manager

Abhijeet Deobhakta

Project Coordinator

Neelkanth Mehta

Indexer

Monica Ajmera

Proofreader

Dirk Manuel

Production Coordinator

Rajni R. Thorat

Cover Work

Rajni R. Thorat

About the Authors

Shea Frederick began his career in web development before the term 'Web Application' became commonplace. By the late 1990s, he was developing web applications for Tower Records that combined a call center interface with inventory and fulfillment. Since then, Shea has worked as a developer for several companies, building and implementing various commerce solutions, content management systems, and lead tracking programs.

Integrating new technologies to make a better application has been a driving point for Shea's work. He strives to use open-source libraries, as they are often the launching pad for the most creative technological advances. After stumbling upon a young user interface library called yui-ext several years ago, Shea contributed to its growth by writing documentation, tutorials, and example code. He has remained an active community member for the modern yui-ext library — Ext JS. Shea's expertise is drawn from community forum participation, work with the core development team, and his own experience as the architect of several large Ext JS-based web applications. He currently lives in Baltimore, Maryland, with his wife and two dogs, and spends time skiing, biking, and watching the Steelers.

> A big loving thanks goes out to my wife Becky for looking over my shoulder to correct the many grammatical errors my fingers produce, and for always being there to support me.

Colin Ramsay began his career building ASP websites as a part-time developer at university. Since then, he's been involved with a range of web technologies and employers in the North East of England, working on everything from flash-in-the-pan web frameworks to legacy applications. Most recently, he has used this experience to provide a springboard for the formation of his UK-based web development company, Plastiscenic Limited. From writing articles and blog posts across the web, Colin has made the leap to book authoring with the patience and kind assistance of his friends and family.

Steve Blades (who goes by the name of 'Cutter'), a Virginia native, raised in Georgia, began his computing career when he started learning BASIC at age 12, hammering out small programs on a Timex Sinclair 1000. As a linguist and Intelligence Analyst for the US Army, Cutter began learning HTML while stationed at the National Security Agency. On leaving the service, Cutter became part-owner of a growing Advertising Specialty company, developing business automation processes for the company by writing MS Office-based applications. From there, Cutter went on to become a Customer Support Technician with a local Internet Service Provider. Upon showing programming aptitude, he was later moved into their Corporate Support department, providing maintenance and rewrites to existing websites and applications. It was here that Cutter began to really dive into web application programming, teaching himself JavaScript, CSS, and ColdFusion programming. Cutter then took the position of IT Director for Seacrets, a large resort destination in Ocean City, Maryland, while also holding the same position for one of its owner's other companies, Irie Radio. Now, Cutter is the Senior Web Developer for Dealerskins, a company that develops and hosts websites for the automobile dealership industry. He lives and works in Nashville, Tennessee with his wife Teresa and daughter Savannah.

Apart from work, side projects, and maintaining his blog (`http://blog.cutterscrossing.com`), Cutter also enjoys spending time with his family, is an avid reader and a videophile, and likes to relive his band days with a mic in hand.

I would like to thank a few people for their support while I have been working on this project. First, thanks to Jack Slocum and the entire Ext JS team for giving us such a great library to write about. Thanks to the Dev Team at Dealerskins for helping proof my chapters. Thanks to my Mom, for buying me my first book on programming. But, most of all, thanks to my wife, Teresa, and my daughter, Savannah, for giving me the time, space, love, and support needed to work on this project. I could never have done it without them.

About the Reviewer

James Kennard is an all-round computer specialist with a particular interest in web-based technologies. He authored the Joomla! CMS book *Mastering Joomla! 1.5 Extension and Framework Development*. He holds a B.Sc. in Computer Science and has worked for organisations such as LogicaCMG. James has recently taken an interest in user interfaces and overall UX—it is this which led him to the truly superb Ext JS project.

Dedicated to our family, friends, and the Ext JS team.

Table of Content

Preface

Ext JS was developed by a unified team of programmers working toward a single goal—to provide a consistent core user interface and interaction library. Because of this, the code used for different functionalities and widgets is more coherent than in some other JavaScript libraries. Ext JS really shines in making web applications easy-to-use and intuitive. If you are a web application developer, it's a great library to have in your arsenal.

We start by outlining how to download and configure the Ext JS library. Covering everything from the simplest alerts to complex grids, layouts, and forms, this book will enable you to start creating rich, interactive web applications.

We will use plenty of real-world examples that can be applied immediately to your ongoing projects. Sample code is broken down to its simplest form, allowing us to concentrate on learning the usage of the library. By the end of this book, we will end up with a sample application that uses the full spectrum of Ext JS components.

What this book covers

Chapter 1 introduces you to the process of installing the required Ext JS library files, and setting up a basic page that displays an alert-style message. This provides us with a way to test whether your setup was done correctly, and whether you're ready to play with some code. We also cover how to set up other base libraries such as jQuery, YUI, and Prototype, to work in conjunction with Ext JS.

Chapter 2 covers how to interact with the web page and the user. With example code that uses simple components, we quickly start to see the level of user interactivity that Ext JS provides right out of the box. We assemble a series of dialogs that appear and modify the existing pages depending upon the users' inputs.

Chapter 3 launches us into using the first major widget—forms. We start by creating a simple form with three fields, explore the different form field types, and then add some simple validation to our form. From there we move on to creating custom validation and database-driven combo-box'es and handling form submissions.

Chapter 4 provides an overview of how to use toolbars and buttons within your application. These components are typically undervalued, yet they provide crucial user interface functions. We jump straight into creating toolbars with buttons, split buttons, and menus, along with adding mechanical elements such as spacers and dividers. Next, we cover customizing the toolbar with stylized icon buttons and form fields.

Chapter 5 covers grids—the most widely-utilized component in the Ext JS library. In this chapter, we learn how to set up a grid panel using both local and remote data, and in both in XML and JSON formats. We also discuss how to prepare different data types and how to create renderers that will style and format the data to your preference. Using the selection model and paging are among the many interesting points covered in this chapter.

Chapter 6 dives into editor grids. Here, we learn how to set up an editor grid using different form field types, and how to save changes made in the grid back to the server or database. We also discuss tactics for adding and removing rows of data to and from our data store, and the server or the database.

Chapter 7 explores the concept of using the layout component to bring all the portions of your application together into a cohesive web application. We start by using a viewport with a border layout to contain the many parts of our application. From there we are able to add other layout features such as tab panels, accordions, and toolbars. We finish up by learning how to nest layouts and make dynamic changes to the layout components.

Chapter 8 discusses the presentation of hierarchical information using the Ext JS Tree support. Using real-world examples of hierarchical data, you will discover how to display and manipulate a Tree view. You will use AJAX techniques to persist the modifications to a server and learn how to tweak the Tree to support advanced scenarios.

Chapter 9 demonstrates how Ext JS can provide attractive user prompts that can either present information or accept input. We then discuss the extension of these dialogs in the form of Ext.Window, a fully-fledged means of creating customizable pop-up windows.

In *Chapter 10*, we take a tour of the visual effects available in the Ext JS effects package. You will learn how to apply animations to create smooth transitions and notifications to enhance the user experience.

Chapter 11 shows how you can harness Ext.dd — the rich drag-and-drop functionality provided by Ext JS. A variety of different demonstrations allow you to understand the concepts behind Ext.dd, and how you can harness its potential within your own applications.

Chapter 12 gets straight to the heart of every application — the data. Ext JS provides several different methods for retrieving data, with each method having its own pros and cons. This chapter will help you to decide what will work for your application, with step-by-step examples to guide you on your way.

Chapter 13 shows the true power of Ext JS, providing an introduction to creating your own custom components by expanding upon Ext JS's extensible architecture. You will see how to create your own components by extending the existing framework, making pieces that you can re-use in your own applications.

Chapter 14 wraps it all up, by showing you that with Ext JS there is more than meets the eye. You will discover some of the invisible architecture that allows you to perform important tasks such as data formatting and application state management. You will also find that you have a broad array of resources at your fingertips, as we show you the rich user community that exists around the library, and introduce you to additional resources to continue your journey in Learning Ext JS.

What you need for this book

At the ground level, this book requires the knowledge to write HTML pages by hand — if you can write an HTML document from memory in Windows Notepad (or in a good text editor) then that will be good enough. Familiarity with including external files such as style sheets and JavaScript files will also be necessary. Only a basic understanding of JavaScript, or another scripting or programming language, will be required.

One of the things that will make life easier is having access to a web server, or a local development web server such as XAMPP or something similar. The XAMPP local web server is developed by Apache Friends (www.apachefriends.org) and comes in an easy-to-use install file. By default, it sets up Apache, PHP, and MySQL, which allows you to perform local web development easily. Running this book's examples from a local web server is useful and can save lots of time.

A good editor and debugger are extremely useful, particularly if they are specific to JavaScript, as Aptana is. The makers of Aptana have created a very powerful tool for developing web applications in JavaScript. Their editor can debug JavaScript, CSS, PHP, and many other languages as you type, and the best part is that you can link the editor up with your libraries and classes to get code auto-completion specific to your development. The debugger can alert you to errors in your code before you get to the browser (enable the JSLint debugger), and can suggest fixes for the errors.

The final point here is an absolute necessity — get Firefox and Firebug installed on your computer! Don't even ask why, because Firebug will soon become the program you just cannot do your job without. Soon, you will be wondering how you ever got any work done before Firebug. What it does is allows you to monitor and interact with the web page in real time. When you start working with single-page web applications and AJAX, you quickly lose the ability to look at the requests and responses for communications such as form submission. One of the things that Firebug provides you with is a way to watch and inspect this communication. The other main thing that it does is allow you to modify the HTML and JavaScript in your web page and watch these changes take effect in real time. The built-in script debugger lets us pause code execution and inspect or even modify code and variables.

Once you are set up with a local (or remote) development web server, your favorite editor and debugger, and Firefox with Firebug, you are ready to start Learning Ext JS.

Who is this book for

This book is written for Web Application Developers who are familiar with HTML, but may have little to no experience with JavaScript application development. If you are starting to build a new web application, or you are revamping an existing web application, then this book is for you.

Conventions

In this book, you will find a number of styles of text that distinguish between different kinds of information. Here are some examples of these styles, and an explanation of their meaning.

Code words in text are shown as follows: "The `config` object used for this dialog has three elements "

A block of code is set as follows:

```
Ext.onReady(function(){
    Ext.Msg.show({
        title: 'Milton',
        msg: 'Have you seen my stapler?',
        buttons: {
            yes: true,
            no: true,
            cancel: true
        }
    });
});
```

When we wish to draw your attention to a particular part of a code block, the relevant lines or items will be shown in bold:

```
{
    xtype: 'datefield',
    fieldLabel: 'Released',
    name: 'released'
}
```

New terms and **important words** are introduced in bold. Words that you see on the screen, in menus or dialog boxes for example, appear in the text like this: "We also have elements that can add space and vertical dividers, like the one used between the **Menu** and the **Split** buttons."

 Warnings or important notes appear in a box like this.

 Tips and tricks appear like this.

Reader feedback

Feedback from our readers is always welcome. Let us know what you think about this book, what you liked or may have disliked. Reader feedback is important for us to develop titles that you really get the most out of.

To send us general feedback, simply drop an email to feedback@packtpub.com, and mention the book title in the subject of your message.

If there is a book that you need and would like to see us publish, please send us a note in the **SUGGEST A TITLE** form on www.packtpub.com or email suggest@packtpub.com.

If there is a topic that you have expertise in and you are interested in either writing or contributing to a book, see our author guide on www.packtpub.com/authors.

Customer support

Now that you are the proud owner of a Packt book, we have a number of things to help you to get the most from your purchase.

Downloading the example code for the book

Visit http://www.packtpub.com/files/code/5142_Code.zip to directly download the example code.

 The downloadable files contain instructions on how to use them.

Errata

Although we have taken every care to ensure the accuracy of our contents, mistakes do happen. If you find a mistake in one of our books—maybe a mistake in text or code—we would be grateful if you would report this to us. By doing this you can save other readers from frustration, and help to improve subsequent versions of this book. If you find any errata, report them by visiting http://www.packtpub.com/support, selecting your book, clicking on the **let us know** link, and entering the details of your errata. Once your errata are verified, your submission will be accepted and the errata added to any list of existing errata. Existing errata can be viewed by selecting your title from http://www.packtpub.com/support.

Piracy

Piracy of copyright material on the Internet is an ongoing problem across all media. At Packt, we take the protection of our copyright and licenses very seriously. If you come across any illegal copies of our works in any form on the Internet, please provide the location address or website name immediately so we can pursue a remedy.

Please contact us at copyright@packtpub.com with a link to the suspected pirated material.

We appreciate your help in protecting our authors, and our ability to bring you valuable content.

Questions

You can contact us at questions@packtpub.com if you are having a problem with any aspect of the book, and we will do our best to address it.

1
Getting Started

In this chapter, we will cover the basics of **Ext** and what it can do for us. If you're accustom to the standard web development, then you'll be excited when you learn about the elegance in the architecture of Ext, just as I was. Unlike other JavaScript libraries, Ext handles the foundation for you, so with only a few lines of code, you can have a fully functional user interface.

In this chapter, we will cover:

- What Ext does and why you'll love using it
- How to get Ext and start using it in your web applications
- Using "adapters" to allow Ext to co-exist with other JavaScript libraries
- Taking advantage of AJAX technology
- Displaying Ext objects in your own language

About Ext

We will be working with the most recent release version of Ext which, at the time of writing, is the 2.x branch. The change from 1.x to 2.x was a major refactoring that included taking full advantage of the newly-created Component model, along with renaming many of the components to provide better organization. These changes have made 1.x code mostly incompatible with 2.x and vice versa (an upgrade guide that explains in more detail what has changed is available on the Ext web site). The 3.x branch is backwards-compatible with 2.x and compatible with everything that we will cover in this book. The Ext development team is dedicated to making future releases backwards-compatible.

The Ext library started out as an extension to the moderately popular, yet very powerful Yahoo User Interface library, providing what the YUI library lacked: an easy to use API (Application Programming Interface), and real world widgets. Even though the Yahoo User Interface tried to focus on the 'User Interface', it didn't contain much that was useful right out of the box.

It wasn't long before Ext had developers and open-source contributors chipping in their knowledge to turn the basic YUI extension into one of the most powerful client-side application development libraries around.

Ext provides an easy-to-use, rich user interface, much like you would find in a desktop application. This lets the web developers concentrate on the functionality of web applications instead of the technical caveats. The examples given on the Ext website speak the loudest about how amazing this library is:

```
http://www.extjs.com/deploy/dev/examples/
```

One of the most striking examples is the **Feed Viewer**. This demonstrates the many aspects of Ext. However, it is a bit too complex to be used as a learning example. So for now, you can just revel in its brilliance.

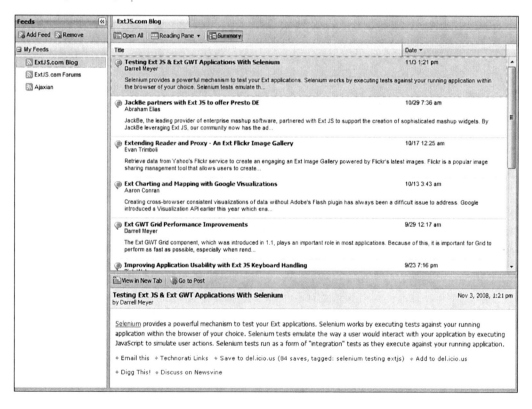

Another excellent example is the **Simple Tasks** task-tracking program, which utilizes a Google Gears database.

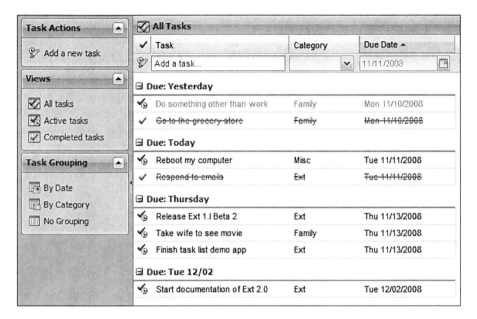

Over the course of this book, you will learn how to build web interfaces as impressive as these.

Ext: Not just another JavaScript library

Ext is not just another JavaScript library — in fact, Ext can work alongside other JavaScript libraries by using adapters. We'll see how to work with adapters later in this chapter.

Typically, we would use Ext in a web site that requires a high level of user interaction — something more complex than your typical web site. A web site that requires processes and a work flow would be a perfect example, or Ext could just be used to make your boss gasp with excitement.

Ext makes web application development simple by:

- Providing easy-to-use cross-browser compatible widgets such as windows, grids, and forms. The widgets are already fine-tuned to handle the intricacies of each web browser on the market, without us needing to change a thing.

- Interacting with the user and browser via the EventManager, responding to the users keystrokes, mouse clicks, and monitoring events in a browser such as a window resize, or font size changes.

- Communicating with the server in the background without the need to refresh the page. This allows you to request or post data to or from your web server using AJAX and process the feedback in real time.

Cross-browser DOM (Document Object Model)

I am sure I don't need to explain the pitfalls of browser compatibility. From the first time you create a DIV tag and apply a style to it, it becomes apparent that it's not going to look the same in every browser unless you are very diligent. When we use Ext widgets, the browser compatibility is taken care of by the Ext library, so that each widget looks exactly the same in most of the popular browsers, which are:

- Internet Explorer 6+
- Firefox 1.5+ (PC, Mac)
- Safari 2+
- Opera 9+ (PC, Mac)

Event-driven interfaces

Events describe when certain actions happen. An event could be a user action such as a click on an element, or it could be a response to an AJAX call. When a user interacts with a button, there is a reaction, with not just one but many events happening. There is an event for the cursor hovering over the button, and an event for the cursor clicking on the button, and an event for the cursor leaving the button. We can add an event listener to execute some code block when any or all of these events take place.

Listening for events is not strictly related to the user interface. There are also system events happening all the time. When we make AJAX calls, there are events attached to the status of that AJAX call to listen for the start, the completion, and the failure.

Ext and AJAX

The term **AJAX** (Asynchronous JavaScript and XML) is an overly-complicated acronym for saying that processes can take place in the background while the user is performing other tasks. A user could be filling out a form while a grid of data is loading—both can happen at the same time, with no waiting around for the page to reload.

Getting Ext

Everything we will need can be downloaded from the Ext website, at
http://www.extjs.com/download. Grab the Ext SDK (Software Development Kit),
which contains a ton of useful examples and the API reference. Most importantly, it
contains the resources that Ext needs to run properly.

Where to put Ext

Once you get the SDK file, uncompress it onto your hard drive, preferably in its own
folder. My approach to folder naming conventions is based on the standard Linux
structure where all libraries go into a lib folder. So for the sake of the examples in
this book, uncompress all of the files in the SDK into a folder named lib.

After extracting everything from the SDK download file, your directory tree should
look like this:

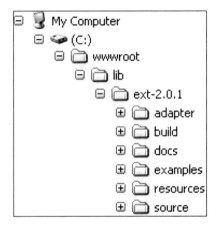

To make it easier when we upgrade our Ext library to the most recently-released
version, let us rename the ext-2.0.1 folder to extjs.

The SDK contains a version of Ext JS that has everything you need included in it,
commonly called ext-all. It also contains a version used for development referred
to as the debug version, which is what we will primarily use. The debug version
makes it easier to locate errors in your code because it's uncompressed and will
report back relevant line numbers for errors. When it's time to release our creation to
the general public, we can switch our application to use the standard ext-all, and
everything will continue to work as it was.

Included in the SDK file are a specification of dependencies, documentation, example code, and more. The `adapter` and `resources` folders shown in **bold** are required for Ext to work properly; everything else is just for development purposes.

- **`adapter`**: Files that allow you to use other libraries along side Ext
- `build`: Files that can be used to custom-build an `ext-all.js`
- `docs`: The documentation center (this will only work when run on a web server)
- `examples`: Plenty of amazing and insightful examples
- **`resources`**: Dependencies of the Ext library, such as CSS and images
- `source`: The complete source code for Ext

When you're ready to host your page on a web server, the `adapter` and `resources` folders will need to be uploaded to the server.

Including Ext in your pages

Before we can use Ext in our pages, we need to reference the Ext library files. To do this, we need to include a few of the files provided in the SDK download in the HEAD portion of our HTML page.

```html
<html>
<head>
   <title>Getting Started Example</title>
   <link rel="stylesheet" type="text/css"
      href="lib/extjs/resources/css/ext-all.css" />
   <script src="lib/extjs/adapter/ext/ext-base.js"></script>
   <script src="lib/extjs/ext-all-debug.js"></script>
</head>
<body>
   <!-- Nothing in the body -->
</body>
</html>
```

The path to the Ext files must be correct and is relative to the location of our HTML file. These files must be included in the following order:

- `ext-all.css`: The main Ext CSS file
- An external `js` library file, if needed (one not used in the examples in this book; however if you need to use an external library it is covered in the 'Adapters' section of this chapter)

- ext-base.js: The Ext 'adapter' — we will learn more about this file later in this chapter
- ext-all.js or ext-all-debug.js: The primary Ext library file
- A theme file could also be included here, or at any point after the main Ext CSS file

What do those files do?

We have included the following three files that Ext requires to run in our page:

- ext-all.css: A stylesheet file that controls the look and feel of Ext widgets. This file must always be included as-is, with no modifications. Any changes to the CSS in this file would break future upgrades. If the look and feel of Ext needs to be adjusted, another stylesheet containing the overrides should be included after the ext-all.css file.
- ext-base.js: This file provides the core functionality of Ext. It's the engine of the Ext car. This is the file that we would change if we wanted to use another library, such as jQuery, along with Ext.
- ext-all-debug.js/ext-all.js: All of the widgets live in this file. The debug version is used for development, and then swapped out for the non-debug version for production.

Once these files are in place, we can start to actually use the Ext library and have some fun.

 If you are working with a server-side language such as PHP or ASP.NET, you might choose to "include" these lines in the header dynamically. For most of the examples in this book, we will assume that you are working with a static HTML page.

Using the Ext library

Now that we've added the Ext library to our page, we can start writing the code that uses the Ext library. In the first example, we will use Ext to display a message dialog. This might not sound like much, but it's a start.

Time for action

We can run some Ext code by adding a script section in the head of our document, right after where the Ext library has been included. Our example will bring up an Ext style alert dialog:

```
<html>
<head>
    <title>Getting Started Example</title>
    <link rel="stylesheet" type="text/css"
        href="lib/extjs/resources/css/ext-all.css" />
    <script src="lib/extjs/adapter/ext/ext-base.js"></script>
    <script src="lib/extjs/ext-all-debug.js"></script>
    <script>
        Ext.onReady(function(){
            Ext.Msg.alert('Hello', 'World');
        });
    </script>
</head>
<body>
    <!-- Nothing in the body -->
</body>
</html>
```

We're not going to cover exactly what our example script is doing yet. First, let's make sure that the Ext library is set up properly. If we open up our page in a web browser, we should be able to see an alert message like the one shown here:

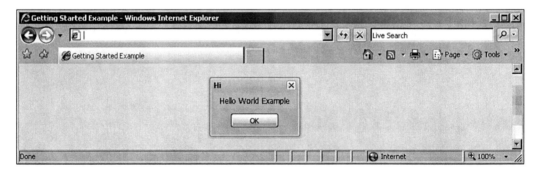

Just like a "real" dialog, you can drag it around, but only within the constraints of the page. This is because this isn't a real dialog; it's a collection of DIV tags and images put together to imitate a dialog. You can also see that the **Close** and **Ok** buttons get highlighted when you move the cursor over them—not bad for one line of code! Ext is taking care of a lot of the work for us here, and throughout this book, we'll see how to get it to do much more for us.

You may have noticed that we are working with an empty document that has no elements in the body. Ext does not require any pre-existing markup for it to function properly; it generates everything it needs on its own.

The example

Let's take a look at that example code we just ran. Every Ext component we use will start with "Ext" and will most likely be contained within an onReady function that we will cover with more detail in the next chapter.

```
Ext.onReady(function(){
    Ext.Msg.alert('Hello', 'World');
});
```

Ext has a very human-readable interface. You can almost read it as a sentence — when Ext is ready, it displays a message box in the alert style with **Hello** for a title and **World** as the body.

Our alert message starts with Ext.Msg, which is the starting point for all message style windows, and is shorthand for "MessageBox". The alert portion tells Ext exactly which style of message window to use.

Not working?

If the library is not set up correctly, we might receive an **'Ext' is undefined** error.

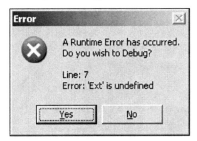

This message means the Ext library was not loaded. Usually, this is caused by having an incorrect path to one or more of the Ext library files that are included in our document. Double-check the paths to the included library files, and make sure they are pointing to the right folders and that the files exist. If everything is in its correct place, you should see an adapter folder along with the files ext-all.js and ext-all-debug.js in your lib/extjs folder.

Another common problem is that the CSS file is either missing or is not referenced correctly, which will result in a page that looks awkward, as shown in the example below:.

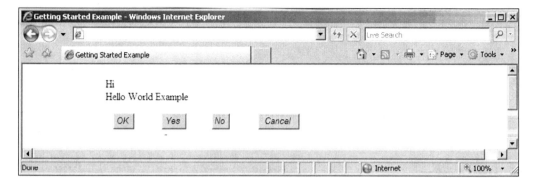

If this happens, check to make sure that you have extracted the `resources` folder from the SDK file, and that your paths are correct. The `resources` folder should reside under the `lib/extjs` folder.

Adapters

When Ext was first being developed (initially called "yui-ext"), it required the YUI library to be in place to do the behind-the-scenes work. Later on, Ext was given the option of using two other frameworks—jQuery or Prototype with Scriptaculous (Protaculous).

This means that if we were using other libraries already or if we felt some other base library was somehow superior or better suited your needs, we could continue using that library in conjunction with Ext by using the appropriate adapter. Either way, Ext will function the same, and all of the components will work identically, no matter which adapter you choose.

Ext also has its own adapter, an adapter to itself. If you have no preference for another library or framework, then go with the Ext built-in the adapter.

Using adapters

To use an adapter, you must first include the external library that you want to use, and then include the related adapter file that is located in the adapters folder of the Ext SDK. Our example code uses the Ext adapter. To use any of the other libraries, just replace the default Ext adapter script include line with the lines for the specific libraries, as shown below:

Default Ext adapter:

```
<script src="lib/extjs/adapter/ext/ext-base.js"></script>
```

For jQuery, include these files in the head of your document:

```
<script src="lib/jquery.js"></script>
<script src="lib/jquery-plugins.js"></script>
<script src="lib/extjs/adapter/jquery/ext-jquery-adapter.js">
                                            </script>
```

For YUI, include these files in the head. The `utilities` file is located in the `build/utilities` folder of the YUI Library download:

```
<script src="lib/utilities.js"></script>
<script src="lib/extjs/adapter/yui/ext-yui-adapter.js"></script>
```

For "Prototype + Scriptaculous", include these files in the head:

```
<script src="lib/prototype.js"></script>
<script src="lib/scriptaculous.js?load=effects"></script>
<script src="lib/extjs/adapter/prototype/
                             ext-prototype-adapter.js"></script>
```

After the adapter and base libraries have been included, we just need to include the `ext-all.js` or `ext-all-debug.js` file.

I'm asynchronous!

The Web 1.0 way of doing things has all of our code happening in succession—waiting for each line of code to complete before moving on to the next. Much like building a house, the foundation must be complete before the walls can be built, then the walls must be complete before the roof is built.

With Ext, we can easily start working on the roof of our house before the foundation has even been thought about. Imagine the roof of our house is being built in a factory, while at the same time we are building the foundation, then the walls, and we come in when all of this is done and set the roof that has already been built on top of it all.

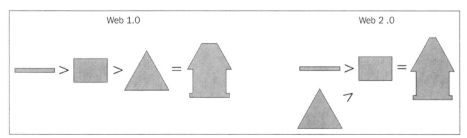

This introduces some things we're not use to having to cope with, such as the roof being complete before the walls are done. No longer are we forced to take a line-by-line approach to web development.

Ext helps us out by giving us events and handlers to which we can attach our functionality. We can set up an event that waits around, watching to see when the walls of the house are built, and then sets the roof on top once this has happened.

This method of thinking about web pages is hard for most people who have grown up in web development. But it won't be long before you are an expert at it.

 Standard JavaScript alert messages pause the code execution, which can cause unexpected results. You should not be using the built in JavaScript alert messages, and instead use Ext's MessageBox widget, which does not pause that code execution.

Localization

Ext objects can be displayed in your specific language, and currently there are over 40 translations (unfortunately, Klingon is not yet available). All of these translations are created by the community — users like you and I who have the need to use Ext in their own native language. The included language files are to be used as a starting point. So let's take the language we want to use and copy it to our lib folder. By copying the language file to our lib folder, we can edit it and add translated text to it without it getting overwritten when we upgrade the Ext library files.

There are three scenarios for localization that require three separate approaches:

- English only
- A single language other than English
- Multiple languages

English only

This requires no modifications to the standard setup, and there are no extra files to include because the English translation is already included in the ext-all.js file.

A language other than English

The second option requires that we include one of the language files from the `build/locale` folder. This option works by overwriting the English text strings, so it should be included after all of the other library files, as shown below:

```
<link rel="stylesheet" type="text/css"
    href="lib/extjs/resources/css/ext-all.css" />
<script src="lib/extjs/adapter/ext/ext-base.js"></script>
<script src="lib/extjs/ext-all-debug.js"></script>
<script src="lib/extjs/build/locale/ext-lang-es.js"></script>
```

I have included the Spanish translations for this example. Let's see what our test page looks like now:

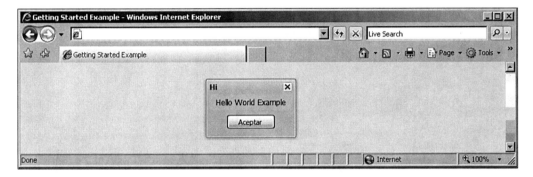

Elements that are part of the UI have been localized — these generally include calendar text, error messages, tool tip info messages, paging info, and loading indicators. Messages that are specific to your application, such as the **Hi** title, and **Hello World Example** text will need to be translated and added to the `ext-lang-XX.js` file (where 'XX' is your two letter language code) or added to a new language file of your own. The preferred method is to create a language file of our own with just the additions and changes we need, this leaves us prepared for upgrades and fixes in the primary language file.

Multiple languages

The third method of switching between different languages is basically the same as the second. We would just need to add some server-side scripting to our page to enable the switching between language files. Unfortunately, switching between languages cannot be done entirely dynamically. In other words, we can't do it in real time and watch it happen on the screen.

Ext JS online community

The online community for Ext is full of quite a few very knowledgeable people, and often, the Ext core developers are answering questions on the forum.

```
http://www.extjs.com/forum/
```

If you run into problems, or run up against a wall, a search of the forum is likely to yield what you are looking for. I would suggest getting the Google forum search tool that is available in the **Learn** section of the Ext web site.

```
http://www.extjs.com/learn/
```

 When asking questions in the forum, be sure to include as much detail about the error(s) as possible. Posting the exact text of an error message and only the relevant portions of your code is the best way to get a response from the community.

Summary

In this chapter, we have covered the basics of what you need to do to get Ext up and running, and what a simple script looks like. It's easy to miss a minor detail and get stuck with an error message that makes no sense. But now, you should be prepared to conquer any initial errors that you might come across.

The example we created showcases what Ext excels at: providing the user interface. We only used dialogs, but, as you now know, a few lines of code are all that are needed to display an Ext widget. The main goal of this chapter was to get Ext installed and working, so we can start creating some really sweet widgets.

2
The Staples of Ext

In this chapter, we will start to use and interact with Ext widgets for the first time, by creating a series of dialogs that interact with each other, the user, and the web page. We will be using the onReady, MessageBox, and get functions to learn how to create different types of dialogs and modify HTML and styles on our page. Furthermore, in this chapter, we will be:

- Finding out how to configure Ext widgets easily
- Waiting for the DOM (Document Object Model) to be made available for interaction
- Using dialogs to figure out what the user wants to do
- Dynamically changing the HTML and CSS on our page in response to the user's inputs

We will start by covering some of the core functions of Ext. We will take a look at how the example given in the first chapter worked, and will expand upon it. The following core functions of Ext will be used on every project that we work on during the course of this book:

- `Ext.onReady`: This function makes sure that our document is ready to be thrashed out
- `Ext.Msg`: This function creates application-style message boxes for us
- `configuration objects`: This function defines how Ext widgets will act
- `Ext.get`: This function accesses and manipulates elements in the DOM

Ready, set, go!

In this section, we'll look at the onReady event—the first thing that you need to deal with when you are working with Ext. We will also see how to display some different types of dialogs, and how to respond to the users' interaction with those dialogs. Before we get to that, we need to cover some ground rules about working with Ext.

Spacer image

Before we proceed any further, we should provide Ext with something it needs—a spacer image. Ext needs a 1 pixel by 1 pixel, transparent, GIF image to stretch in different ways, giving a fixed width to its widgets. We need to set the location of this spacer image using the following line:

```
Ext.onReady(function(){
    Ext.BLANK_IMAGE_URL = 'images/s.gif';
});
```

You're probably wondering why we need a spacer image at all. The user interface of Ext is created using CSS, but the CSS needs underlying HTML elements to style so that it can create the look and feel of Ext components. The one HTML element that is an exact, predictable size across all browsers is an image. So an image is used to define how an Ext component is drawn. This is a part of how Ext maintains its cross-browser compatibility.

Widget

Ext has many "widgets". These include components such as a message box, grid, window, and pretty much everything else that serves a particular user interface function. I prefer to view components like onReady more as core functions, and only refer to components that provide a specific user interface role as a "widget"—like the grid that is used to present tabular data to the user.

Time for action

Let's create a new page (or just modify the 'getting started' example page) and add the code to display a dialog when the page is ready:

```
Ext.onReady(function(){
    Ext.BLANK_IMAGE_URL = 'images/s.gif';
    Ext.Msg.show({
        title: 'Milton',
        msg: 'Have you seen my stapler?',
        buttons: {
            yes: true,
            no: true,
            cancel: true
        }
    });
});
```

As we did in the previous chapter, we have placed our code insi(
function. We can then start to code our dialog and configure it u
The `config` object used for this dialog has three elements, the l
nested object for the three buttons.

Here is how our code now looks in a browser:

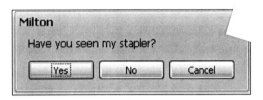

This displays what appears to be a very minimal dialog, but if we start clicking on things, the built-in functionality of Ext becomes apparent. The dialog can be dragged around the screen by grabbing the title bar, just like the dialog in a typical desktop application. There is a close button built-in, and pressing the *Escape* key when the dialog has focus, or clicking on the **Cancel** button will close the dialog.

What just happened?

Let's take a closer look at the two core Ext functions we have just used:

- `Ext.onReady`: This function provides a way to make our code wait until the DOM is available, before doing anything. This is needed because JavaScript starts executing as soon as it is encountered in the document, at which point, our DOM elements might not exist.

- `Ext.Msg.show`: This is the core function used for the creation of a dialog. It takes care of everything needed to have a working dialog. There are some shortcuts that can be used for common dialog types, which will help you save time. We will cover these in just a minute.

Using onReady

It's time to examine the code we just used to display our dialog.

```
Ext.onReady(function(){
    Ext.Msg.show({
        title: 'Milton',
        msg: 'Have you seen my stapler?',
        buttons: {
            yes: true,
```

```
            no: true,
            cancel: true
        }
    });
});
```

The onReady function is what we use to make our code wait until the document is ready. The argument passed to onReady is a function, which can be passed in as a function name, or created in-line, as we have done in the example code. This method of creating a function in-line is referred to as an anonymous function, which is used when you plan on calling a particular function only once.

If we were executing a function that will be used again, then we could define and call it like this:

```
Function stapler(){
    Ext.Msg.show({
        title: 'Milton',
        msg: 'Have you seen my stapler?',
        buttons: {
            yes: true,
            no: true,
            cancel: true
            }
    });
}


    Ext.onReady(stapler());
```

When we start to make our application bigger, we are not likely to use many anonymous functions, and will probably opt for creating re-usable functions.

 The buttons record can also specify the text to display on the button. Instead of passing a boolean value, just pass it the text you want, for example, {yes: 'Maybe'}.

More widget wonders

Let's get back to making our little application as annoying as possible by adding an icon and buttons! This can be done by adding a style for the icon, and modifying the config to have an icon record along with a buttons record.

First, let's discuss the CSS we need. Add the following code into the head of the document, within a style tag:

```
.milton-icon {
    background: url(milton-head-icon.png) no-repeat;
}
```

Also, we will make some changes to our widgets configuration. The `icon` record just needs our style name as the value, `milton-icon`. We have also included a function to be executed when a user clicks on any of the buttons in the dialog. This function is created as an anonymous function, and in this case, it is merely used to pass variables:

```
Ext.Msg.show({
    title: 'Milton',
    msg: 'Have you seen my stapler?',
    buttons: {
        yes: true,
        no: true,
        cancel: true
    },
    icon: 'milton-icon',
    fn: function(btn) {
        Ext.Msg.alert('You Clicked', btn);
    }
});
```

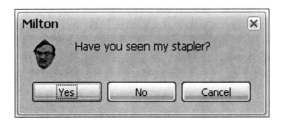

In our case, the function has only one argument, which is the name of the button that was clicked. So if our user was to click the **Yes** button, the `btn` variable would contain a value of `yes`. Using the example code, we are taking the name of the button clicked, and passing it to alert, as the message.

 The built-in functionality takes care of making sure the **Cancel** button, the **close** icon in the upper right corner, and the *Esc* key are all tied together to perform the cancel action. This is one of the many ways in which Ext makes the coding of web applications easier for us.

Meet JSON and the config object

In our example, we are utilizing what's called a `config` object, which is the primary way to get Ext to do what you want. This is what provides the configuration of the different options that are available for the function that is being used.

The old way

We used to call functions with a pre-determined set of arguments. This means that we had to remember the order of the arguments every time the function was used.

```
var test = new TestFuntion(
    'three',
    'fixed',
    'arguments'
);
```

This old way of using functions can create many problems:

- It requires us to remember the order of the arguments
- It does not describe about what the arguments represent
- It provides less flexibility in dealing with optional arguments

The new way—config objects

Using a `config` object, we are able to have a larger level of flexibility, and can tell what our variables are in descriptive plain text. The order of our arguments no longer matters — `firstWord` could be the last item, and `thirdWord` could be the first, or they could be in any random order. With the `config` object method of passing arguments to your functions, the arguments no longer needs to be tied down to a specific place.

```
var test = new TestFunction({
    firstWord: 'three',
    secondWord: 'fixed',
    thirdWord: 'arguments'
});
```

This method also allows for unlimited expansion of our function's arguments. Using fewer arguments or adding new arguments is simple. Another great result that comes by using a `config` object is that the prior usage of your functions will not be harmed by the addition or subtraction of arguments at a later point.

```
var test = new TestFunction({
    secondWord: 'three'
});
```

```
var test = new TestFunction({
    secondWord: 'three',
    fourthWord: 'wow'
});
```

What is a config object?

If you are familiar with CSS or JSON, you'll notice that a `config` object looks similar to these, mostly because they are all the same. Config objects are just ways of structuring data so that it can easily be read by programming languages—in our case, JavaScript.

For an example, let's take a look at the `config` portion of our example code:

```
{
    title: 'Milton',
    msg: 'Have you seen my stapler?',
    buttons: {
        yes: true,
        no: true,
        cancel: true
    },
    icon: 'milton-icon',
    fn: function(btn) {
        Ext.Msg.alert('You Clicked', btn);
    }
}
```

The particular `config` that we are using here may appear complex at first, but once we get to know it, it becomes an extremely fast way of configuring widgets. Just about every Ext widget uses a configuration object, so this is something that we will want to become very familiar with. The `config` object will become our new best friend.

Here are some key things to remember when working with a `config` object:

- Curly brackets wrap around your whole record set, which symbolizes the records inside the brackets as being part of an object—`{records}`.

- Each record consists of a set of name/value pair, with the name and value separated by a colon, and pairs separated by commas—`{name0: value0, name1: value1}`.

- The records' values can contain any type of data, including boolean, array, function, or even another object—`{ name0: true, name1: { name2: value2 } }`.

- Square brackets identify an array — {name: ['one', 'two', 'three'] }. An array can also contain objects with records, values, or any number of other things.

The best thing about using JSON to configure our widgets is that if we want more options, we just start typing them out. Presto! Unlike a typical function call, the order of your config options has become irrelevant, and there can be as few or as many as necessary.

How does JSON work?

Sometimes, you will hear people talk about eval, which generally refers to JSON. The eval function is what JavaScript uses to interpret a JSON string, converting it into the objects, arrays, and functions that we are using.

Time for action

Ok! So now we've seen how to get our Ext JS party started and ask the user a question. Now let's see what we can do with their answers. Let's add to our dialog's function so that we can decide what to do in response to each of the button-clicks. A switch statement can take care of deciding what to do in each case:

```
fn: function(btn) {
    switch(btn){
        case 'yes':
            Ext.Msg.prompt('Milton', 'Where is it?');
        break;
        case 'no':
            Ext.Msg.alert('Milton',
                        'Im going to burn the building down!');
        break;
        case 'cancel':
            Ext.Msg.wait('Saving tables to disk...','File Copy');
        break;
    }
}
```

Remember those built in dialog types I mentioned earlier? Well we just used some of them. They let us accomplish some common tasks without spending time writing the config needed for each standard scenario.

Click **OK** and you get a prompt. A **prompt** is the common name for a small window that allows you to enter a single value, and is a standard element in almost every user interface.

Click **No** and you get an alert. I'm sure you are familiar with the standard **alert** dialog in JavaScript. I remember the first time I used an alert dialog in JavaScript. I was so excited to have an alert message on my home page that I made it pop up and say "Click OK if you are a moron".

Click the **Cancel** button(or click the close button or press the *Escape* key) and you will get a wait message that's using a progress dialog.

The progress dialog we are using can be controlled by Ext and be notified when it should disappear. But for the sake of simplicity, in this example, we are letting it run forever.

Button focus and tab orders are built into Ext. Typically the **OK** or **Yes** button will be the default action. So pressing *Enter* on your keyboard will trigger that button, and pressing *Tab* will move you through the buttons and other items in the dialog.

Lighting the fire

Now, we can start causing some reactions in our page, based on the users' responses to the dialogs. We are going to add to our `switch` statement, which takes care of a **Yes** button click. The `prompt` function can handle a third argument, which is the function to be executed after the **Yes** button has been clicked. We are defining this so that the function will check to see if the value entered into our prompt dialog is equal to the `office` and then write this text to a DIV in our page if it is, and a default text of **Dull Work** if it does not. The code also applies a style to the same DIV, which uses a "Swingline" stapler background image.

```
case 'yes':
    Ext.Msg.prompt('Milton', 'Where is it?', function(btn,txt)
{
        if (txt.toLowerCase() == 'the office') {
            Ext.get('my_id').dom.innerHTML = 'Dull Work';
        }else{
            Ext.get('my_id').dom.innerHTML = txt;
        }
        Ext.DomHelper.applyStyles('my_id',{
          background: 'transparent
              url(images/stapler.png) 50% 50% no-repeat'
        });
    });
break;
```

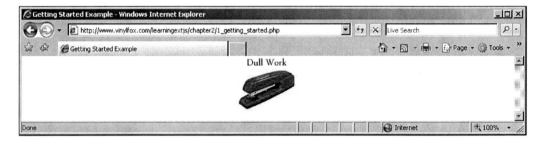

The `no` case will display an alert message, which also styles the document when the **No** button is clicked.

```
case 'no':
    Ext.Msg.alert('Milton',
      'Im going to burn the building down!',
      function() {
        Ext.DomHelper.applyStyles('my_id',{
          'background': 'transparent
              url(images/fire.png) 0 100% repeat-x'
        });
```

```
Ext.DomHelper.applyStyles(Ext.getBody(),{
    'background-color': '#FF0000'
});
Ext.getBody().highlight('FFCC00',{
    endColor:'FF0000',
    duration: 6
});
});
break;
```

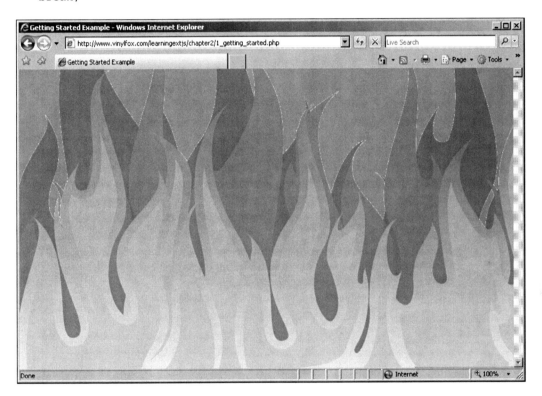

The workhorse—Ext.get

Ext is able to work so well, because it has a foundation that provides access to the DOM, and to many functions that allow manipulation of the DOM. Of these functions, get is one of the most used.

```
Ext.get('my_id');
```

This gives us access to an element in the document with the ID, my_id. If we take a look at the first example, it is using getBody , which retrieves the body element and applies our effect to that. Let's switch that around to use my_id instead. But first, we will need to create a my_id element in our document:

```
<div id='my_id'
    style='width:200px;height:200px;'>test</div>
```

If we add this to the body section of our document, and change our effect to reference this instead of the body, then our effect will happen only to the my_id div we created:

```
Ext.get('my_id').highlight('FF0000',{
    endColor:'0000FF', duration: 3
});
```

If we now looked at our document in a browser, we would see a 200-pixel square box changing color, instead of the entire body of the document changing color.

Bear in mind that IDs are unique. So once we have used my_id, we cannot use this ID again in our document. If duplicate IDs exist in your document, then the last one found will be used. But this should be considered as a bug, and not a design practice. For the most part, Ext creates and tracks its own IDs, and most of the time, we will default to Ext's tracking of the document elements and not create them on our own.

 Having duplicate IDs in your document can lead to strange behavior, such as a widgets always showing up in the upper left corner of the browser, and is therefore best avoided.

Speed tip

This isn't exactly a speed tip, but is more about conserving memory by using something called a "flyweight" to perform simple tasks, which results in higher speed by not clogging up the browser's memory.

The same highlight effect we just used, could be written using a flyweight instead:

```
Ext.fly('my_id').highlight('FF0000',{
    endColor:'0000FF', duration: 3
});
```

This is used when we want to perform an action on an element in a single line of code, and we do not need to reference that element again. The flyweight re-uses the same memory over and over each time it is called.

Here is an example of using a flyweight incorrectly:

```
var my_id = Ext.fly('my_id');
Ext.fly('another_id');
my_id.highlight('FF0000',{
    endColor:'0000FF', duration: 3
});
```

Because the flyweight re-uses the same memory each time it is called, by the time we run the highlight function on our `my_id` reference, the memory has changed to actually contain a reference to `another_id`.

Summary

Using only a few lines of code, we have created a fun program that will keep you entertained for hours! Well, maybe not for hours, but for at least a few minutes. Nonetheless, we have the beginnings of the basic functionality and user interface of a typical desktop application.

We have learned the basics of using configuration objects, and I'm sure this will make even more sense after we have had the chance to play with some more Ext widgets. But the real point here is that the configuration object is something that is very fundamental when using Ext. So the quicker you can wrap your head around it, the better off you will be.

Don't worry if you are not entirely comfortable with the configuration object yet. We have plenty of time to figure it out. For now, let's move on to one of my favorite things—forms.

3
Forms

In this chapter, we will learn how to create Ext forms, which are similar to the HTML forms that we use, without the usability restrictions and boring user interface.

We use some different form field types to create a form that validates and submits asynchronously. Then we will create a database-driven, drop-down menu (ComboBox), and add some more complex field validation and masking. We will then finish it off with a few advanced topics that will give our forms some serious 'wow' factor.

The goals of this chapter include:

- Creating a form that uses AJAX submission
- Validating field data and creating custom validation
- Loading form data from a database

The core components of a form

The possibilities are endless with Ext forms. Key listeners, validation, error messages, and value restrictions are all built in with simple config options. Extending a form option for your own specific needs can be done easily, which is something we will cover later on in this chapter. Here are some of the core form components that you should become familiar with:

- `Ext.form.FormPanel`: Groups fields together in a panel, much as the FORM tag does for a standard HTML form
- `Ext.form.Field`: As the primary handler of form field creation and interaction, it can be compared to the INPUT tag in HTML

't form

's create a form with multiple field types, a date picker, validation,
ıd AJAX submission—just a simple one for our first try.

ır fields will be created using a `config` object instead of an
_.form.Field component. This method will work just fine, will take
_ ıo code, and will help our code run faster. A basic HTML page like the one
._ used in the previous example will be used as a starting point. The standard Ext
library files need to be included and, as with everything we create in Ext, our code
will need to be wrapped in the `onReady` function.

```
Ext.onReady(function(){
    var movie_form = new Ext.FormPanel({
        url: 'movie-form-submit.php',
        renderTo: document.body,
        frame: true,
        title: 'Movie Information Form',
        width: 250,
        items: [{
            xtype: 'textfield',
            fieldLabel: 'Title',
            name: 'title'
        },{
            xtype: 'textfield',
            fieldLabel: 'Director',
            name: 'director'
        },{
            xtype: 'datefield',
            fieldLabel: 'Released',
            name: 'released'
        }]
    });
});
```

When we run this code in a browser, we end up with a form panel that looks
like this:

Nice form—how does it work?

The `FormPanel` is very similar to an HTML form. It acts as the container for our form fields. Our form has a `url` config so the form knows where to send the data when it is submitted. It also has a `renderTo` config, which defines where the form is displayed on the page.

The `items` config element is the important one as it contains all of our form fields. The `items` config element is an array of fields. Each field element has an `xtype` that defines which type of Ext component will be used: text, date, or number. This could even be a grid or some other type of Ext component.

Form fields

Now we know that each type of field is defined by its `xtype`. But where do `xtypes` come from, and how many of them are there? An `xtype` is just a reference to a particular Ext component, so a 'textfield' `xtype` is the same as its `Ext.form.TextField` counterpart. Here are examples of some of the `xtypes` that are available to us:

- textfield
- timefield
- numberfield
- datefield
- combo
- textarea

Because these are all just Ext components, we could easily be using a grid, toolbar, or button—pretty much anything! A recurring theme in Ext components is that everything is interchangeable, and everything shares the same core functions. This ensures that just about any scenario can be handled with the Ext library.

Our basic field config is set up like this:

```
{
    xtype: 'textfield',
    fieldLabel: 'Title',
    name: 'title'
}
```

Of course, we have the `xtype` that defines what type of a field it is—in our case it is a `textfield`. The `fieldLabel` is the text label that is displayed to the left of the field, although this can also be configured to be displayed on the top or the right side of the field. The `name` config is just the same as its HTML counterpart and will be used as the variable name when sending the form data to the server.

mes of most of the config options for Ext components match
    ınterparts in HTML. This is because Ext was created by web
    rs, for web developers.

]

sn't much different from making the text field. Change the
    nd we're done.

```
_ype: 'datefield',
    fieldLabel: 'Released',
    name: 'released'
}
```

Validation

A few of our sample fields could have validations that present the users with errors
if the user does something wrong. Let's add some validation to our first form. One of
the most commonly-used types of validation is checking to see if the user has entered
any value at all. We will use this for our movie `title` field. In other words, let's
make this field a required one:

```
{
    xtype: 'textfield',
    fieldLabel: 'Title',
    name: 'title',
    allowBlank: false
}
```

Setting up an `allowBlank` config option and setting it to `false` (the default is `true`)
is easy enough. Most forms we build will have a bunch of required fields just
like this.

Each type of Ext field also has its own set of specialized validations that are specific
to the data type of that field. For instance, a `date` field has ways to disable certain
days of the week, or to use a regular expression to disable specific dates. The
following code disables every day except Saturday and Sunday:

```
{
    xtype: 'datefield',
    fieldLabel: 'Released',
    name: 'released',
    disabledDays: [1,2,3,4,5]
}
```

In this example, everyday except Saturday and Sunday is disabled. Keep in mind that the week starts on 0 for Sunday, and ends on 6 for Saturday.

When we use other types of fields, we have different validations, like number fields that can restrict the size of a number or how many decimal places the number can have. The standard validation options for each field type can be found in the API reference.

Built-in validation—vtypes

Another more complex type of validation is the vtype. This can be used to validate and restrict user input, and report back error messages. It will work in just about any scenario you can imagine because it uses regular expressions to do the grunt work.

Here are some built-in vTypes that can come in handy:

- email
- url
- alpha
- alphanum

These built-in vtypes are intended to be simplistic, and mostly used as a starting point for creating your own vtypes.

Here is an alpha vtype being used with a QuickTips balloon error message:

```
Ext.onReady(function(){
    var movie_form = new Ext.FormPanel({
        url: 'movie-form-submit.php',
        renderTo: document.body,
        frame: true,
        title: 'Movie Information Form',
        width: 250,
        items: [{
            xtype: 'textfield',
            fieldLabel: 'Title',
            name: 'title',
            allowBlank: false
        },{
            xtype: 'textfield',
            fieldLabel: 'Director',
            name: 'director',
            vtype: 'alpha'
        },{
            xtype: 'datefield',
            fieldLabel: 'Released',
            name: 'released',
            disabledDays: [1,2,3,4,5]
        }]
    });
});
```

All we did was add a vtype to the director field. This will validate that the value entered is composed of only alphabetic characters.

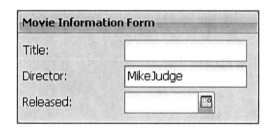

Now we're starting to see that the built-in vtypes are very basic. The built-in alpha vtype restricts our fields to alphabet characters only. In our case, we want the user to enter a director's name, which would usually contain only alphabet characters, with just one space or a hyphen. Capitalizing the first characters in the names could possibly make them look pretty.

 A search of the Ext forum is likely to come back with a vType that someone else has created that is either exactly what you need, or close enough to use as a starting point for your own requirements.

Styles for displaying errors

Forms are set up by default with a very bland error display which shows any type of error with a squiggly red line under the form field. This error display closely mimics the errors shown in programs like Microsoft Word when you spell a word incorrectly. We do have other options for displaying our error messages, but we will need to tell Ext JS to use it.

The preferred option is to display the error message in a balloon. This utilizes the standard squiggly line, but also adds a balloon message that pops up when you mouse over the field.

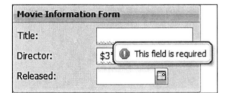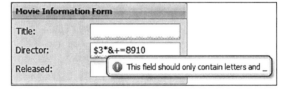

We just need to add a line of code before our form is created that will initialize the balloon messages. Typically this is the first line within the OnReady function.

For example:

```
Ext.onReady(function(){
        Ext.QuickTips.init();
        // our form here
});
```

This is all that needs to happen for your form fields to start displaying error messages in a fancy balloon.

Custom validation—create your own vtype

If you're like me, regular expressions can leave you in a stupefied gaze at your monitor, so I always try to find something that is close to what I need and then modify it, rather than start from scratch.

To create our own vtype, we need to add it to the vtype definitions. Each definition has a value, mask, error text, and a function used for testing:

- xxxVal: This is the regular expression to match against
- xxxMask: This is the masking to restrict user input
- xxxText:This is the error message that is displayed

As soon as we figure out the regular expressions we need to use, it's fairly straight forward creating our own vType—so lets try one out. Here is a validation for our director's name field. The regular expression matches a pair of alpha strings, separated by a space, and each starting with a capital letter. Sounds like a good way to validate a name—right?

```
Ext.form.VTypes['nameVal']  = /^[A-Z][A-Za-z\-]+
                              [A-Z][A-Za-z\-]+$/;
Ext.form.VTypes['nameMask'] = /[A-Za-z\- ]/;
Ext.form.VTypes['nameText'] = 'In-valid Director Name.';
Ext.form.VTypes['name']     = function(v){
    return Ext.form.VTypes['nameVal'].test(v);
}
```

It's hard to look at this all at once, so let's break it down into its main parts. We first start with the regular expression that validates the data entered into our form field:

```
Ext.form.VTypes['nameVal'] = /^([A-Z]{1})[A-Za-z\-]+
                             ([A-Z]{1})[A-Za-z\-]+/;
```

Next, we add the masking, which defines what characters can be typed into our form field. This is also in the form of a regular expression:

```
Ext.form.VTypes['nameMask'] = /[A-Za-z]/;
```

Then, we have the text to be displayed in a balloon if there is an error:

```
Ext.form.VTypes['nameText'] = 'In-valid Director Name.';
```

And finally, the part that pulls it all together—the actual function used to test our field value:

```
Ext.form.VTypes['name'] = function(v){
    return Ext.form.VTypes['nameVal'].test(v);
}
```

Put all this together and we have our own custom `vtype` without much effort, and that can be used over and over again.

Masking—don't press that key!

Masking is used when a particular field is forced to accept only certain keystrokes, such as numbers only, or letters only, or just capital letters. The possibilities are limitless, because regular expressions are used to decide what keys to filter out.

This mask example would allow an unlimited string of capital letters:

```
maskRe: /[A-Z]/
```

Instead of using the masking config, consider creating a `vType` to accomplish your masking. If the formatting requirements should happen to change, it will be centrally-located for easy changing.

So when the day arrives where your boss comes to you freaking out and tells you, "Remember those product codes that I said would always be ten numbers, well it turns out they will be eight letters instead", you can make the change to your `vType`, and go play Guitar Hero for the rest of the day!

Radio buttons and check boxes

Radio buttons and check boxes are a necessary evil. They are clumsy, and hard to work with. I try to use them only as a last resort, when nothing else will do the job. But let's add them to our form just so we can say that we did.

It's not a button, it's a radio button

Lets first add a set of radio buttons to our form:

```
{
    xtype: 'radio',
    fieldLabel: 'Filmed In',
    name: 'filmed_in',
    boxLabel: 'Color'
}, {
    xtype: 'radio',
    hideLabel: false,
    labelSeparator: '',
    name: 'filmed_in',
    boxLabel: 'Black & White'
}
```

These radio buttons work much like their HTML counterparts. Give them all the same name, and they will work together for you. I also like to hide the labels for the trailing radio buttons by setting `hideLabel` to true and `labelSeparator` to an empty value. This gives the form a cleaner look.

X marks the check box

Sometimes, we need to use check boxes for boolean values — sort of an on/off switch.

```
{
    xtype: 'checkbox',
    fieldLabel: 'Bad Movie',
    name: 'bad_movie'
}
```

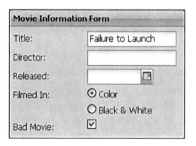

The ComboBox

The ComboBox, or SELECT as its known in HTML, also called a drop-down menu, is a highly-useful form element. It reduces the users' need to touch the keys on their keyboards. The Ext ComboBox has a ton of practical uses, and just as many configuration options to keep track of.

First, let's make a combo using local data. To do this, we need to create a data store. There are a few different types of data store, each of which can be used for different situations. However, for this one, we are going to use a simple store:

```
var genres = new Ext.data.SimpleStore({
    fields: ['id', 'genre'],
    data : [['1','Comedy'],['2','Drama'],['3','Action']]
});
```

Just like the other fields in our form, we add it to the items config. A few other config options are needed when we are setting up a combo box. The store is the obvious one-this is the data that populates the options for our combo. The other things we need are the mode, which determines if the data is coming from a local source or a remote source, and the displayField, which determines which column of data is displayed in the combo options:

```
{
    xtype: 'combo',
    name: 'genre',
    fieldLabel: 'Genre',
    mode: 'local',
    store: genres,
    displayField:'genre',
    width: 120
}
```

This gives us a combo box that uses local data, which is good for small lists, or lists that don't change often. What happens when our list needs to be pulled up from a database?

Database-driven ComboBox

The biggest change that needs to happen is on the server side—getting your data and formatting it into a JSON string that the combo box can use. Whatever server-side language is used, we will need a JSON library to 'encode' the data. If we're using PHP 5.1 or higher, this is built in.

To check our version of PHP, we can either execute a command in a terminal window or run a single line of PHP code. If we have access to this command line we can run php -v to check our version, otherwise, running a script that just has the single line <?php phpinfo(); ?> will do the job.

This is what we would use to generate our JSON data using PHP 5.1 or higher:

```
<?php
// connection to database goes here

$result = mysql_query('SELECT id, genre_name FROM genres');

If (mysql_num_rows($result) > 0) {
    while ($obj = mysql_fetch_object($result)) {
        $arr[] = $obj;
    }
}
Echo '{rows:'.json_encode($arr).'}';

?>
```

When we use remote data, there are a few more things that need to happen. First, the data store needs to know what format the data is in. We specify this by using a data reader—in our case, it's the JSON Reader.

```
var genres = new Ext.data.Store({
    reader: new Ext.data.JsonReader({
        fields: ['id', 'genre_name'],
        root: 'rows'
    }),
    proxy: new Ext.data.HttpProxy({
        url: 'data/genres.php'
    })
});
```

The first argument for the data reader is an object containing the configuration of our reader—specifically, which fields will be read and what the root element is. The fields list is simply an array of field names; notice that we left out sort_order—this field will not be available to our data set. Our root is the element that contains our array of data, in this case it's rows, but could just as easily be bobs-crab-shack, or whatever you felt like:

```
{rows:[
    {
        "id":"1",
        "genre_name":"Comedy",
        "sort_order":"0"
    },{
```

```
        "id":"2",
        "genre_name":"Drama",
        "sort_order":"1"
    },{
        // snip...//
    }]
}
```

We have also set up the proxy — typically this will be an HTTP Proxy that retrieves data from the same domain as the web page. This is the most common method, but there is also a `ScriptTagProxy` that can be used to retrieve data from a different domain. All we need to provide for our proxy is the URL to fetch our data from.

 Whenever we specify a 'proxy' we are actually using AJAX. This requires that you have a web server running, otherwise AJAX will not work. Simply running your code from the file system in a web browser will not work.

Let's throw in a call to the `load` function at the end, so the data is loaded into our combo box before the user starts to interact with it.

```
genres.load();
```

This gives us a combo box that's populated from our database, and should look like this:

Another way to pre-load the data store is to set the `autoLoad` option to `true` in our data store configuration:

```
var genres = new Ext.data.Store({
    reader: new Ext.data.JsonReader({
        fields: ['id', 'genre_name'],
        root: 'rows'
    }),
    proxy: new Ext.data.HttpProxy({
        url: 'data/genres.php'
    }),
    autoLoad: true
});
```

TextArea and HTMLEditor

We are going to add a text field to our movie information form, and Ext has a couple of options for this. We can either use the standard `textarea` that we were familiar with from using HTML, or we can use the HTMLEditor field, which provides rich text editing:

- `textarea`: Similar to a typical HTML `textarea` field
- `htmleditor`: A rich text editor with a button bar for common formatting tasks

If we set `hideLabel` to `true` and clear out the label separator then we can have a `textarea` that spans the entire width of our form panel. This gives a nice look to the form:

```
{
    xtype: 'textarea',
    name: 'description',
    hideLabel: true,
    labelSeparator: '',
    height: 100,
    anchor: '100%'
}
```

By changing just the `xtype`, as shown below, we now have a fairly simple HTML editor with built-in options for font face, size, color, italics, bold, and so on. This is the first Ext component we have used that requires the `QuickTips` component to be initialized before we can use it.

```
{
    xtype: 'htmleditor',
    name: 'description',
    hideLabel: true,
    labelSeparator: '',
    height: 100,
    anchor: '100%'
}
```

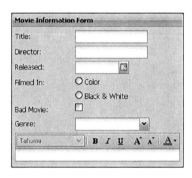

Listening for form field events

Ext makes it extremely simple to listen for particular user actions, such as clicking on an element or pressing a particular key.

A common task would be listening for the *Enter* key to be pressed, and then submitting the form. So let's see how this is accomplished:

```
{
    xtype: 'textfield',
    fieldLabel: 'Title',
    name: 'title',
    allowBlank: false,
    listeners: {
        specialkey: function(f,e){
            if (e.getKey() == e.ENTER) {
                movie_form.getForm().submit();
            }
        }
    }
}
```

The `specialkey` listener is called whenever a key related to navigation is pressed. This listener is also called every time the arrow keys are pressed, along with *Tab*, *Esc*, and so on. That's why we have to check to see if it was the *Enter* key before we take action.

Now the form will only be submitted when you press *Enter*.

ComboBox events

It seems that combo boxes commonly need to have events attached to them. Let's take our `genre` combo box and attach a listener to it that will run when an item in the list is selected.

First let's add a dummy item to our data as the first item in the list and call it New Genre:

```
var genres = new Ext.data.SimpleStore({
    fields: ['id', 'genre'],
    data : [
        ['0','New Genre'],
        ['1','Comedy'],
        ['2','Drama'],
        ['3','Action']
    ]
});
```

Then, we add the listener to our combo:

```
{
    xtype: 'combo',
    name: 'genre',
    fieldLabel: 'Genre',
    mode: 'local',
    store: genres,
    displayField:'genre',
    width: 130,
    listeners: {
        select: function(f,r,i){
            if (i == 0){
                Ext.Msg.prompt('New Genre','Name',Ext.emptyFn);
            }
        }
    }
}
```

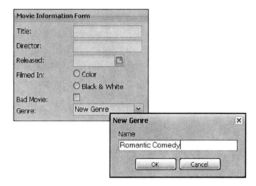

The listener is set up to wait for a `select` event and then run the function that is specified. Each listener type has its own set of variables that is passed to the function—these can be looked up in the API reference.

For the `select` event, our function is passed three things:

- The form field
- The data record of the selected combo item
- The index number of the item that was clicked on

Once the list item is selected, we can see which item in the list was selected. The third argument in our listener function is the index of the item that was clicked. If that has an index of zero (the first item in the list), then we will prompt the user to enter a new genre using the prompt dialog we learned about in the previous chapter.

Just about every component in Ext has a listener. A list of valid events for these listeners can be found at the bottom of the API documentation page for each component.

Buttons and form action

Now, we have quite a mess of a form with only one problem – it doesn't send data to the server, which was the actual point behind creating our form in the first place. To do, this we are going to add some buttons.

Our buttons are added to a `buttons` config object, similar to the way that the form fields were added. These buttons really only need two things: the text to be displayed on the button, and the function(which is called the handler) to execute when the button is clicked.

```
buttons: [{
    text: 'Save',
    handler: function(){
        movie_form.getForm().submit({
            success: function(f,a){
                Ext.Msg.alert('Success', 'It worked');
            },
            failure: function(f,a){
                Ext.Msg.alert('Warning', 'Error');
            }
        });
    }
}, {
    text: 'Reset',
    handler: function(){
        movie_form.getForm().reset();
    }
}]
```

The handler is provided with a function – or a reference to a function – that will be executed once the button is clicked. In this case, we are providing an anonymous function.

Form submission

Our `FormPanel` has a `url` option that contains the name of the file that the form data will be sent to. This is simple enough – just like an HTML form, all of our fields will be posted to this `url`, so they can be processed on the server side.

Inside our **Save** button, we have an anonymous function that runs the following code. This will run the actual submission function for our form, which sends the data to the server using AJAX. No page refresh is needed to submit the form. It all happens in the background, while the page you are looking at remains the same:

```
movie_form.getForm().submit({
    success: function(f,a){
        Ext.Msg.alert('Success', 'It worked');
    },
    failure: function(f,a){
        Ext.Msg.alert('Warning', 'Error');
    }
});
```

 In order for our form submission to work properly, it must be run from a web server.

`success` and `failure` options provided to the `submit` call handle the server's response. These are also anonymous functions, but could just as easily be references to functions created earlier on in the code.

Did you notice that the functions have a pair of arguments passed to them? These will be used to figure out what response the server gave. But first, we need to discuss how to provide that response on the server side.

Talking back—the server responses

When our form is submitted to the server, a script on the server side will process the post data from the form, and decide if a `true` or `false` 'success' message should be sent back to the client side. Error messages can be sent back along with our response, and these can contain messages that correspond to our form field names.

When using forms and server-side validation, a `success` boolean value is required. An example of a response from the server would look like this:

```
{
    success: false,
    errors: {
        title: "Sounds like a Chick Flick"
    }
}
```

When the `success` flag is set to `false`, it triggers the Ext form to read in the error messages and apply them to the form's validation to present the user with error messages.

Server-side validation of our form submission gives us a way to look up information on the server side, and return errors based on this. Let's say we have a database of bad movie names, and we don't want users to submit them to our database. We can submit the form to our script, which checks the database and returns a response based on the database lookup of that name.

If we wanted to filter out `chick flicks` the response could look something like this:

```
{
    success: false,
    errors: {
        title: "Sounds like a Chick Flick"
    },
     errormsg: "That movie title sounds like a chick flick."
}
```

The `false` success response triggers the forms error messages to be displayed. An `errors` object is passed with the response. The form uses this object to determine each of the error messages. A name/value pair exists in the `errors` object for each form field's error.

Our example response also passes an `errormsg`, which is not used by the form, but is going to be accessed separately to present our own error message.

Let's take the extra error message that we were passing back, and display it in a message box.

```
buttons: [{
    text: 'Save',
    handler: function(){
        movie_form.getForm().submit({
            success: function(f,a){
                Ext.Msg.alert('Success', 'It worked');
            },
            failure: function(f,a){
                Ext.Msg.alert('Warning', a.result.errormsg);
            }
        });
    }
}, {
    text: 'Reset',
    handler: function(){
        movie_form.getForm().reset();
    }
}]
```

Our `submit` form action passes information back to the `success` and `failure` handlers. The first argument is an Ext form object, and the second is an Ext action object. Let's take a look at what's available in the Ext action object:

Option		Description
failureType	String	Reports both client-side and server-side errors
response	Object	Contains raw information about the server's response, including useful header information
result	Object	Parsed JSON object based on the response from the server
type	String	The type of action that was performed–either submit or load

Now that we know what is available to the failure handler, we can set up some simple error checking:

```
failure: function(f,a){
    if (a.failureType === Ext.form.Action.CONNECT_FAILURE)
        {Ext.Msg.alert('Failure', 'Server reported:
        '+a.response.status+' '+a.response.statusText);
    }
    if (a.failureType === Ext.form.Action.SERVER_INVALID){
        Ext.Msg.alert('Warning', a.result.errormsg);
    }
}
```

By checking the failure type, we can determine if there was a server connection error and act accordingly, even providing details about the server's specific error message by using the result property.

Loading a form with data

There are three basic ways in which forms are used in a user interface:

- To input data for a separate action – say, Google search
- To create new data
- To change existing data

It's the last option that we are interested in now. To accomplish this, we need to learn how to load that data from its source (static or database) into our user interface.

Static data load

We can take data from somewhere in our code, and display it as the value in a form field. This single line of code sets a fields value:

```
movie_form.getForm().findField('title').
                setValue('Dumb & Dumber');
```

Once we start working with more complex forms, this method becomes a hassle. That's why we also have the ability to load our data via an AJAX request. The server side would work much as it did when we loaded the combo box:

```php
<?php
// connection to database goes here

$result = mysql_query('SELECT * FROM movies WHERE id = '.$_
REQUEST['id']);

If (mysql_num_rows($result) > 0) {
    $obj = mysql_fetch_object($result);
    Echo '{success: true, data:'.json_encode($obj).'}';
}else{
    Echo '{success: false}';
}


?>
```

This would return a JSON object containing a success flag, and a data object that would be used to populate the values of the form fields. The returned data would look something like this:

```
{
    success: true,
    data:{
        "id":"1",
        "title":"Office Space",
        "director":"Mike Judge",
        "released":"1999-02-19",
        "genre":"1",
        "tagline":"Work Sucks",
        "coverthumb":"84m.jpg",
        "price":"19.95",
        "available":"1"
    }
}
```

To trigger this, we need to use the form's load handler:

```
movie_form.getForm().load({
    url:'data/movie.php',
    params:{
        id: 1
    }
});
```

Providing it with a `url` and `params` config will do the trick. The `params` config represents what is sent to the server side script as post/get parameters. By default, these are sent as post parameters.

Object reference or component config

Throughout these first few chapters, we have started to use more and more configuration objects to set up our Ext JS components, instead of instantiating them. Let's do a quick comparison of the two methods.

Instantiated

```
var test = new Ext.form.TextField({
    fieldLabel: 'Title',
    name: 'title',
    allowBlank: false
});
```

Here, the component has been created and memory used right away, even if it is not displayed on the screen yet. Depending on how your end users work with your application, they might never even need or use this particular text field. However, when it is the time to display this field to the end users, it shows up really fast.

Component config

```
{
    xtype: 'textfield',
    fieldLabel: 'Title',
    name: 'title',
    allowBlank: false
}
```

With the component config, we have a 'description' of what has to happen when it is time to use the field. No memory is used right away. It's only when the user needs it that the memory is used. At that point, the field is rendered after the user has clicked on or interacted with something else, which can slow the initial display slightly.

This method of setting up components has many other advantages; one of them is being able to send configurations 'over the wire'. The method of sending configurations 'over the wire' means that server-side code can generate a configuration to create a client-side component.

Summary

We have taken the foundation of the classic web application—forms—and injected them with the power of Ext JS, creating a uniquely-flexible and powerful user interface. The form created in this chapter can validate user input, load data from a database, and send that data back to the server. From the methods outlined in this chapter, we can go on to create forms for use in simple text searches, or a complexly validated data entry screen.

4
Buttons, Menus, and Toolbars

The unsung heroes of every application are the simple things like buttons, menus, and toolbars. In this chapter, we will cover how to add these items to our applications.

Our example will contain a few different types of buttons, both with and without menus. A button can simply be an icon, or text, or both. Toolbars also have some mechanical elements such as spacers and dividers that can help to organize the buttons on your toolbars items.

We will also cover how to make these elements react to user interaction.

A toolbar for every occasion

Just about every Ext component—panels, windows, grids can accept a toolbar on either the top or the bottom. The option is also available to render the toolbar standalone into any DOM element in our document. The toolbar is an extremely flexible and useful component that will no doubt be used in every application.

- `Ext.Toolbar`: The main container for the buttons
- `Ext.Button`: The primary handler for button creation and interaction
- `Ext.menu`: A menu

Toolbars

Our first toolbar is going to be rendered standalone in the body of our document. We will add one of each of the main button types, so we can experiment with each:

- Button—`tbbutton`: This is the standard button that we are all familiar with.
- Split Button—`tbsplit`: A split button is where you have a default button action and an optional menu. These are used in cases where you need to have many options in the same category as your button, of which there is a most commonly used default option.

- Menu — tbbutton+menu: A menu is just a button with the menu config filled in with options.

```
Ext.onReady(function(){
    new Ext.Toolbar({
        renderTo: document.body,
        items: [{
            xtype: 'tbbutton',
            text: 'Button'
        },{
            xtype: 'tbbutton',
            text: 'Menu Button',
            menu: [{
                text: 'Better'
            },{
                text: 'Good'
            },{
                text: 'Best'
            }]
        },{
            xtype: 'tbsplit',
            text: 'Split Button',
            menu: [{
                text: 'Item One'
            },{
                text: 'Item Two'
            },{
                text: 'Item Three'
            }]
        }]
    });
});
```

Button   Menu Button ▾   Split Button ▾

As usual, everything is inside our onReady event handler. The items config holds all of our toolbars elements — I say elements and not buttons because the toolbar can accept many different types of Ext components including form fields — which we will be implementing later on in this chapter.

> The default xtype for each element in the items config is tbbutton. We can leave out the xtype config element if tbbutton is the type we want, but I like to include it just to help me keep track.

The button

Creating a button is fairly straightforward; the main config option is the text that is displayed on the button. We can also add an icon to be used alongside the text if we want to.

Here is a stripped-down button:

```
{
    xtype: 'tbbutton',
    text: 'Button'
}
```

Menu

A menu is just a button with the menu config populated—it's that simple. The menu items work along the same principles as the buttons. They can have icons, classes, and handlers assigned to them. The menu items could also be grouped together to form a set of option buttons, but first let's create a standard menu.

This is the config for a typical menu config:

```
{
    xtype: 'tbbutton',
    text: 'Button',
    menu: [{
        text: 'Better'
    },{
        text: 'Good'
    },{
        text: 'Best'
    }]
}
```

As we can see, once the `menu` array config is populated, the menu comes to life. To group these menu items together, we would need to set the `group` config and the boolean `checked` value for each item:

```
menu: [{
    text: 'Better',
    checked: true,
    group: 'quality'
}, {
    text: 'Good',
    checked: false,
    group: 'quality'
}, {
    text: 'Best',
    checked: false,
    group: 'quality'
}]
```

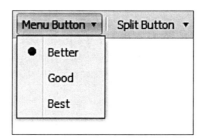

Split button

The split button sounds like a complex component, but it's just like a button and a menu combined, with a slight twist. By using this type of button, you get to use the functionality of a button while adding the option to select an item from the attached menu. Clicking the left portion of the button that contains the text triggers the button action. However, clicking the right side of the button, which contains a small down arrow, triggers the menu.

```
{
    xtype: 'tbsplit',
    text: 'Split Button',
    menu: [{
        text: 'Item One'
    },{
        text: 'Item Two'
    },{
        text: 'Item Three'
    }]
}
```

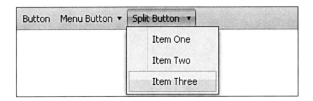

Toolbar item alignment, dividers, and spacers

By default, every toolbar aligns elements to the leftmost side. There is no alignment config for a toolbar, so if we want to align all of the toolbar buttons to the rightmost side, we need to add a fill as the first item in the toolbar. If we want to have items split up between both the left and right sides, we can also use a fill:

```
{
    xtype: 'tbfill'
}
```

Pop this little guy in a tool-bar wherever you want to add space and he will push items on either side of the fill to the ends of the tool bar, as shown below:

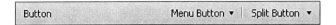

We also have elements that can add space or vertical dividers, like the one used between the **Menu Button** and the **Split Button**.

The spacer adds a few pixels of empty space that can be used to space out buttons, or move elements away from the edge of the toolbar:

```
{
    xtype: 'tbspacer'
}
```

A divider can be added in the same way:

```
{
    xtype: 'tbseparator'
}
```

Shortcuts

Ext has many shortcuts that can be used to make coding faster. Shortcuts are a character or two that can be used in place of a configuration object. For example, consider the standard toolbar filler configuration:

```
{
    xtype: 'tbfill'
}
```

The shortcut for a toolbar filler is a hyphen and a greater than symbol:

```
'->'
```

Not all of these shortcuts are documented. So be adventurous, poke around the source code, and see what you can find. Here is a list of the commonly-used shortcuts:

Component	Shortcut	Description
Fill	'->'	The fill that is used to push items to the right side of the toolbar.
Separator	'-' or 'separator'	A vertical bar used to visually separate items.
Spacer	' '	Empty space used to separate items visually. The space is two pixels wide, but can be changed by overriding the ytb-spacer CSS class.
TextItem	'Your Text'	Add any text or HTML directly to a toolbar by simply placing it within quotes.

Icon buttons

The standard button can act as an icon button like the ones you see used in text editors to make text bold or italic. Two steps need to be taken to make an icon button—defining an image to be used as the icon and applying the appropriate class to the button.

```
{
    xtype: 'tbbutton',
    cls: 'x-btn-icon',
    icon: 'images/bomb.png'
}
```

This could just as easily be an icon beside text by changing the style class and adding the text config.

```
{
    xtype: 'tbbutton',
    cls: 'x-btn-text-icon',
    icon: 'images/bomb.png',
    text: 'Tha Bomb'
}
```

Button handlers—click me!

A button needs to do more than just look pretty—it needs to react to the user. This is where handlers come in. A handler is a function that is executed when a button or menu item is clicked.

The handler config is where we add our function:

```
{
    xtype: 'tbbutton',
    text: 'Button',
    handler: function(){
        Ext.Msg.alert('Boo', 'Here I am');
    }
}
```

This code will pop up an alert message when the button is clicked. Sometimes, we need to make changes to the button when it's clicked, so each button handler passes a reference to itself for this purpose. The first argument of our handler is a reference to the component that triggered the event.

```
{
    xtype: 'tbbutton',
    text: 'Button',
    handler: function(f){
        f.disable();
    }
}
```

We can take this reference to the button—a reference to itself—and access all of the properties and functions of that button. For this sample, we have called the disable function which grays out the button and makes it unselectable.

We can have more fun than just disabling a button. Why don't we try something more useful?

Load content on menu item click

Lets take our button click and do something more useful with it. For this example, we are going to add a `config` option to each menu item that will be used to determine what content file to load in the body of our page:

```
{
    xtype: 'tbsplit',
    text: 'Help',
    menu: [{
        text: 'Genre',
        helpfile: 'genre',
        handler: Movies.showHelp
    },{
        text: 'Director',
        helpfile: 'director',
        handler: Movies.showHelp
    },{
        text: 'Title',
        helpfile: 'title',
        handler: Movies.showHelp
    }]
}
```

Note the `helpfile` config option that we have added to each of the menu items config. We have made this config property up so that we have a way to store a variable that is unique to each menu item. This is possible because `config` properties can be anything we need them to be, and can be created on the fly. In this case, we are using a config property as a variable that holds the name of the file we want to load.

The other new thing we are doing is creating a collection of functions to handle the menu item click. These functions are all organized into a `Movies` class.

```
var Movies = function() {
    return {
        showHelp : function(btn){
            var helpbody = Ext.get('helpbody');
            if (!helpbody) {
                Ext.DomHelper.append(Ext.getBody(), {
                    tag:'div',
                    id:'helpbody'
                });
            }
            Movies.doLoad(btn.helpfile);
        },
```

```
      doLoad : function(file){
         Ext.get('helpbody').load({
            url: 'html/' + file + '.txt'
         });
      }
   };
}();
```

I don't want to get bogged down with too much detail about this `Movies` class just yet, but essentially all it does is handle our menu item clicks. This class will load a text file into the body of our web page via an AJAX request—which text file it loads is related to which menu item is clicked. So once this `Movies` class is in place in our page, we will be able to bring up this page in our browser and click on each menu item to load the relevant help file into the body of the page.

Next, we will try using a text field to perform this same type of action.

Form fields in a toolbar

Like most things in Ext, a tool bar can accept just about any Ext component. Naturally, form fields and combo boxes are very useful items to have on a toolbar.

```
{
   xtype: 'textfield'
}
```

In the same way as we created form fields in the last chapter, we have added the form fields to the items array, which will place the form fields within the toolbar. Now let's make the form field do something useful, by having it perform the same functionality as our help menu, but in a more dynamic way.

```
{
   xtype: 'textfield',
   listeners: {
      specialkey: Movies.doSearch
   }
}
```

This listener is added directly to the form field's config. For this, we are using a `specialkey` listener, which we used in the previous chapter. This is the listener that is used to capture edit keystrokes, such as *Enter* and *Delete* among others. The `handler` function will be added to our small `Movies` class created earlier:

```
doSearch : function(frm,evt){
    if (evt.getKey() == evt.ENTER) {
        Movies.doLoad(frm.getValue());
    }
}
```

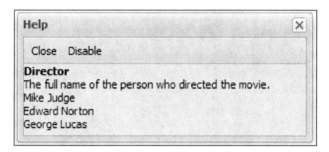

Now we have a text field in our toolbar that enables us to type in the name of the text file to load. Try some of the samples used in our menu, such as **director** or **title**.

Toolbars in windows, grids, and panels

All of the toolbars we have been working with have an `items` config. If we want to place one of these toolbars into another Ext component, such as a panel or a window, we can simply take the contents of the items config for a toolbar, and place it within one of the two pre-set containers that exist for panel-type components.

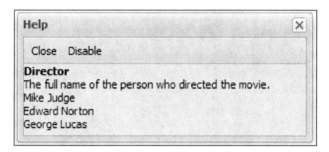

Panel-type components, such as the window and the grid, have a top and bottom toolbar config:

- `tbar`: The top toolbar
- `bbar`: The bottom toolbar

If we wanted to place a toolbar at the top of a window, filling the `tbar` config with an array of toolbar items would give us what we wanted:

```
new Ext.Window({
    title: 'Help',
    id: 'helpwin',
    width: 300,
    height: 300,
    tbar: [{
        text: 'Close',
        handler: function(){
            Ext.getCmp('helpwin').close();
        }
    },{
        text: 'Disable',
        handler: function(t){
            t.disable();
        }
    }],
    autoLoad: 'html/' + btn.helpfile + '.txt'
}).show();
```

Ext also has a custom toolbar for paged grids that contains all of the buttons for moving through pages of results. We will cover this special toolbar in the grid chapter later in this book.

Summary

In this chapter, we had the chance to play with a couple of different ways to create toolbar items, including using a config object or its shortcut. The many options available for toolbars make them a useful component for everything from the simplest button bar, to a complex combination of buttons, menus, and form fields. Interacting with the buttons, menus and form fields is easy using the built-in handlers.

5
Displaying Data with Grids

The grid is, without doubt, one of the most widely-used components of Ext. We all have data, and this needs to be presented to the end user in an easy-to-understand manner. The spreadsheet (a.k.a.: grid) is the perfect way to do this—the concept has been around for quite a while because it works. Ext takes that concept and makes it flexible and downright amazing!

In this chapter we shall be:

- Using a GridPanel to display structured data in a user-friendly grid
- Reading data from the server (or database) to display in the grid
- Working with a grid's events and manipulating the grid's features
- Using some advanced data formatting techniques for grids
- Paging data in a grid

We will cover how to define the rows and columns, but more importantly, we will learn how to make the grid flashier. We can do this by adding custom rendered cells that contain images, and change styles based on data values. In doing this we are adding real value to our grid by breaking out of the boundaries of spreadsheets!

What is a grid anyway?

Ext grids are similar to a spreadsheet; there are two main parts to each spreadsheet:

- Columns
- Rows

Here our columns are **Title, Released, Genre,** and **Price**. Each of the rows contains movies such as **The Big Lebowski, Super Troopers,** and so on. The rows are really our data; each row in the grid represents a record of data.

Displaying structured data with a GridPanel

Displaying data in a grid requires two Ext components:

- A `store` that acts like an in-memory database, keeping track of the data we want to display
- A `grid panel` that provides a way to display the data stored in a data store

Before we start to create each of these, let's look at some of the terminology that will be used, because this can be confusing at first:

- Columns: This refers to a whole column of data, and would contain information only relevant to the display of data down through the entire column, including the heading. In Ext JS, this information is part of the `Column Model`.

- Fields: This also refers to an entire column of data, but is refers to the actual data values. With Ext JS, this is used in the `reader`, for loading data.

Setting up a data store

The first thing we need to do is set up our data, which will be placed into a data store. The data store types available in Ext give us a consistent way of reading different data formats such as XML and JSON, and reading this data in a consistent way throughout all of the Ext widgets. Regardless of whether this data it is JSON, XML, an array, or even a custom data type of your own, it's all accessed in the same way thanks to the data store.

Some data stores available, by default, in Ext are:

- Simple (Array)
- XML
- JSON

A custom data store could be created to read data that does not fit into these categories. The Ext JS forums provide user-contributed data readers for things such as CSV and ColdFusion formats of data.

Adding data to our data store

In our first attempt, we are going to create a grid that uses simple local array data. The data we're using below is taken from a very small movie database of some of my favorite movies, and is similar to the data that will be pulled from an actual database later in this chapter.

The data store needs two things: the data itself, and a description of the data—or what could be thought of as the fields. A `reader` will be used to read the data from the array, and this is where we define the fields of data contained in our array. The `reader` acts as an interpreter of sorts; it knows how to interpret a string of data as rows of data to be used with Ext JS.

ng code should be placed inside the Ext OnReady function:

```
ore = new Ext.data.Store({
   : [

         1,
         "Office Space",
         "Mike Judge",
         "1999-02-19",
         1,
         "Work Sucks",
         "19.95",
         1
      ], [
         3,
         "Super Troopers",
         "Jay Chandrasekhar",
         "2002-02-15",
         1,
         "Altered State Police",
         "14.95",
         1
      ]
      //...more rows of data removed for readability...//
   ],
   reader: new Ext.data.ArrayReader({id:'id'}, [
      'id',
      'title',
      'director',
      {name: 'released', type: 'date', dateFormat: 'Y-m-d'},
      'genre',
      'tagline',
      'price',
      'available'
   ]
});
```

If we viewed this code in a browser we would not see anything—that's because a data store is just a way of loading and keeping track of your data. The web browser's memory has our data in it. Now we need to decide how to display it to the user.

Defining your data for the data store

The reader needs to know which fields to read in as data for our data store, so we will need to define these.

Fields are defined using an array of objects — or if the data is to be read verbatim, just a string specifying the field name. All except one of our fields in this example can be defined with a simple name. For example, the `title` field could be defined using an object like this:

```
{name: 'title'}
```

However, in our case, because we are just reading in the data as a string, we can simply pass the field name and save some typing:

```
'title'
```

The `released` field is different because we want to treat its data appropriately, as a `date` type. For each field format type, there may be options to define the format of the data more explicitly. With the `date` type, there is a `dateFormat` string that needs to be defined. If you have used PHP, these date format strings will look familiar, because Ext uses the same date format strings that PHP does.

```
{name: 'released', type: 'date', dateFormat: 'Y-m-d'}
```

Specifying data types

Ext JS has many ways to properly read in particular data types. They are shown here:

Field Type	Description	Information
string	String data	
int	Number	Uses JavaScripts `parseInt` function
float	Floating point number	Uses JavaScripts `parseFloat` function
boolean	True/False data	
date	Date data	`dateFormat` config needed

Below are a few useful data types that I take advantage of very often:

Field Type	Description	Usage
date	Data containing a date	You also have to specify the `dateFormat`. This tells Ext how to turn text data into dates
		Y-m-d means 'full 4 digit year-numbered month-numbered day'
		`dateFormat` in Ext is the same as in PHP, and there's a handy reference to different date formats online here: `http://www.php.net/date`

Field Type	Description	Usage
int	Numeric data	Treats the value as an integer — this is useful when you plan on making comparisons of your data to perform other actions, such as adding two columns together
boolean or bool	True/False data	Takes care of reading the different ideas of what boolean values are, such as converting a string to an actual boolean value, or translating zero and one to boolean values

If we were to display the data just as the reader sees it, we would end up with something like this:

Movie Database			
Released	Price	Avail	
Fri Feb 19 1999 00:00:00 GMT-0700 (Mountain Standard Time)	19.95	true	
Fri Feb 15 2002 00:00:00 GMT-0700 (Mountain Standard Time)	14.95	true	
Fri Oct 01 1999 00:00:00 GMT-0600 (Mountain Daylight Time)	19.95	true	
Fri Mar 06 1998 00:00:00 GMT-0700 (Mountain Standard Time)	21.9	true	
Fri Oct 15 1999 00:00:00 GMT-0600 (Mountain Daylight Time)	19.95	true	

Now that is ugly — here's a breakdown of what happened:

- The released date has been type set properly as a date, and interpreted from the value in our data. It's provided in the standard ugly JavaScript date format — luckily Ext has ways to make this look pretty.
- The **Price** column has been type set as a floating point number. Note that there is no need to specify the decimal precision.
- The **Avail** column has been interpreted as a true boolean value, even if the raw data was not a true boolean value.

This is why it's useful to specify the type of data that is being read, and apply any special options that are available.

Displaying the GridPanel

The thing that pulls everything together is the GridPanel, which takes care of placing the data into columns and rows, along with adding column headers, and boxing everything together in a neat little package.

The movie data isn't much good to anybody just sitting in the computer'
Let's display it in a grid:

1. Add your data store to the following GridPanel code:

```
Ext.onReady(function(){

    // add your data store here

    var grid = new Ext.grid.GridPanel({
      renderTo: document.body,
      frame:true,
      title: 'Movie Database',
       height:200,
       width:500,
       store: store,
       columns: [
           {header: "Title", dataIndex: 'title'},
           {header: "Director", dataIndex: 'director'},
           {header: "Released", dataIndex: 'released',
            renderer: Ext.util.Format.dateRenderer('m/d/Y')},
           {header: "Genre", dataIndex: 'genre'},
           {header: "Tagline", dataIndex: 'tagline'}
       ]
    });

});
```

2. Load it in a browser, and here's what you will see:

Title	Director	Released	Genre	Tagline
Office Space	Mike Judge	02/19/1999	1	Work Sucks
Super Troopers	Jay Chandrasekhar	02/15/2002	1	Altered State Police
American Beauty	Sam Mendes	10/01/1999	2	... Look Closer
The Big Lebowski	Joel Coen	03/06/1998	1	The "Dude"
Fight Club	David Fincher	10/15/1999	3	How much can you

Movie Database

How did that work?

Our data store is passed into the grid along with a column model that determines how the columns and column headers are to be displayed. This is different from the field data used in the reader, which was defined so that the reader knew how to read data.

Configuring the GridPanel

The GridPanel is the widget that ties everything together:

```
Ext.grid.GridPanel
```

Only a few basic things are needed to set up the `GridPanel`:

Field type	Description	Usage
renderTo	Where should the grid panel be displayed?	This needs to be a valid DOM object, or the ID of a DOM element. Later on, we will pass the GridPanel directly into the other widgets to be rendered. So this config option will become obsolete.
frame	Frames the grid panel	This just adds a nice border around the GridPanel along with a title bar. It's not required, but looks good when rendered to the page.
height and width	Size in pixels	A height is almost always required when using a grid, as the grid itself cannot determine its own height. When we get into using grids in a layout, this will no longer be needed.
store	Our data	This is a reference to a valid data store where our data lives.
columns	Column model	This is an array of objects defining the columns of our grid.
stripeRows	Stripe rows	This is set to `true` to alternate the colors in the rows of data.

Our basic setup for a grid panel will look something like this:

```
var grid = new Ext.grid.GridPanel({
    renderTo: Ext.getBody(),
    frame:true,
    title: 'Movie Database',
    height:200,
    width:500,
    store: store,
    columns: [ insert columns here ]
});
```

We can almost read through the configuration like a sentence:

> Render our grid into the body of the document, frame it, and give it a title of 'Movie Database'. The height will be 200 and the width 500; it will use our 'store' data store and have the columns specified.

The one reason why I love object-based configuration so much is that it is human readable. We never have to go to the manual to look up what argument 3 of function x is; we simply say "make it 200 tall and 500 wide".

Defining a Grids column model

To define our grid's columns, we need to create an array of objects that define how these columns are to be displayed and treated.

```
columns: [
   {header: 'Title', dataIndex: 'title'},
   {header: 'Director', dataIndex: 'director'},
   {header: 'Released', dataIndex: 'released'},
   {header: 'Genre', dataIndex: 'genre'},
   {header: 'Tagline', dataIndex: 'tagline'}
]
```

This will create grid column headers that look like this:

Title	Director	Released	Genre	Tagline

The object defining each column can have many config options, but requires that at least a `header` and `dataIndex` be defined. The `header` config is simply the text to be displayed in the column header. The `dataIndex` config is the name of the data field to be used in that column. We defined these when we set up the data stores reader.

Here are some other useful config options for the column model:

Option	Description	Usage
renderer	Specifies how the data should be displayed	Can be used to format the data for this column into your preferred format. Any type of data can be transformed. We will learn about these in the next few pages.
hidden	Hides the column	Boolean value defining whether or not the column should be displayed.

Option	Description	Usage
width	Specifies the column width in pixels	The width of the column. Default is 100 pixels; overflowing content is hidden.
sortable	Specifies whether the column is sortable	Boolean value specifying whether or not the column can be sorted.

Using cell renderers

We can do some pretty neat things with cell rendering. There are few limitations to stop us from making the cell look like or contain whatever we want. All that needs to be done is to specify one of the built-in cell formatting functions provided by Ext JS, such as usMoney, or create our own cell renderer that returns a formatted value. Let's take a look at using the built-in cell renderers first. Then we can look at creating our own.

Formatting data using the built-in cell renderers

Many built-in formatting functions exist to take care of common rendering requirements. One that I use quite often is the date renderer:

```
renderer: Ext.util.Format.dateRenderer('m/d/Y')
```

Some other renderers include some commonly-required formatting, such as money, capitalize, and lowercase.

Here are some renderers that most people find useful:

Renderer	Description	Usage
dateRenderer	Formats a date for display	Can be used to format the data for this column into your preferred date format. Any type of date can be transformed.
uppercase lowercase	Upper and lower case conversion	Converts the string to completely upper or lower case text.
capitalize	Pretty text	Formats a text string to have correct capitalization.

Creating lookup data stores—custom cell rendering

We're going to start by taking the 'genre' column, which has a numeric value, and looking up that value in the data store we created in the *Forms* chapter to find the textual representation of our genre number.

First, we add a config option to the column model that tells it which function to use for rendering the cell's content.

```
{header: 'Genre', dataIndex: 'genre', renderer: genre_name}
```

Now let's create that function. The function call is passed the value of its cell as the first argument. The second argument is a cell object, while the third is the data store for that grid—neither of which we will use for this renderer. So let's just leave them.

```
function genre_name(val){
   return genres.queryBy(function(rec){
      if (rec.data.id == val){
        return true;
      }else{
        return false;
      }
   }).itemAt(0).data.genre;
}
```

The renderer function is passed the value of the current cell of data. This value can be tested, and actions can be performed on it—whatever value is returned by the function is rendered to the grid cell. A `queryBy` handler is used to filter the data from our store. It accepts a function that performs a comparison against each row of data, and returns `true` to use the row that matches.

Just for good measure, here is a compacted version of the same function. It's not as easy to read as the first version, but accomplishes the same result.

```
function genre_name(val){
   return genres.queryBy(function(rec){
      return rec.data.id == val;
   }).itemAt(0).data.genre;
}
```

Combining two columns

The lookup data store is a very useful renderer. However, it's more common for developers to combine two columns to form a single cell, for example, to perform a calculation on a pair of columns to figure out a total, percentage, remainder, and so on or to concatenate two or more text fields.

Let's just take the title of our movie, and append the tagline field underneath the title. The first step will be to hide the tagline column, since it will be displayed along with the title field – we don't need it shown in two places. Hiding the column can be done in our column model.

```
{header: 'Tagline', dataIndex: 'tagline', hidden: true}
```

The next step is our `renderer` function that will take care of combining the fields.

```
function title_tagline(val, x, store){
   return '<b>'+val+'</b><br>'+store.data.tagline;
}
```

I went ahead and bolded the title as well, to provide some contrast between the two pieces of data. As you can see, HTML tags work just fine within grid cells. The next step would be to add the renderer config to our column model, referencing the `title_tagline` function that we just created.

```
{header: 'Title', dataIndex: 'title', renderer: title_tagline}
```

This will make the `title` column look like this:

Generating HTML and graphics

Let's get some visuals by placing an image into each row, which will show the cover art for each movie title. As we just found out, we can use plain HTML within the cell. So all that needs to happen is to create a renderer that grabs our field containing the filename of the image and write that into an IMG tag as the SRC attribute.

```
function cover_image(val){
   return '<img src=images/'+val+'>';
}
```

With this fairly straightforward function, and setting a column renderer, we have an image in our grid:

```
{header: 'Cover', dataIndex: 'coverthumb', renderer:
                                    cover_image}
```

If you make all these renderer additions, the grid should now look like this:

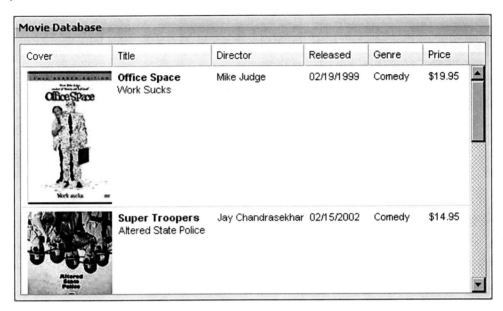

Built-in features

Ext has some very nice built-in features to help complete the spreadsheet-like interface. Columns have a built-in menus that provide access to sorting, displaying, and hiding columns.

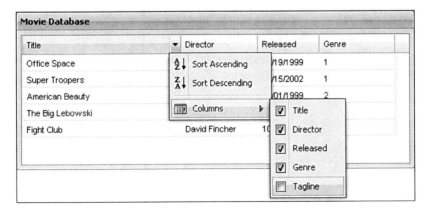

Client-side sorting

Unless specified as a server-side (remotely) sorted grid, an Ext grid is able to sort columns on the client side. Server-side sorting should be used if the data is paged, or if the data is in such a format that client-side sorting is not possible. Client-side sorting is quick, easy, and built-in:

```
{header: 'Tagline', dataIndex: 'tagline', sortable: true}
```

We can also accomplish this after the grid has been rendered:

```
var colmodel = grid.getColumnModel();
colmodel.getColumnById('tagline').sortable = true;
```

Our column model controls the display of columns and column headers. If we grab a reference to the column model by asking for it from the grid, then we can make changes to the columns after it has been rendered. We do this by using the getColumnById handler that the column model provides us with, and which accepts the column ID as the argument.

Hidden/visible columns

Using the column header menu, columns can be hidden or shown. This can also be changed at a config level, to have columns hidden by default, as shown below:

```
{header: "Tagline", dataIndex: 'tagline', hidden: true}
```

The more exciting way is to do this after the grid has been rendered, by using the functions Ext provides:

```
Var colmodel = grid.getColumnModel();
colmodel.setHidden(colmodel.getIndexById('tagline'),true);
```

Grabbing a reference to the column model again will allow us the make this change.

Column reordering

Dragging a column header will allow the user to reorder the entire column into a new order within the grid. All of this is enabled by default as part of the built-in functionality of the grid.

Any column can be dragged to a different order in the grid . This screenshot shows the **Price** column being moved to between the **Title** and **Director** columns.

We can disable this functionality entirely by setting a config option in the GridPanel:

```
enableColumnMove: false
```

This move event—and many other events in the grid—can be monitored and responded to. For example, we could monitor the movement of columns and pop up a message based on where the column was moved to:

```
grid.getColumnModel().on('columnmoved',
    function(cm,oindex,nindex) {
        var title = 'You Moved '+cm.getColumnHeader(nindex);
        if (oindex > nindex){
            var dirmsg = (oindex-nindex)+' Column(s) to the Left';
        }else{
            var dirmsg = (nindex-oindex)+' Column(s) to the Right';
        }
        Ext.Msg.alert(title,dirmsg);
    }
);
```

Many different events can be monitored using the same technique. The grid, data store, and column model each have their own set of events that can be monitored, all of which we will learn about in more detail later in this chapter.

Displaying server-side data in the grid

With Ext we can pull data into our web page in many ways. We started by pulling in local array data for use in the grid. Now we are going to pull the data in from an external file and a web server.

Loading the movie database from an XML file

We have this great movie database now, but each time I want to add a new movie I have to edit the JavaScript array. So why not store and pull our data from an XML file instead? This will be easier to update, and the XML file could even be generated from a database query or a custom script.

Lets take a look at an example of how our XML file would be laid out like:

```xml
<?xml version="1.0" encoding="UTF-8"?>
<dataset>
    <row>
        <id>1</id>
        <title>Office Space</title>
        <director>Mike Judge</director>
        <released>1999-02-19</released>
        <genre>1</genre>
        <tagline>Work Sucks</tagline>
        <coverthumb>84m.jpg</coverthumb>
        <price>19.95</price>
        <active>1</active>
    </row>
    <row>
        <id>3</id>
        <title>Super Troopers</title>
        <director>Jay Chandrasekhar</director>
        <released>2002-02-15</released>
        <genre>1</genre>
        <tagline>Altered State Police</tagline>
        <coverthumb>42m.jpg</coverthumb>
        <price>14.95</price>
        <active>1</active>
    </row>
   //...more rows of data removed for readability...//
</dataset>
```

The other change we would need to make is to alter the data reader, and set the location of our XML file so that the data store knows where to fetch the data from.

There are four basic changes that need to happen when moving from local to remote data:

- The `url` config option, specifying the location of our data, needs to be added — this will replace the `data` config option that we used to store local data

- The reader is changed from an `ArrayReader` to an `XmlReader` to deal with the differences involved in reading from an XML format instead of an array format

- The `XmlReader` is told which element contains a record or row of data by setting the `record` config option

- A call needs to be added to the `load` function that tells our data store to pull in the data from the file and parse it into memory

```
var store = new Ext.data.Store({
  url: 'movies.xml',
  reader: new Ext.data.XmlReader({
    record:'row',
    id:'id'
  }, [
    'id',
    'coverthumb',
    'title',
    'director',
    {name: 'released', type: 'date', dateFormat: 'Y-m-d'},
    'genre',
    'tagline',
    {name: 'price', type: 'float'},
    {name: 'available', type: 'bool'}
  ])
});

store.load();
```

Try making these changes and see if your grid still works — there should be no noticeable difference when changing data sources or formats.

Note that to make the change from local to remote data, and from an array format to an XML format, the only changes we needed to make were to the data store. Ext isolates these types of changes by using a common data store that is able to use an external reader to read many formats.

Loading the movie database from a JSON file

We're in the same boat as XML with this data format. Just changing the reader and setting up some config options will take care of everything.

The JSON rows of data are expected to be in the form of an array of objects — our `movies.json` file will therefore contain data like this:

```
{
   success:true,
   rows:[
      {
         "id":"1",
         "title":"Office Space",
         "director":"Mike Judge",
         "released":"1999-02-19",
         "genre":"1",
         "tagline":"Work Sucks",
         "coverthumb":"84m.jpg",
         "price":"19.95",
         "active":"1"
      },{
         "id":"3",
         "title":"Super Troopers",
         "director":"Jay Chandrasekhar",
         "released":"2002-02-15",
         "genre":"1",
         "tagline":"Altered State Police",
         "coverthumb":"42m.jpg",
         "price":"14.95",
         "active":"1"
      }
      //...more rows of data removed for readability...//
   ]
}
```

The main difference between setting up a JSON reader versus an XML reader, is that the JSON reader needs to know the name of the root element that holds our array objects (the data). So instead of specifying a `record` config, we need to specify a `root` config:

```
var store = new Ext.data.Store({
   url: 'movies.json',
   reader: new Ext.data.JsonReader({
      root:'rows',
```

```
      id:'id'
    }, [
      'id',
      'coverthumb',
      'title',
      'director',
      {name: 'released', type: 'date', dateFormat: 'Y-m-d'},
      'genre',
      'tagline',
      {name: 'price', type: 'float'},
      {name: 'available', type: 'bool'}
    ])
  });

  store.load();
```

This grid will have an identical look and the same functionality as the array and the XML grids that we created earlier.

 JSON is a format native to JavaScript, and will end up being the quickest format for the data store to read, which means that our grid will be displayed much faster.

Loading data from a database using PHP

The setup for our GridPanel stays the same. But instead of grabbing a static file with the JSON data, we can pull the data from a PHP script that will fetch the data from a database, and format it into JSON that Ext is able to read:

```php
<?php
// connect to database

$sql = "SELECT * FROM movies";
$arr = array();

If (!$rs = mysql_query($sql)) {

  Echo '{success:false}';

}else{

  while($obj = mysql_fetch_object($rs)){
    $arr[] = $obj;
  }

  Echo '{success:true,rows:'.json_encode($arr).'}';

}

?>
```

The PHP code used in these examples is meant to be the bare minimum needed to get the job done. In a production environment you would want to account for security against SQL injection attacks, other error checking, and probably user authentication—which the example code does not account for.

Programming the grid

Most of the code we have written so far concerns configuring the grid prior to it being displayed. Often, we will want the grid to do something in response to user input. One of the common interactions in a grid is to select or move the rows of data. Ext JS refers to this interaction and how it's handled as the "selection model". Let's see how to set one up.

Working with cell and row selections

Ext grids provide ways of monitoring user interaction with the grids rows, cells and columns with a thing called the selection model. The selection model is used to determine how rows, columns, or cells are selected, and how many items can be selected at a time. This allows us to create listeners for these selection events, along with giving us a way to query which rows have been selected.

Some of the selection models are:

- `CellSelectionModel`: This lets the user to select a single cell from the grid
- `RowSelectionModel`: This lets the user select an entire row from the grid
- `ColumnSelectionModel`: This lets the user select an entire column from the grid
- `CheckBoxSelectionModel`: This one uses a checkbox to enable row selections

Choosing a selection model is something that depends on your project's requirements. For our movie database, we will use a row selection model, which is the most commonly used type of selection model.

The selection model is defined in the GridPanel config by using the `sm` config option.

```
sm: new Ext.grid.RowSelectionModel({
   singleSelect: true
})
```

We will also pass the selection model a config that specifies single row selections only. This stops the user from selecting multiple rows at the same time.

Listening to our selection model for selections

Listeners for a grid can be included in many different places depending on the desired interaction. Earlier, we applied a listener to our column model because we wanted to listen for column activity.

Here, we will add a `listener` to the selection model because we want to know when a user has selected a `movie`.

```
sm: new Ext.grid.RowSelectionModel({
    singleSelect: true,
    listeners: {
        rowselect: {
            fn: function(sm,index,record) {
                Ext.Msg.alert('You Selected',record.data.title);
            }
        }
    }
})
```

Selecting a row now brings up an alert dialog. Let's take a look at what is happening here:

- A listener is set for the `rowselect` event. This waits for a row to be selected, and then executes our function when this happens.

- Our function is passed a selection model, the numeric index of the row selected (starting with zero for the first row), and the data record of the row that was selected.

- Using the data record that our function received, we can grab the `title` of the movie selected and put it into a message dialog.

Manipulating the grid (and its data) with code

Many functions are available for manipulating the grid and the data in the grid. These can be tied into other Ext widgets to create pretty much any functionality needed.

Altering the grid at the click of a button

Here, we are going to add a top toolbar, which will have a button that brings up a prompt allowing the movie title to be edited.

```
tbar: [{
  text: 'Change Title',
  handler: function(){
    var sm = grid.getSelectionModel();
    if (sm.hasSelection()){
      var sel = sm.getSelected();
      Ext.Msg.show({
      title: 'Change Title',
          prompt: true,
          buttons: Ext.MessageBox.OKCANCEL,
          value: sel.data.title,
          fn: function(btn,text){
            if (btn == 'ok'){
              sel.set('title', text);
            }
          }
        });
    }
  }
}]
```

All we are really doing here is changing the data store. The data in our database on the web server has stayed the same, and the web server has no idea whether anything has changed. It's up to us to communicate this change to the server via an AJAX request or via some other method you may prefer to use.

Let's take a quick look at what's happening here:

- `sm`: The selection model is retrieved from our grid
- `sel`: We used the selection model to retrieve the row that has been selected
- `sel.data`: Using the data object of the selected item, we can grab its data

This basic method can be used to create many fun user interactions. Our limitation is that there are only 24 hours in a day, and sleep catches up with everyone!

Advanced grid formatting

Because we are in the mood to create some user-grid interactions, let us add some more buttons that do fun stuff.

Here is a button we can add to the top toolbar to allow us to hide or show a column. We will also change the text of the button based on the visibility of the column:

```
{
  text: 'Hide Price',
  handler: function(btn){
    var cm = grid.getColumnModel();
    var pi = cm.getIndexById('price');
    if (cm.isHidden(pi)){
      cm.setHidden(pi,false);
      btn.setText('Hide Price');
    }else{
      cm.setHidden(pi,true);
      btn.setText('Show Price');
    }
    btn.render();
  }
}
```

We use a new handler here—getIndexById, which, as you can imagine, gets the column index, and will be a number from zero to one less than the total number of columns. This number is an indicator of where that column is in relation to the other columns. In our grid code, the column price is the fourth column, which means that the index is 3 because indexes start at zero.

Paging the grid

Paging requires that we have a server-side element (script) that will break up our data into pages. Let's start with that. PHP is well-suited to this, and the code is easy to understand and interpret into other languages. So we will use PHP for our example.

When a paging grid is paged, it will pass start and limit parameters to the server-side script. This is typical of what's used with a database to select a subset of records. Our script can read in these parameters and use them pretty much verbatim in the database query.

Here is a typical PHP script that would handle paging. We will name the file movies-paging.php.

```
<?php
// connect to database

$start = ($_REQUEST['start'] != '') ? $_REQUEST['start'] : 0;
$limit = ($_REQUEST['limit'] != '') ? $_REQUEST['limit'] : 3;

$count_sql = "SELECT * FROM movies";
$sql = $count_sql . " LIMIT ".$start.", ".$limit;
```

```
$arr = array();

If (!$rs = mysql_query($sql)) {

  Echo '{success:false}';

}else{

  $rs_count = mysql_query($count_sql);
  $results = mysql_num_rows($rs_count);

  while($obj = mysql_fetch_object($rs)){
    $arr[] = $obj;
  }

  Echo '{success:true,results:'.$results.',
        rows:'.json_encode($arr).'}';

}

?>
```

This PHP script will take care of the server-side part of paging. So now we just need to add a paging toolbar to the grid — it's really quite simple!

Earlier we had used a top toolbar to hold some buttons for messing with the grid. Now we are going to place a paging toolbar in the bottom toolbar slot (mostly because I think paging bars look dumb on the top).

The following code will add a paging toolbar:

```
bbar: new Ext.PagingToolbar({
   pageSize: 3,
   store: store
})
```

And of course we need to change the url of our data store to the url of the PHP server-side paging code. A totalProperty is also required when paging data. This is the variable name that holds the total record count of rows in the database.

```
var store = new Ext.data.Store({
   url: 'movies-paged.php',
   reader: new Ext.data.JsonReader({
     root:'rows',
     totalProperty: 'results',
     id:'id'
   }, [
     // data column model removed for readability
   ])
});
```

Grouping

Grouping grids are used to provide a visual indication that sets of rows are similar to each other. It also provides us with sorting that is confined to each group. So if we were to sort by the price column, the price would sort only within each group of items.

Grouping store

A special store is required, which is called...wait for it...the GroupingStore...tada!

The setup is similar to a standard store. We just need to provide a few more configuration options, such as the sortInfo and the groupField. No changes to the actual data are needed because Ext JS takes care of grouping on the client side.

```
var store = new Ext.data.GroupingStore({
   url: 'movies.json',
   sortInfo: {
     field: 'genre',
     direction: "ASC"
   },
   groupField: 'genre',
   reader: new Ext.data.JsonReader({
```

```
        root:'rows',
        id:'id'
    }, // reader column model here //)
});
```

We also need to add a `view` configuration to the grid panel. This view helps the grid to visually account for grouped data.

```
var grid = new Ext.grid.GridPanel({
    renderTo: document.body,
    frame:true,
    title: 'Movie Database',
    height:400,
    width:520,
    store: store,
    autoExpandColumn: 'title',
    columns: // column model goes here //,
    view: new Ext.grid.GroupingView()
});
```

After making the changes needed for a grouping grid, we end up with something that looks like this:

If you now expand the context menu for the column headings, you will see a new item in the menu for Group By This Field that will allow the user to change the grouping column on the fly.

Summary

We have learned a lot in this chapter about presenting data in a grid. With this new-found knowledge we will be able to organize massive amounts of data into easy to understand grids.

Specifically, we covered:

- Creating data stores and grids for display
- Reading XML and JSON data from a server and displaying it in a grid
- Rendering cells of data for a well formatted display
- Altering the grid based on user interaction

We also discussed the intricacies of each of these elements, such as reading data locally or from a server—along with paging. We also covered formatting cells using HTML, images, and even lookups into separate data stores.

Now that we've learned about standard grids, we're ready to take it to the next level, by making our grid cells editable just like a spreadsheet—which is the topic of the next chapter.

6
Editor Grids

In the previous chapter we learned how to display data in a structured grid that users could manipulate. But one major limitation was that there was no way for the users to edit the data in the grid in-line. Fortunately, Ext provides an `EditorGridPanel`, which allows the use of form field type editing in-line—and we will learn about it in this chapter. This works much like Excel, allowing the user to click on and edit cell data immediately.

In this chapter you will learn to:

- Present the user with editable grids that are connected to a data store
- Send edited data back to the server, enabling users to update server-side databases using the Ext JS editor grid
- Manipulate the grid from program code, and respond to events
- Use tricks for advanced formatting and creating more powerful editing grids

But first, let's see what you can do with an editable grid.

What can I do with an editable grid?

The `EditorGridPanel` is very similar to the forms we were working with earlier. In fact, an editor grid uses the exact same form fields as our form. By using form fields to perform the grid cell editing we get to take advantage of the same functionality that a form field provides. This includes restricting input, and validating values. Combine this with the power of an Ext `GridPanel`, and we are left with a widget that can do pretty much whatever we want.

Movie Database				
Add Movie Remove Movie				
Title	Director	Released	Genre	Tagline
Office Space	Mike Judge	02/19/1999	Comedy	Work Sucks
Super Troopers	Jay Chandrasekhar	02/15/2002	Comedy	Altered State Police
American Beauty	Sam Mendes	10/01/1999	Drama	... Look Closer
The Big Lebowski	Joel Coen	03/06/1998	Comedy	The "Dude"
Fight Club	David Fincher	10/15/1999	Action	How much can you

All of the fields in this table can be edited in-line using form fields such as the text field, date picker, and combo box.

Working with editable grids

The change from a non-editable grid to an editable grid is quite a simple process to start with. The complexity comes into the picture when we start to create a process to handle edits and send that data back to the server. But once you learn how to do it, that part can be quite simple as well.

Let's see how you would update the grid we created at the start of Chapter 5 to make the title, director, and tagline editable. Here's what the modified code will look like:

```
var title_edit = new Ext.form.TextField();

var director_edit = new Ext.form.TextField({vtype: 'name'});

var tagline_edit = new Ext.form.TextField({
    maxLength: 45
});

var grid = new Ext.grid.EditorGridPanel({
    renderTo: document.body,
    frame:true,
    title: 'Movie Database',
    height:200,
    width:520,
    clickstoEdit: 1,
    store: store,
    columns: [
        {header: "Title", dataIndex: 'title',
```

```
        editor: title_edit},
     {header: "Director", dataIndex: 'director',
        editor: director_edit},
     {header: "Released", dataIndex: 'released',
        renderer: Ext.util.Format.dateRenderer('m/d/Y')},
     {header: "Genre", dataIndex: 'genre',
        renderer: genre_name},
     {header: "Tagline", dataIndex: 'tagline',
        editor: tagline_edit}
   ]
});
```

There are four main things that we need to do to make our grid editable. These are:

- The grid definition changes from being Ext.grid.GridPanel to Ext.grid. EditorGridPanel
- We add the clicksToEdit option to the grid config—this option is not required, but defaults to two clicks
- Create a form field for each column that we would like to be editable
- Pass the form fields into our column model via the editor config

The editor can be any of the form field types that already exist in Ext JS, or a custom one of your own. We start by creating a text form field that will be used when editing the movie title.

```
var title_edit = new Ext.form.TextField();
```

Then add this form field to the column model as the editor:

```
{header: "Title", dataIndex: 'title', editor: title_edit}
```

The next step will be to change from using the GripPanel component to using the EditorGridPanel component, and to add the clicksToEdit config:

```
var grid = new Ext.grid.EditorGridPanel({
   renderTo: document.body,
   frame:true,
   title: 'Movie Database',
   height:200,
   width:520,
   clickstoEdit: 1,
   // removed extra code for clarity
})
```

Making these changes has turned our static grid into an editable grid. We can click on any of the fields that we set up editors for, and edit their values.

Movie Database				
Title	Director	Released	Genre	Tagline
Office Space The Musical	Mike Judge	02/19/1999	Comedy	Work Sucks
Super Troopers The Musical	Jay Chandrasekhar	02/15/2002	Comedy	Altered State Police
American Beauty The Musical	Sam Mendes	10/01/1999	Drama	... Look Closer
The Big Lebowski	Joel Coen	03/06/1998	Comedy	The "Dude"
Fight Club	David Fincher	10/15/1999	Action	How much can you kn

Here we see some changes have been made to the titles of a few of the movies, turning them into musicals. The editor gets activated with a single click on the cell of data; pressing *Enter*, the *Tab* key, or clicking away from the field will save the change, and pressing the *Escape* key will discard any changes. This works just like a form field, because, well… it is a form field.

The little red tick that appears in the upper-left corner indicates that the cell is 'dirty', which we will cover in just a moment. First, let's make some more complex editable cells.

Editing more cells of data

For our basic editor grid, we started by making a single column editable. To set up the editor, we created a reference to the form field:

```
var title_edit = new Ext.form.TextField();
```

Then we used that form field as the editor for the column:

```
{header: "Title", dataIndex: 'title', editor: title_edit}
```

That's the basic requirements for each field. Now let's expand upon this knowledge.

Edit more field types

Now we are going to create editors for the other fields. Different data types have different editor fields and can have options specific to that field's needs.

Any form field type can be used as an editor. These are some of the standard types:

- `TextField`
- `NumberField`
- `ComboBox`
- `DateField`
- `TimeField`
- `CheckBox`

These editors can be extended to achieve special types of editing if needed, but for now, lets start with editing the other fields we have in our grid – the release date and the genre.

Editing a date value

A `DateField` will work perfectly for editing the release date column in our grid. So let's use that. We first need to set up the editor field and specify which format to use:

```
release_edit = new Ext.form.DateField({
    format: 'm/d/Y'
});
```

Then we apply that editor to the column, along with the renderer that we used earlier:

```
{header: "Released", dataIndex: 'released', renderer:
    Ext.util.Format.dateRenderer('m/d/Y'), editor: release_edit}
```

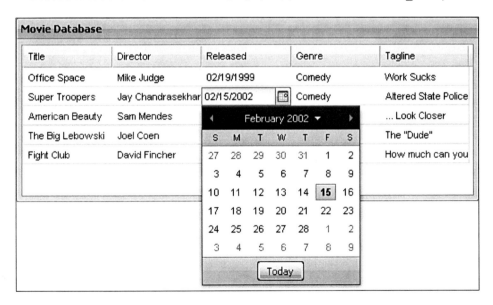

This column also takes advantage of a renderer, which will co-exist with the editor. Once the editor field is activated with a single click, the renderer passes the rendering of the field to the editor and vice versa. So when we are done with editing the field, the renderer will take over formatting the field again.

Edit with a ComboBox

Let's set up an editor for the genres column that will provide us with a list of the valid genres to select from — sounds like a perfect scenario for a combo box.

```
var genre_edit = new Ext.form.ComboBox({
  typeAhead: true,
  triggerAction: 'all',
  mode: 'local',
  store: genres,
  displayField:'genre',
  valueField: 'id'
});
```

Simply add this editor to the column model, like we did with the others:

```
{header: "Genre", dataIndex: 'genre', renderer: genre_name,
                                    editor: genre_edit}
```

Now we end up with an editable field that has a fixed selection of options.

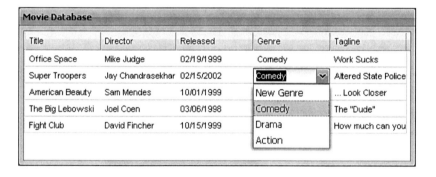

Reacting to a cell edit

Of course, we now need to figure out how to save all of this editing that we have been doing. I am sure the end user would not be so happy if we threw away all of their changes. We can start the process of saving the changes by listening for particular edit events, and then reacting to those with our own custom handler. Before we start coding this, we need to understand a bit more about how the editor grid works.

What's a dirty cell?

A field that has been edited and has had its value changed is considered to be 'dirty' until the data store is told otherwise. This 'dirty' value has been saved to a temporary data store that contains a version of our data with all of the changes made. Our original data store stays unchanged.

We can save the changes to the primary data store by calling the `commit` function, or we can discard the changes by calling the `reject` handler. These handlers can be called for the entire grid, for a single cell of data, or as the result of an event that is happening.

Let's imagine e is an edit event object. We could reject a record by calling the `reject` handler:

```
e.record.reject();
```

Alternatively, we can save our change by committing it:

```
e.record.commit();
```

Reacting when an edit occurs

To save our changes to the data store, we are going to listen for an edit being completed, which is accomplished by listening for the `afteredit` event.

The listener we need is added to the grid panel:

```
var grid = new Ext.grid.EditorGridPanel({
  // more config options clipped //,
  title: 'Movie Database',
  store: store,
  columns: // column model clipped //,
  listeners: {
    afteredit: function(e){
      if (e.field == 'director' && e.value == 'Mel Gibson'){
        Ext.Msg.alert('Error','Mel Gibson movies not allowed');
        e.record.reject();
      }else{
        e.record.commit();
      }
    }
  }
});
```

As with other listeners in Ext, the editor grid listeners are given a function to execute when the event occurs. The function for `afteredit` is called with a single argument: an object, which has a number of useful properties. We can use these properties to make a decision about the edit that just happened.

Property	Description
grid	The grid that the edit event happened in
record	The entire record that's being edited; other column values can be retrieved using this objects 'data' property
field	The name of the column that was edited
value	A string containing the new value of the cell
originalValue	A string containing the original value of the cell
row	The index of the row that was edited
column	The index of the column that was edited

For instance, if we wanted to make sure that movies directed by Mel Gibson never made it into our database, we could put a simple check in place for that scenario:

```
if (e.field == 'director' && e.value == 'Mel Gibson'){
   Ext.Msg.alert('Error','Mel Gibson movies not allowed');
   e.record.reject();
}else{
   e.record.commit();
}
```

First, we check to see that the director field is the one being edited. Next, we make sure the new value entered for this field is not equal to Mel Gibson. If either of these is false, we commit the record back to the data store. This means that once we call the commit handler, our primary data store is updated with the new value.

```
e.record.commit();
```

We also have the ability to reject the change—sending the changed value into the black hole of space, lost forever.

```
e.record.reject();
```

Of course, all we have done so far is update the data that is stored in the browsers' memory. I'm sure you're just dying to be able to update a web server. We will get to that soon enough.

Deleting and adding in the data store

We are going to create two buttons to allow us to alter the data store—to add or remove rows of data. Let us set up a top toolbar (tbar) in the grid to house these buttons:

```
var grid = new Ext.grid.EditorGridPanel({
   // more config options clipped //,
```

```
  tbar: [{
    text: 'Remove Movie'
  }]
}
```

Removing grid rows from the data store

Let's add a **remove** button to the toolbar in our grid. When this button is clicked, it will prompt the user with a dialog that displays the movie title. If the **Yes** button is clicked, then we can remove the selected row from the data store, otherwise we will do nothing.

```
{
  text: 'Remove Movie',
  icon: 'images/table_delete.png',
  cls: 'x-btn-text-icon',
  handler: function() {
    var sm = grid.getSelectionModel();
    var sel = sm.getSelected();
    if (sm.hasSelection()){
      Ext.Msg.show({
        title: 'Remove Movie',
        buttons: Ext.MessageBox.YESNOCANCEL,
        msg: 'Remove '+sel.data.title+'?',
        fn: function(btn){
          if (btn == 'yes'){
            grid.getStore().remove(sel);
          }
        }
      });
    };
  }
}
```

Let's take a look at what is happening here. We have defined some variables that we will use to determine if there were selections made, and what the selections were:

- `sm`: The selection model is retrieved from our grid
- `sel`: We used the selection model to retrieve the row that has been selected
- `grid.getStore().remove(sel)`: Passing the `data stores remove` function, a row will remove that row from the store and update the grid

It's as simple as that. The local data store that resides in the browser's memory has been updated. But what good is deleting if you can't add anything—just be patient, grasshopper!

Adding a row to the grid

To add a row we have a bit of a twist. We need to have a definition of what the data looks like in order to be able to create a new row—just like it was created for the data reader.

```
var ds_model = Ext.data.Record.create([
    'id',
    'coverthumb',
    'title',
    'director',
    {name: 'released', type: 'date', dateFormat: 'Y-m-d'},
    'genre',
    'tagline',
    {name: 'price', type: 'float'},
    {name: 'available', type: 'bool'}
]);
```

Once we have this definition of the data, we can insert a new row fairly easily. A button can be added to the same top toolbar that will be used to insert the row:

```
{
    text: 'Add Movie',
    icon: 'images/table_add.png',
    cls: 'x-btn-text-icon',
    handler: function() {
        grid.getStore().insert(
            0,
            new ds_model({
                title:'New Movie',
                director:'',
                genre:0,
                tagline:''
```

```
            })
        );
        grid.startEditing(0,0);
    }
}
```

The first argument to the `insert` function is the point at which to insert the record. I have chosen zero, so the record will be inserted at the very top. If we wanted to insert the row at the end we could simply retrieve the row count for our data store. Because the row index starts at zero, and the count at one, incrementing the count is not necessary because the row count will always be one greater than the last item in the index.

```
grid.getStore().insert(
    grid.getStore().getCount(),
    new ds_model({
        title:'New Movie',
        director:'',
        genre:0,
        tagline:''
    })
);
grid.startEditing(grid.getStore().getCount()-1,0);
```

Movie Database

Add Movie (First)	Add Movie (Last)	Remove Movie		
Title	Director	Released	Genre	Tagline
Office Space	Mike Judge	02/19/1999	Comedy	Work Sucks
Super Troopers	Jay Chandrasekhar	02/15/2002	Comedy	Altered State Police
American Beauty	Sam Mendes	10/01/1999	Drama	... Look Closer
The Big Lebowski	Joel Coen	03/06/1998	Comedy	The "Dude"
Fight Club	David Fincher	10/15/1999	Action	How much can you
New Movie|			New Genre	

Now we are back to inserting a row. The second argument is the new record definition, which can be passed with some default values.

```
new ds_model({
    title:'New Movie',
    director:'',
    genre:0,
    tagline:''
})
```

After inserting the new row, we call a function that will activate a cells editor. This function just needs a row and column index number to activate the editor for that cell.

```
grid.startEditing(0,0);
```

This gives our user the ability to start typing the movie title directly after clicking the **Add Movie** button.

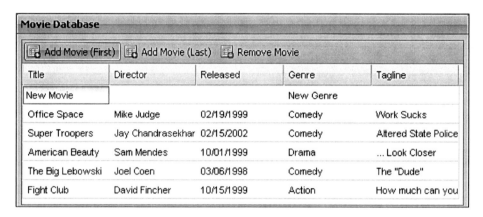

Saving edited data to the server

Everything we have done so far is related to updating the local data store residing in the memory of the web browser. More often that not, we will want to save our data back to the server to update a database, file system, or something along those lines.

This section will cover some of the more common requirements of grids used in web applications to update server-side information.

- Updating a record
- Creating a new record
- Deleting a record

Sending updates back to the server

Earlier, we had set up a listener for the `afteredit` event. We will be using this `afteredit` event to send changes back to the server on a cell-by-cell basis.

To update the database with cell-by-cell changes, we need to know three things:

- `field`: What field has changed
- `Value`: What the new value of the field is
- `record.id`: Which row from the database the field belongs to

This gives us enough information to be able to make a distinct update to a database. We communicate with the server (using AJAX) by calling the connection request method.

```
listeners: {
    afteredit: function(e){
        var conn = new Ext.data.Connection();
        conn.request({
            url: 'movie-update.php',
                params: {
                action: 'update',
                id: e.record.id,
                field: e.field,
                value: e.value
            },
            success: function(resp,opt) {
                e.commit();
            },
                failure: function(resp,opt) {
                e.reject();
            }
        });
    }
}
```

This will send a request to the `movie-update.php` script with four parameters in the form of post headers. The `params` that we pass as a config object into the data connection are all sent through the headers to our script on the server side.

The `movie-update.php` script should be coded to recognize the 'update' action and then read in the `id`, `field`, and `value` data and then proceed to update the file system or database, or whatever else we need to make it happen.

This is what's available to us when using the `afteredit` event:

Option	Description
grid	Reference to the current grid
record	Object with data from the row being edited
field	Name of the field being edited
value	New value entered into the field
originalValue	Original value of the field
row	Index of the row being edited — this will help in finding it again
column	Index of the column being edited

Deleting data from the server

When we want to delete data from the server, we can handle it in very much the same way as an update — by making a call to a script on the server, and telling it what we want done.

For the delete trigger, we will use another button in the grids toolbar.

```
{
  text: 'Remove Movie',
  icon: 'images/table_delete.png',
  cls: 'x-btn-text-icon',
  handler: function() {
    var sm = grid.getSelectionModel();
    var sel = sm.getSelected();
    if (sm.hasSelection()){
      Ext.Msg.show({
          title: 'Remove Movie',
          buttons: Ext.MessageBox.YESNOCANCEL,
          msg: 'Remove '+sel.data.title+'?',
          fn: function(btn){
            if (btn == 'yes'){
              var conn = new Ext.data.Connection();
              conn.request({
                url: 'movie-update.php',
                params: {
                    action: 'delete',
                    id: e.record.id
                },
                success: function(resp,opt) {
                    grid.getStore().remove(sel);
```

```
                },
                failure: function(resp,opt) {
                    Ext.Msg.alert('Error',
                    'Unable to delete movie');
                }
            });
        }
    }
    });
    };
    }
}
```

Just as with edit, we are going to make a request to the server to have the row deleted. The `movie-update.php` script would see that the action is `delete` and execute the appropriate action.

Saving new rows to the server

Here we are going to add another button that will add a new row. It sends the request to the server with the appropriate parameters and reads the `insert id` from the server's response. Using this `insert id`, we are able to add the row to our data store with the unique identifier generated on the server side for that row.

```
{
    text: 'Add Movie',
    icon: 'images/table_add.png',
    cls: 'x-btn-text-icon',
    handler: function() {
        var conn = new Ext.data.Connection();
        conn.request({
            url: 'movies-update.php',
            params: {
                action: 'insert',
                title:'New Movie'
            },
            success: function(resp,opt) {
                var insert_id = Ext.util.JSON.decode(
                    resp.responseText
                ).insert_id;
                grid.getStore().insert(0,
                    new ds_model({
                        id:insert_id,
                        title:'New Movie',
                        director:'',
                        genre:0,
                        tagline:''
```

```
            })
        );
        grid.startEditing(0,0);
    },
    failure: function(resp,opt) {
        Ext.Msg.alert('Error','Unable to add movie');
    }
    });
    }
}
```

Much like editing and deleting, we are going to send a request to the server to have a new row inserted. This time, we are actually going to take a look at the response to get the `insert id` (the unique identifier for that row) to pass back to our grid so that when we start editing that row, it will be easy to save our changes.

```
success: function(resp,opt) {
    var insert_id = Ext.util.JSON.decode(
        resp.responseText
    ).insert_id;
    grid.getStore().insert(0,
        new ds_model({
            id:insert_id,
            title:'New Movie',
            director:'',
            genre:0,
            tagline:''
        })
    );
    grid.startEditing(0,0);
}
```

Our success handler function has a couple of arguments, the first is the response object, which contains the response text from our `movie-update.php` script. Because that response is in a JSON format, we're going to decode it into a usable object and grab the `insert id` value.

```
var insert_id = Ext.util.JSON.decode(
    resp.responseText
).insert_id;
```

When we insert this row into our data store, we can use the `insert id` that was retrieved.

Summary

The Ext JS grid functionality is one of the most advanced portions of the framework. With the backing of the Ext.data package, the grid can pull information from a remote server in an integrated manner—this support is built into the grid class. Thanks to the array of configuration options available, we can present this data easily in a variety of forms, and set it up for manipulation by our users.

In this chapter, we've seen how the data support provided by the grid offers an approach to data manipulating that will be familiar to many developers. The amend-and commit approach allows fine-grained control over the data that is sent to the server when used with a validation policy, along with the ability to reject changes. As well as amending the starting data, we've seen how the grid provides functionality to add and remove rows of data.

We've also shown how standard Ext JS form fields such as the ComboBox can be integrated to provide a user interface on top of this functionality. With such strong support for data entry, the grid package provides a very powerful tool for application builders.

In the next chapter, we'll demonstrate how components such as the grid can be integrated with other parts of an application screen by using the extensive layout functionality provided by the Ext JS framework.

Layouts

A layout turns your forms, grids, and other widgets into a true web application. The most widely-used layout styles can be found in operating systems such as Microsoft's Windows, which uses border layouts, resizable regions, accordions, tabs, and just about everything else you can think of.

To keep looks consistent between browsers, and to provide common user interface features, Ext JS has a powerful layout management system. The sections are manageable, and can be moved or hidden, and they can appear at the click of a button, right when and where you need them to.

In this chapter you will learn to:

- Lay out an application style screen
- Create tabbed sections
- Manage Ext widgets within a layout
- Learn advanced and nested layouts

What are layouts, regions, and viewports?

Ext uses **Panels**, which are the basis of most layouts. We have used some of these, such as FormPanel and GridPanel, already. A **viewport** is a special panel-like component that encloses the entire layout, fitting it into the whole visible area of our browser. For our first example, we are going to use a viewport with a border layout that will encapsulate many panels.

A viewport has regions that are laid out in the same way as a compass, with **North**, **South**, **East** and **West** regions — the **Center** region represents what's left over in the middle. These directions tell the panels where to align themselves within the viewport and, if you use them, where the resizable borders are to be placed:

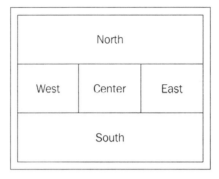

The example we're creating will look like the following image, and combines many of the previous examples we have created:

This layout is what's called a 'border' layout, which means that each region is separated by a somewhat three dimensional border bar that can be dragged to resize the regions. This example contains four panel regions:

- **North**: The toolbar
- **West**: A form
- **Center**: Grid in a tab panel
- **East**: A plain panel containing text

Note that there is no 'South' panel in this example – not every region needs to be used in every layout.

Our first layout

Before we create our layout that uses only four regions let's go ahead and create a layout that utilizes all the regions, and then remove the South panel. We are going to create all of the regions as 'panels', which can be thought of as blank canvases to which we will add text, HTML, images, or even Ext JS widgets.

```
var viewport = new Ext.Viewport({
  layout: 'border',
  renderTo: Ext.getBody(),
  items: [{
    region: 'north',
    xtype: 'panel',
    html: 'North'
  },{
    region: 'west',
    xtype: 'panel',
    split: true,
    width: 200,
    html: 'West'
  },{
    region: 'center',
    xtype: 'panel',
    html: 'Center'
  },{
    region: 'east',
    xtype: 'panel',
    split: true,
    width: 200,
    html: 'East'
  },{
    region: 'south',
    xtype: 'panel',
    html: 'South'
  }]
});
```

Each region is defined as one of the four compass directions—East, West, North, and South. The remainder in the middle is called the center region, which will expand to fill all of the remaining space. Just to take up some blank space in each region and to give a visual indicator as to where the panels are, we defined an 'HTML' config that has just text. (This could also contain complex HTML if needed, but there are better ways to set the contents of panels which we will learn about soon.)

 Ext JS provides an easy, cross-browser compatible, speedy way to get a reference to the body element, by using `Ext.getBody()`.

If everything works out ok, you should see a browser that looks like this:

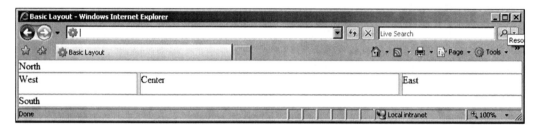

Now we have a layout with all five regions defined. These regions can have other text widgets added into them, seamlessly, by using the `xtype` config. Alternatively they can be divided up separately into more nested regions—for instance, the center could be split horizontally to have its own South section.

 A 'Center' region must always be defined. If one is not defined, the layout will produce errors and appear as a jumbled set of boxes in the browser.

Splitting the regions

The dividers are set up for each panel by setting the `split` flag—the positioning of the dividers is determined automatically based on the region the panel is in.

```
split: true
```

For this page, we have set the West and East regions as 'split' regions. This, by default, makes the border into a resizing element for the user to change the size of that panel.

I want options

Typically, when a split is used, it's combined with a few other options that make the section more useful, such as `width`, `minSize`, and `collapseMode`.

Here are some of the more commonly-used options:

Option	Value	Description
split	true/false	Boolean value that places a resizable bar between the sections
collapsible	true/false	Boolean value that adds a button to the title bar which lets the user collapse the region with a single click
collapseMode	Only option is mini mode, or undefined for normal mode	When set to 'mini', this adds a smaller collapse button that's located on the divider bar, in addition to the larger collapse button on title bar; the panel also collapses into a smaller space
title	String	Title string placed in the title bar
bodyStyle	CSS	CSS styles applied to the body element of the panel.
minSize	Pixels, ie: 200	The smallest size that the user can drag this panel to
maxSize	Pixels, ie: 250	The largest size that the user can drag this panel to
margins	In pixels: top, right, bottom, left, i.e.,: 3 0 3 3	Can be used to space the panel away from the edges or away from other panels; spacing is applied outside of the body of the panel
cmargins	In pixels: top, right, bottom, left, i.e.,: 3 0 3 3	Same idea as margins, but applies only when the panel is collapsed

Let's add a couple of these options to our `west` panel:

```
{
    region: 'west',
    xtype: 'panel',
    split: true,
    collapsible: true,
    collapseMode: 'mini',
    title: 'Some Info',
    bodyStyle:'padding:5px;',
    width: 200,
    minSize: 200,
    html: 'West'
}
```

Adding these config options to our `west` panel would give us the following look:

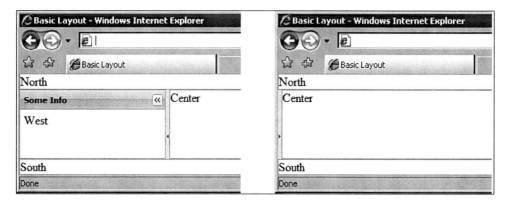

Normal/Expanded   Collapsed

 Expanding and collapsing a panel that does not have a width specified can produce rendering problems. Therefore, it's best to specify a width for panels — of course this is not needed for the center, as this panel automatically fills the remaining space.

Tab panels

With Ext JS, tab panels are also referred to as a "card" layout because they work much like a deck of cards where each card is layered directly above or below the others and can be moved to the top of the deck, to be visible. We also get pretty much the same functionality in our tab panel as a regular panel, including a title, toolbars, and all the other usual suspects (excluding tools).

Adding a tab panel

If the Ext JS component is a panel type component, for instance `GridPanel` and `FormPanel`, then we can add it directly to the layout using its `xtype`. Let's start by creating a `tabPanel`:

```
{
    region: 'center',
    xtype: 'tabpanel',
    items: [{
        title: 'Movie Grid',
        html: 'Center'
    }]
}
```

The `items` config is an array of objects that defines each of the tabs contained in this `tabpanel`. The `title` is the only option that's actually needed to give us a tab, and right now `html` is just being used as a placeholder, to give our empty tab some content.

We will also need to add an `activeTab` config that is set to zero to our tab panel. This is the index of the tabs in the panel left to right starting with zero and counting up for each tab. This tells the tab panel at position zero to make itself active by default, otherwise, we would have no tabs displayed, resulting in a blank section until the user clicked a tab.

```
{
    region: 'center',
    xtype: 'tabpanel',
    activeTab: 0,
    items: [{
        title: 'Movie Grid',
        html: 'Center'
    }]
}
```

If we take a look at this in a browser, we should see a tab panel in the center section of our layout.

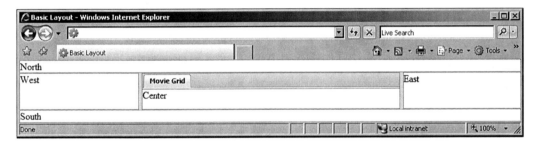

Adding more tabs is as easy as adding more items into the `items` array. Each tab item is basically its own panel, which is shown or hidden, based on the tab title that has been clicked on the tab panel.

```
{
    region: 'center',
    xtype: 'tabpanel',
    activeTab: 0,
    items: [{
        title: 'Movie Grid',
```

```
      html: 'Center'
   },{
      title: 'Movie Descriptions',
      html: 'Movie Info'
   }]
}
```

Both the `Movie Grid` and `Movie Descriptions` tabs are just plain panels right now. So let's add some more configuration options and widgets to them.

Widgets everywhere

Earlier, I mentioned that any type of panel widget could be added directly to a layout, just as we had done with the tabs. Let's explore this by adding another widget to our layout—the grid.

Adding a grid into the tabpanel

As we now have these tabs as part of our layout, let's start by adding a grid panel to one of the tabs. Adding the `xtype` config option to the grid config code you created in Chapter 5, will produce a grid that fills one entire tab:

```
{
   region: 'center',
   xtype: 'tabpanel',
   activeTab: 0,
   items: [{
      title: 'Movie Grid',
      xtype: 'gridpanel',
      store: store,
      autoExpandColumn: 'title',
      columns: // add column model //,
      view: // add grid view spec //
   },{
      title: 'Movie Descriptions',
      html: 'Movie Info'
   }]
}
```

> `xtypes` offer a quick way to instantiate a new component with minimal typing. This is sometimes referred to as 'lazy rendering' because the components sit around waiting to be displayed before they actually execute any code. This method can help conserve memory in your web application.

As we are adding this grid to a tab—which is essentially just a panel—there are some things that we no longer need (like the `renderTo` option, width, height, and a frame). The size, title, and border for the grid are now handled by our tab panel.

Now we should have a layout that looks like this:

Accordions

The **accordion** is a very useful layout that works somewhat like a tab panel, where we have multiple sections occupying the same space, with only one showing at a time. This type of layout is commonly used when we're lacking the horizontal space needed for a tab panel, but instead have more vertical space available. When one of the accordion panels is expanded, the others will collapse. Expanding and collapsing the panels can be done either by clicking the panel's title bar or by clicking the plus/minus icons along the rightmost side of the panel.

Nesting an accordion layout in a tab

We can nest a layout within a panel to create a more complex layout. For this example, we will nest an accordion panel within one of our tabs.

By setting the layout to 'accordion' and adding three items, we will end up with three panels in our accordion.

```
{
  title: 'Movie Descriptions',
  layout: 'accordion',
  items: [{
    title: 'Office Space',
    autoLoad: 'html/1.txt'
  },{
    title: 'Super Troopers',
    autoLoad: 'html/3.txt'
  },{
    title: 'American Beauty',
    autoLoad: 'html/4.txt'
  }]
}
```

This gives us a tab that has within it three accordion panels, which will load text files into their body sections. Note that the config on this is very similar to a tab panel — the consistency between widgets in Ext JS makes it easy to set up different types of widgets without having to look at the API reference for each one.

Now we should have a layout that looks like, this when we switch to the **Movie Descriptions** tab:

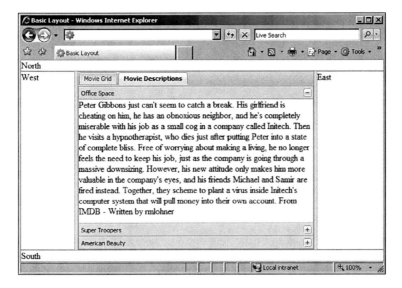

Each panel now has a description of the movie, which was loaded from a text file on the web server. Let's take a closer look at that.

```
autoLoad: 'html/1.txt'
```

This loads the file from the URL specified into the body section of the panel. The file loaded can contain any type of HTML, which will show up just as if it were in a browser by itself. As this is done via AJAX, if you're running the examples from your file system instead of a local web server they will not load.

 Note that the JavaScript contained within the loaded content will not be executed and any HTML will be ignored.

Placing a toolbar in your layout

Next, let's add a toolbar to the North section of our layout. We can use the toolbar for menus, buttons, and a couple of form fields, or maybe just a blinking marquee with our name scrolling across it. We can change these easily later.

Let's take our toolbar items we used in the example code in Chapter 4 — *Buttons, Menus, and Toolbar* — and add them to this toolbar. We should also copy over the `Movies` class we created in the toolbar chapter, if we want the buttons to work.

By changing the `xtype` to `toolbar` and copying the array of toolbar items over, we will end up with a snazzy menu bar at the top of the screen.

```
{
  region: "north",
  xtype: 'toolbar',
  items: [{
    xtype: 'tbspacer'
  },{
    xtype: 'tbbutton',
    text: 'Button',
    handler: function(btn){
      btn.disable();
    }
  },{
    xtype: 'tbfill'
  },
  // more toolbar items here //]
}
```

This gives us a toolbar that fits nicely into the top of our layout—like an application toolbar or menu bar that you would typically see in desktop applications.

You should end up with something that looks like this:

Even though this toolbar does not contain a blinking marquee with my name in it, it will be quite useful for our application. All of the navigation for your application can be placed in it, which might trigger new tabs to be added to the center region, or be used used to search for movie titles, or whatever else that is needed.

A form to add new movies

A form panel will fit nicely into that currently-empty West region, and since it's a panel type component, it can be added directly to our layout. Let's add the movie form that we used in the forms chapter to the West section. But instead of instantiating it, let's use the `xtype` config to perform lazy instantiation for the entire form panel.

```
{
    region: 'west',
    xtype: 'form',
    items: // form fields //
    buttons: // form panel buttons //
}
```

The `items` config holds all of our form fields:

```
items: [{
    xtype: 'textfield',
    fieldLabel: 'Director',
    name: 'director',
    anchor: '100%',
    vtype: 'name'
},{
    xtype: 'datefield',
    fieldLabel: 'Released',
    name: 'released',
    disabledDays: [1,2,3,4,5]
},{
    xtype: 'radio',
    fieldLabel: 'Filmed In',
    name: 'filmed_in',
    boxLabel: 'Color'
}, // more fields go here //]
```

 Many xtypes exist, and the names are not exactly what you would guess—for a full reference, look under the **Component** section in the API reference.

After adding the form items and buttons, our layout should look like this:

Tricks and advanced layouts

Some of the more complex web applications will need to do things that are not as simple as setting a few configuration values, for example nesting one layout within another layout, or adding icons to your tabs. But with Ext JS these kinds of things are made easy.

Nested layouts

When we nest one layout within another layouts region, we will occupy that entire region's body so it cannot be used any more. Instead, the nested layout regions are used for content.

For example, if we wanted the center region split into two horizontal regions, we could add a nested layout with center and North regions. This is typical of an application where you have a data panel (Center) to list email messages and a reader panel (South) to preview the entire email when it's selected in the list in the North panel.

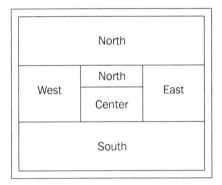

A couple of things are needed for a nested layout—the layout type must be set, and in this case, we are turning off the border so we don't get a doubled-up border, as the container has its own border. Each of the items represents one of our nested regions:

```
{
    title: 'Nested Layout',
    layout: 'border',
    border: false,
    items: [{
      region: 'north',
      height: 100,
      split: true,
      html: 'Nested North'
    },{
      region: 'center',
      html: 'Nested Center'
    }]
}
```

This produces a layout that would look like this:

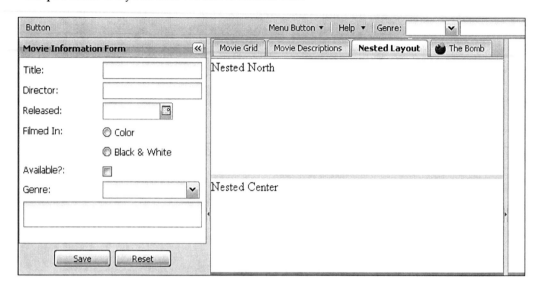

 Percentages are not allowed in border type layouts. There must always be a 'center' region that fills the remaining space not taken up by the other regions', which are all defined in pixel sizes.

Icons in tabs

Don't you just love it when you can have a visual indicator to show which tab does what? That's where icons come into play. The icons on tabs work much like the icons we added to the buttons in an earlier chapter. All we need to do is create a style with the icon and add that style to our tabs configuration.

The style would look like this:

```
bomb {
    background-image:url(images/bomb.png) !important;
}
```

The tab config will need to have the iconCls property set to the style we've just created:

```
{
    title: 'The Bomb',
    iconCls: 'bomb',
    html: 'Boom!'
}
```

Don't click on that tab too quickly, it might go off!

Programmatically manipulating a layout

We have the ability to modify just about anything, after the layout has been rendered. For example, we can, like add new tabs, hide, and display panels and change the content of any of the panels. Let's experiment with a couple of different things we can do.

Now you see me, now you don't

Expanding and collapsing sections of your layout programmatically is a requirement in most applications. So it should be no surprise by now that this can be done in Ext JS as well.

The first thing we need to do is give our panel and viewport ids, so that we can locate them. We can do this by setting the id config option in our layout and panel configurations:

```
var viewport = new Ext.Viewport({
  layout: 'border',
  id: 'movieview',
  renderTo: document.body,
  items: [{
    // extra code removed //
    region: 'east',
    xtype: 'panel',
    id: 'moreinfo'
    // extra code removed //
  }
});
```

Now that both the layout and the panel have been given unique ids, we can use the ids to interact with these components by using getCmp.

```
var moreinfo = Ext.getCmp('movieview').findById('moreinfo');

if (!moreinfo.isVisible()){
  moreinfo.expand();
}
```

This little bit of code will check to see if the panel is visible (expanded), and if its not will expand it.

Give me another tab

Adding a tab is as easy as creating a single tab. We first need to locate the tab panel within our layout. Luckily we just need to add an `id` config to our tab panel so that we can easily locate it.

```
{
    region: 'center',
    xtype: 'tabpanel',
    id: ' movietabs',
    activeTab: 0,
    items: [{
        title: 'Movie Grid',
        // extra code removed //
    },{
        title: 'Movie Descriptions',
        html: 'Movie Info'
    }]
}
```

Then we can call the add handler for our tab panel and pass a basic config into it:

```
Ext.getCmp('movieview').findById('movietabs').add({
  title: 'Office Space',
  html: 'Movie Info'
});
```

This will add a tab that is titled `Office Space` to the `movietabs` tab panel.

The `add` function is a way to add new items to a layout or a widget. Typically, anything that you can pass into the `items` config of a component can also be passed to the `add` handler.

Summary

In this chapter, we have been able to use many of the components outlined in the previous chapters, within a layout. The layout really takes the various components of Ext JS and uses them to create a true web application. We have seen that the layout can integrate the different components of Ext JS into one fluid application. We also learned how to change the state of panels, create nested layouts, and load content dynamically.

8
Ext JS Does Grow on Trees

Hierarchical data is something that most developers are intimately familiar with. The root-branch-leaf structure is the underlying feature for many user interfaces, from the file and folder representations in Windows Explorer to the classic family tree showing children, parents, and grandparents. The `Ext.tree` package enables developers to bring these data structures to the user with only a few lines of code, and provides for a range of advanced cases with a number of simple configuration options.

Although the default Ext JS icon set shows tree nodes as files and folders, it is not restricted to the file system concept. The icons and text of the items, or nodes in your tree, can be changed based on the dynamic or static data used to populate it—and without requiring custom code. How about a security screen showing permission groups containing a number of users, with icons showing a photo of each user, or a gallery showing groups of photos, or image previews in the icons? Ext JS's tree classes puts all of these scenarios within your grasp.

Planting for the future

Ultimately, the Ext JS tree doesn't care about the data you're displaying, because it's flexible enough to deal with any scenario that you can come up with. Data can be instructed to load up-front, or in logical bursts, which can become a critical feature when you've got a lot of information to load. You can edit data directly in the tree, changing labels and item positions, or you can modify the appearance of the overall tree or of each individual node, all of which will contribute to a customized end-user experience.

The Ext JS tree is built on top of the Component model, which underlies the whole Ext JS framework. This means that developers receive the benefits of working with the familiar Component system, that users get a consistent and integrated interface experience, and that you can be sure your tree will work seamlessly with the rest of your application.

From tiny seeds...

In this chapter, we'll see how you can build a tree from first principles with a minimal of code. We'll also discuss the unique data structure that is used to populate the tree, and the way in which clever use of that data can let you harness important configuration options. The Ext JS tree natively supports advanced features such as sorting, and drag-and-drop, so we'll be discussing those as well. But if you need a truly bespoke tree, we'll also explore the way in which configuration options, methods, and events can be overridden or augmented to provide it.

The tree itself is created via the `Ext.tree.TreePanel` class, which in turn contains many `Ext.tree.TreeNodes` classes. These two classes are the core of the Ext JS tree support, and as such will be the main topics of discussion throughout this chapter. However there are a number of other relevant classes that we'll also cover. Here's the full list from the `Ext.tree` package:

AsyncTreeNode	Allows `TreeNode` children to be loaded asynchronously
DefaultSelectionModel	Standard single-select for the `TreePanel`
MultiSelectionModel	Provides support for multiple node selection
RootTreeNodeUI	Specialized `TreeNode` for the root of `TreePanel`
TreeDragZone	Provides support for `TreeNode` dragging
TreeDropZone	Provides support for `TreeNode` dropping
TreeEditor	Allows node labels to be edited
TreeFilter	Filter support for `TreePanel` child nodes
TreeLoader	Populates a `TreePanel` from a specified URL
TreeNode	The main class representing a node within a `TreePanel`
TreeNodeUI	Provides the underlying interface for the `TreeNode`
TreePanel	A tree-like representation of data — the main tree class
TreeSorter	Supports sorting of nodes within a `TreePanel`

Ouch! Fortunately, you don't have to use all of them all at once. `TreeNode` and `TreePanel` provide the basics, and the rest of the classes are bolted on to provide extra functionality. We'll cover each of them in turn, discussing how they're used, and showing a few practical examples along the way.

Our first sapling

By now, you're probably thinking of the various possibilities for the Ext JS tree, and want to get your hands dirty. Despite the fact that the `Ext.tree` classes are some of the most feature-rich available in the framework, you can still get everything up and running with only a few lines of code.

In the examples that follow, we'll assume that you have a blank-slate HTML page ready and waiting, with all of the Ext JS dependencies included. Most of the code we will use builds on what came before, to make sure that we're only working with bite-sized pieces. Bear this in mind when you look at them in isolation.

It is best practice to put the JavaScript in a separate file and wrap it in an Ext. onReady call. However, you can also do it according to your individual coding style.

Preparing the ground

First, we need to create a containing `<div>` element on our HTML page. We will be rendering our TreePanel into this container. So we have to set it to the size we want our tree to be:

```
<div id="treecontainer" style="height:300px; width:200px;"></div>
```

The JavaScript for the tree can be broken down into three parts. Firstly, we need to specify the manner in which it's going to be populated. The Ext.tree. TreeLoader class provides this functionality, and here we're going to use it in the simplest manner:

```
var treeLoader = new Ext.tree.TreeLoader({
    dataUrl:'http://localhost/samplejson.php'
});
```

The dataUrl configuration parameter specifies the location of the script that is going to supply the JavaScript Object Notation (JSON) used to populate our tree. I'm not going to go into the details of the structure of JSON now; let's save that for later.

Each tree requires a root node, which acts as a great-granddaddy for all of its descendants. To create that root node, we use the Ext.tree.AsyncTreeNode class:

```
var rootNode = new Ext.tree.AsyncTreeNode({
    text: 'Root'
});
```

The reason we're using AsyncTreeNode, rather than the basic TreeNode that is also available, is because we're fetching our nodes from the server and are expecting child nodes to be populated branch-by-branch rather than all at once. This is the most typical scenario for a tree.

 AsyncTreeNode uses AJAX on-the-fly to ensure your users aren't waiting too long for your data to load and for the first nodes to be rendered.

Finally, we create the tree itself, using the `Ext.tree.TreePanel` class:

```
var tree = new Ext.tree.TreePanel({
    renderTo:'treecontainer',
    loader: treeLoader,
    root: rootNode
});
```

This is just a matter of passing the root node and the `TreeLoader` in as configuration options, as well as using the `renderTo` config to specify that we'd like the `TreePanel` rendered into our `treeContainer` element.

Again, you should remember that you need to wrap all of this code in a call to `Ext.onReady`, to make sure that the DOM is available when our code runs.

A tree can't grow without data

We've seen that it only takes eleven lines of code to create a tree interface using Ext JS. You can see an example of the finished product here:

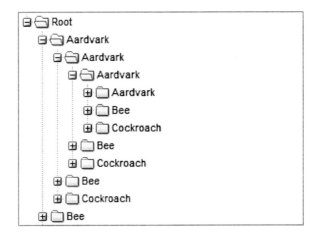

I guess it doesn't look like much, but we've got quite a bit of functionality for our eleven lines of code. We've got a consistent and attractive look and feel, with asynchronous remote loading of child nodes. To be fair, it's not as simple as that, because we skimmed over a crucial part of building an Ext JS tree—the data.

JSON

The standard `TreeLoader` supports JSON in a specific format—an array of node definitions. Here's a cut-down example:

```
[
    { id: '1', text: 'No Children', leaf: true },
    { id: '2', text: 'Has Children',
      children: [{
          id: '3',
          text: 'Youngster',
          leaf: true
      }]
    }
]
```

The `text` property is the label of the node as it appears in the tree. The `id` property is used to uniquely identify each node, and will be used to determine which nodes are selected or expanded. Using the `id` property can make your life a whole lot easier if you're using some of the advanced features of the `TreePanel`, which we'll see later. The `children` property is optional. The `leaf` property can be thought of as marking a node as either a folder or a file. As a `leaf`, the file is contained within the folder. In the tree, `leaf` nodes will not be expandable and won't have the plus icon which identifies folders.

A quick word about ID

By default, `TreeNodes` are assigned an automatically-generated ID, meaning that the ID configuration property is actually optional. The generated ID is a text string in the form ynode-xx, with xx being replaced by a number. IDs can be useful for retrieving a node you have previously referenced. However, it is quite likely that you'd want to assign the ID value yourself. Whenever you expand a node with children to trigger an asynchronous load of data from the server, your server script needs to know exactly which node was clicked in order to send its children back. By explicitly setting the ID, you'll find it a lot easier to match nodes with their actions when you're working with the server.

Extra data

Although the id, text, and leaf properties are the most commonly-used properties, the way in which they are populated by JSON isn't exclusive to them. In fact, any configuration property of a TreeNode can be initialised by JSON, which will prove to be a useful trick when we begin to explore the other features of the tree. You're also able to include application-specific data; perhaps your nodes are products and you want to hold the price of them. Any property that isn't recognized as a TreeNode config option will still be included on the TreeNode.attributes property for later access.

XML

XML is not natively supported by the tree. However, it is possible to use Ext JS's data support to make this happen. Generally, using JSON will ease your pain, although some applications may use XML as their data transport. So it's worth discussing some general approaches.

We can use Ext.data.HttpProxy to pull in the data, but we need to transform the XML as it is being read:

```
var xmltree = new Ext.tree.TreePanel({el: 'treeContainer'});
var proxy = new Ext.data.HttpProxy({url:
                    'http://localhost:81/ext/treexml.php'});
proxy.load(null, {
   read: function(xmlDocument) {
      parseXmlAndCreateNodes(xmlDocument);
   }
}, function(){ xmltree.render(); });
```

We create a new TreePanel and HttpProxy, and specify that when the proxy loads we want an Ext.data.Reader to handle the incoming XML data. We then tell the reader to pass the XML to parseXmlAndCreateNodes. In this function, you would create a root TreeNode and children based on the XML data, which is pretty straightforward given that HttpProxy is XML-aware and passes you a true XML document rather than a plain string.

JavaScript is fully capable of handling XML data, although you may be more comfortable approaching it as you would approach traversing the DOM of an XHTML document. By navigating and reading the XML document you can build up a TreeNode hierarchy, incorporating XML attributes as extra data for each node, and using textnodes as the text label. Because you have access to the raw XML nodes in this manner, you have full control over the resultant tree structure and the TreeNodes that comprise it.

Tending your trees

We're now going to discuss the main features that you can bolt on to your tree to make it a little bit more useful. Drag-and-drop, sorting, and node editing, are the kinds of things that lift the `TreePanel` from being a clever way of displaying data, to being a great way of manipulating it.

Drag and drop

Ext JS takes care of all of the drag-and-drop UI for you when you're using a `TreePanel`. Just add `enableDD: true` to your configuration, and you'll be able to rearrange nodes with a drop target graphic, and add them to folders, with a green plus icon to indicate what you're about to do.

> The `TreePanel` doesn't care about just its own nodes. If you've got more than one `TreePanel` on the page, then you can happily drag-and-drop branches or leaves between them.

But that's only half the story. When you refresh your page, all of your rearranged nodes will be back to their starting positions. That's because the `TreePanel` doesn't automatically know how you want to persist your changes, and in order to educate it, we've got to hook into some events.

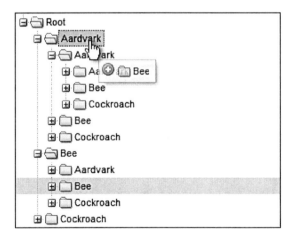

The `TreePanel`'s `beforemovenode` event fires at just the right time for us—after the mouse button is released to signify we want to do a drop, but before the `TreePanel` UI is updated to reflect that. We are most likely to add code such as the following to tell the server about node move events:

```
tree.on('beforemovenode', function(tree, node,
                                oldParent, newParent, index) {
    Ext.Ajax.request({
        url: 'http://localhost/node-move.php',
        params: {
            nodeid: node.id,
            newparentid: newParent.id,
            oldparentid: oldParent.id,
            dropindex: index
        }
    });
});
```

Augmenting our previous code, we're adding a new event handler for the `beforemovenode` event. The handler function is called with a few useful arguments:

1. `tree`: The `TreePanel` that raised the event
2. `node`: The `TreeNode` being moved
3. `oldParent`: The previous parent of the node being moved
4. `newParent`: The new parent of the node being moved
5. `index`: The numerical index where the node was dropped

We use these arguments to form the parameters of an AJAX call to the server. As you can pull out pretty much any information you need about the current state of the tree, your server-side script can perform any action that it needs to.

In some cases, that could include canceling the move action. If the logic you place within the `beforemovenode` handler fails, you need to roll back your changes. If you're not doing an AJAX call, this is pretty straightforward—just return `false` at the end of the handler and the action will be canceled. For AJAX though, it's more difficult, because the `XMLHttpRequest` happens asynchronously, and the event handler will proceed with its default action, which is to allow the move.

In these circumstances, you need to make sure that you provide a failure handler for your AJAX request, and pass enough information back to that failure handler to allow it to manually return the tree to its previous state. Because `beforemovenode` provides a lot of information through its arguments, you can pass the necessary data to take care of these error events.

Sorting

We can sort nodes in a `TreePanel` in a very flexible manner by using the `TreeSorter`. Again, building on our previous code, we can create a `TreeSorter` such as this:

```
new Ext.tree.TreeSorter(tree, {
    folderSort: true,
    dir: "asc"
});
```

Because `TreeSorter` assumes a couple of defaults — specifically, that your leaf nodes are marked with a property called `leaf` and that your labels are in a property called `text` — we can perform an alphabetical sort very easily. The `dir` parameter tells the `TreeSorter` to sort in either ascending (with the `asc` value) or descending (`desc`) order, and the `folderSort` parameter indicates that it should sort leaf nodes that are within folders — in other words, the whole tree hierarchy.

If you've got data that isn't simple text, you can specify a custom method of sorting with the `sortType` configuration option. `sortType` takes a function as its value, and that function will be called with one argument: a `TreeNode`.

The purpose of the `sortType` function is to allow you to cast a custom property of the `TreeNode` — presumably something you've passed from the server and that is specific to your business needs — and convert it to a format that Ext JS can sort, in other words, one of the standard JavaScript types such as integer, string, or date.

This feature can be useful in cases where data passed to the tree is in a format that isn't conducive to normal searching. Data generated by the server might serve multiple purposes, and hence may not always be right for a particular purpose. For example, we may need to convert dates into a standard format — from US style MM/DD/YY to YYYYMMDD format that is suitable for sorting — or maybe we need to strip extraneous characters from a monetary value so that it can be parsed as a decimal.

```
sortType: function(node) {
    return node.attributes.creationDate
}
```

In the above example, we return some custom data from our node, and because this value is a valid JavaScript date, Ext JS will be able to sort against it. This is a simple demonstration of how the `sortType` option can be used to allow the `TreeSorter` to work with any kind of server data.

Editing

There are many scenarios in which editing the value of your nodes could be useful. When viewing a hierarchy of categorized products, you may wish to rename either the categories or the products in-line, without navigating to another screen. We can enable this simple feature by using the `Ext.tree.TreeEditor` class:

```
var editor = new Ext.tree.TreeEditor(tree);
```

The defaults of the `TreeEditor` mean that this will now give your tree nodes a `TextField` editor when you double-click on their label. However, as with basic drag-and-drop functionality, enabling this feature doesn't automatically mean that your changes will be persisted to the server. We need to handle the event that fires when you've finished editing the node:

```
editor.on('beforecomplete', function(editor, newValue, originalValue)
{
    // Possible Ajax call?
});
```

The `beforecomplete` event handler gets called with three arguments:

1. `editor`: The editor field used to edit the node
2. `newValue`: The value that was entered
3. `originalValue`: The value before you changed it

However, it is important to note that the editor parameter is no ordinary `Ext.form.Field`. It is augmented with extra properties, the most useful of which is `editNode`, a reference to the node that was edited. This allows you to get information such as the node ID, which would be essential in making a server-side call to synchronize the edited value in the database.

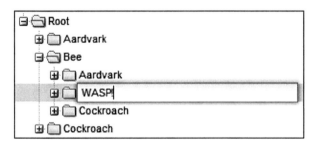

As with the `TreePanel`'s `beforemovenode` event, `beforecomplete` allows cancellation of the edit action by returning False at the end of its handler processing; AJAX requests will need to provide a failure handler to manually restore the edited value.

This has been a quick overview of how to create a very simple in-line editor. There are also means of using this class to create more complicated features. The `TreeEditor` constructor can take up to two optional parameters on top of the single mandatory parameter shown in the example above. These are a field configuration object and a configuration object for the `TreeEditor`. The field config can be one of two things: a field `config` object to be applied to the standard `TextField` editor, or an already-created instance of a different form field. If it is the latter, it will be used instead of the default, which means that you can add `NumberField`, `DateField` or another `Ext.form.Field` in a similar manner.

The second parameter allows you to configure the `TreeEditor`, and is more for fine-tuning rather than introducing any exciting functionality. For example, we can use `cancelOnEsc` to allow the user to cancel any editing by pressing the *Escape* key, or use `ignoreNoChange` to avoid firing completion events if a value has not changed after an edit.

Trimming and pruning

There a few other tricks that the `TreePanel` supports, which assist in the creation of rich applications. Varying selection models, node filtering, and context menus are commonly-used features in many solutions. So let's take a look at these now.

Selection models

In our previous example code, we dragged and edited `TreeNodes` to alter them immediately. But nodes can also be selected for further processing. The `TreePanel` uses a single-selection model by default. In our previous code, we've already done everything we need to enable node selection. As with many aspects of the tree, simply selecting the node doesn't do anything; instead we need to hook in to some of the features provided to manipulate the selection.

A great example of this would be to select a node and have an information panel automatically populated with further details of that node. Perhaps you have a tree of named products, and clicking a node will display the price and stock level of the selected product. We can use the `selectionchange` event to make this happen. Again, using our previous code as a starting point, we could add the following:

```
tree.selModel.on('selectionchange', function(selModel, node) {
    var price = node.attributes.price;
});
```

The second node argument that is passed to the `selectionchange` event makes it very easy to grab any custom attributes in your node data.

What if we want to allow multiple nodes to be selected? How can we do that, and how can we handle the `selectionchange` event in that configuration? We can use `Ext.tree.MultiSelectionModel` when creating our `TreePanel`:

```
var tree = new Ext.tree.TreePanel({
        renderTo:'treeContainer',
        loader: treeLoader,
        root: rootNode,
        selModel: new Ext.tree.MultiSelectionModel()
    });
```

Configuration is as simple as that. Although handling the `selectionchange` event is very similar to the default selection model, there is an important difference. The second argument to the event handler will be an *array* of nodes rather than a single node.

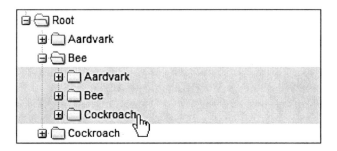

Selection models don't just expose the means of retrieving selection information. They also allow manipulation of the current selection. For example, the `MultiSelectionModel.clearSelections()` method is useful for wiping the slate clean after you have finished handling an event involving multiple nodes. `DefaultSelectionModel` has methods (`selectNext` and `selectPrevious`) for navigating the tree, moving up or down the node hierarchy as required.

Round-up with context menus

We've already covered a lot of the functionality that the `TreePanel` can provide, so let's consolidate a little bit with a practical example. Adding a context menu that appears when you right-click a `TreeNode` is a trivial task with Ext JS. However, it can be an extremely useful means of adding shortcuts to your interface. We'll be building on the code that has been used in the previous sections. First, let's create the menu, and then we'll hook it up to the `TreePanel`:

```
var contextMenu = new Ext.menu.Menu({
    items: [
        { text: 'Delete', handler: deleteHandler },
```

```
        { text: 'Sort', handler: sortHandler }
    ]
});
tree.on('contextmenu', treeContextHandler);
```

The `TreePanel` provides a `contextmenu` event which fires when the user right-clicks on a node. Note that our listeners are not anonymous functions as they have been in the previous examples—instead they have been split off for easy reading.

First, the `treeContextHandler` that handles the `contextmenu` event:

```
function treeContextHandler(node) {
    node.select();
    contextMenu.show(node.ui.getAnchor());
}
```

The handler gets called with a node argument, so we need to select the node to allow us to act upon it later. We then pop up the context menu by calling the `show` method with a single parameter that tells the pop-up menu where to align itself—in this case it's the text of the `TreeNode` we've clicked on.

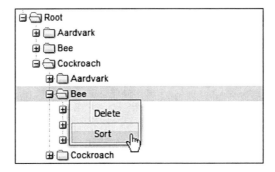

Handling the menu

We've got two context menu entries—**Delete** and **Sort**. Let's first take a look at the handler for **Delete**:

```
function deleteHandler() {
    tree.getSelectionModel().getSelectedNode().remove();
}
```

Using our previous knowledge of selection models, we get the node that we selected in the `treeContextHandler`, and simply call its remove method. This will delete the node and all of its children from the `TreePanel`. Note that we're not dealing with persisting this change to the server, but if this was something that you needed to do, `TreePanel` has a remove event that you could use a handler for to provide that functionality.

The handler for our **Sort** menu entry is given here:

```
function sortHandler() {
    tree.getSelectionModel().getSelectedNode().sort(
        function (leftNode, rightNode) {
            return (leftNode.text.toUpperCase() < rightNode.text.
toUpperCase() ? 1 : -1);
        }
    );
}
```

Again, we use the selection model to get the selected node. Ext JS provides a `sort` method on the `TreeNode` that takes a function as its first parameter. This function gets called with two arguments: the two nodes to compare. In this example, we are sorting by the node's `text` property in descending order, but you can sort by any custom node attribute you like.

 You can use this sorting method in conjunction with a `TreeSorter` without issues. That's because `TreeSorter` only monitors the `beforechildrenrendered`, `append`, `insert`, and `textchange` events on the `TreePanel`. Any other changes will be unaffected.

The **Delete** context menu action will completely remove the selected node from the `TreePanel`, while the **Sort** action will order its children according to their text label.

Filtering

The `Ext.tree.TreeFilter` class is marked as "experimental" in Ext JS 2.2, so I'm going to touch upon it only briefly. It's designed for scenarios where the user needs to search for nodes based on a particular attribute. This attribute could be the text, the ID, or any custom data that was passed when the node was created. Let's take the context menu that we just built and use it to demonstrate filtering. First, we have to create the `TreeFilter`:

```
var filter = new Ext.tree.TreeFilter(tree);
```

You need to go back to the configuration for the context menu and add a new entry to the `items` configuration property:

```
{ text: 'Filter', handler: filterHandler }
```

We now need to create a `filterHandler` function that performs the filter action:

```
function filterHandler() {
    var node = tree.getSelectionModel().getSelectedNode();
    filter.filter('Bee', 'text', node);
}
```

As with our other handler functions, we start by getting the currently-selected node in the tree, and then call the `filter` function. This function takes three arguments:

1. The value to filter by
2. The attribute to filter on; this is optional and defaults to `text`
3. The starting node for the filter

We pass the selected node as the starting node for the filter, which means that the node we right-clicked on in order to to pop up the menu will have its children filtered by the specified value.

Our aardvark, bee, and cockroach examples don't really require this level of filtering, but there are other situations in which this could prove to be a useful user feature. Online software documentation, with multiple levels of detail, could be represented in a tree and a `TreeFilter` could be used to search by topic. In a more advanced scenario, you could use checkboxes or pop-up dialogs to get the user's input for the filter, providing a much more flexible experience.

The roots

Although we've demonstrated a number of powerful techniques using the Ext tree support, its real strength lies in the wealth of settings, methods, and hook points that the various classes expose. We've already reviewed a number of ways of configuring the `TreePanel` and `TreeNode` classes, which give access to a number of powerful features. However, there are more configuration options that can be used to tweak and enhance your tree, and we're going to review some of the more interesting ones now.

TreePanel tweaks

By default, there are a number of graphical enhancements enabled for the `TreePanel` which, depending on your application requirements, may not be desirable. For example, setting `animate` to `false` will prevent the smooth animated effect being used for the expansion and contraction of nodes. This can be particularly useful in situations where nodes will be repeatedly expanded and collapsed by a user and slower animated transitions can be frustrating.

Because `TreePanel` extends from `Ext.Panel`, it supports all of the standard `Panel` features. This is easy to remember, because it means that support for toolbars at the top and the bottom (via the `tbar` and `bbar` config options), separate header and footer elements, and expand/collapse functionality for the `Panel` are all supported. The `TreePanel` can also be included in any `Ext.ViewPort` or `Ext.layout`.

Cosmetic

In terms of purely cosmetic options, `TreePanel` provides the `lines` option, which, when set to `false`, will disable the guide-lines that show the hierarchy of the TreeNodes within the panel. This can be useful if you're creating a very simple tree for which lines would just clutter the interface.

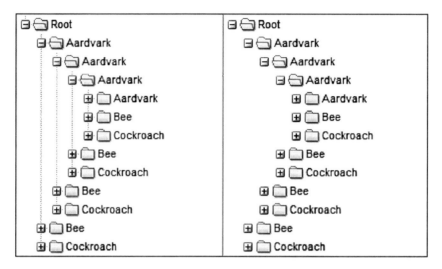

`hlColor` is applicable for drag-and-drop enabled trees, and controls the start color for the fading highlight (supplied as a hex string, such as 990000) which is triggered when a node is dropped. This can be completely disabled by setting `dlDrop` to `false`. Setting `trackMouseOver` to `false` will disable the highlight that appears when you hover over a node.

Tweaking TreeNode

In many cases, you won't be manually creating `TreeNodes`, other than your root node, so you might think that the configuration options aren't of much use to you. Not so, because it's not just the `id` and `text` properties from your JSON that are used when generating nodes—any property in your JSON that matches with a `config` option on the `TreeNode` will be used to create the node. If you have a JSON that like this:

```
[
    { text: 'My Node', disabled: true, href: 'http://extjs.com'}
]
```

You'll get a node that starts off as disabled, but when enabled will act as a link to the Ext JS website.

This feature is extremely useful for passing application-specific information to your `TreeNodes`. For example, your server logic may dictate that particular nodes cannot have children. Setting `allowChildren:false` means that the node can't be used as a drop target for a node that is being dragged. Similarly , you can set individual nodes to be disallowed for dragging by using the `draggable: false` option. We can set the status of a checkbox on the node by using `checked: true`. In fact, simply specifying the `checked` option — whether `true` or `false` — will cause the checkbox to appear next to the node. These configuration options allow you to set the behavior of your nodes based on some server logic, but do not require any manual handling in order to see your preferences enacted.

There are a few other useful configuration options available for `TreeNode`. You can provide custom icons by using the `icon` option, or provide a CSS styling hook by using the `cls` option. The `qtip` option lets you provide a pop-up tooltip, perhaps providing a description of the node, while the text label shows its name.

Manipulating

Once the `TreePanel` is configured, we can begin to work with its nodes. The panel mostly allows for navigation of the hierarchy, starting at a selected node and moving to a parent or child, or up and down the current branch. We can also select nodes or expand them by their path, which could be used to search for specific nodes.

The `expandAll` and `collapseAll` methods are pretty self-explanatory, and can be useful for resetting the tree to a default state. Each method takes a single Boolean parameter to state whether the change should be animated or not.

The `expandPath` method's first parameter is the "path" of a node. The path uniquely identifies the node within the hierarchy, and takes the form of a string which fully qualifies the location of a node in the tree. For example, a path could look like this:

```
/n-15/n-56/n-101
```

Here, we have a representation of the location of the node with the ID `n-101`. `n-15` is the root node, with a child `n-56`; and `n-101` is in turn a child of `n-56`. If you're familiar with XPath, then this notation will be well-known to you. If you're not familiar with XPath then you can think of it as a postal address or a web IP address — a unique way of referring to this node.

By passing this value to `expandPath`, the tree will drill down to the specified node, expanding branches as necessary. Imagine the following code:

```
Ext.Msg.prompt('Node', 'Please enter a product name',
               function(btn, text){
    if (btn == 'ok'){
        var path = GetNodePathFromName(text);
      tree.expandPath(path);
    }
});
```

The `GetNodePathFromName` function could perform a server lookup and return the node ID, enabling quick navigation of the tree based on the user's input. Alternatively, `TreePanel.getNodeById` could be used in a similar way. Rather than expand to the node, further manipulation could occur.

In some circumstances, you may need to perform the reverse action, that is, you have a node but you need to get the path for it. `TreeNode.getPath` is provided for just this purpose, and can be used as a means of storing the location of a node.

Further methods

The `TreeNode` has a number of other useful methods as well. We've already covered `sort` and `remove`, but now we can add some basic utility methods such as `collapse` and `expand`, `enable` and `disable`, as well as some handy extras such as `expandChildNodes` and `collapseChildNodes`, which can traverse all child nodes of an arbitrary root, and change their expansion states. The `findChild` and `findChildBy` methods allow both simple and custom searching of child nodes, as shown in the following example where we search for the first node with a price attribute of `300`:

```
var node = root.findChild('price', 300);
```

In some cases you may need to mass-manipulate the attributes of your node hierarchy. You can do this by using the `TreeNode.eachChild` method:

```
root.eachChild(function(currentNode) {
    currentNode.attributes.price += 30;
});
```

Because the first parameter to `eachChild` is a function, we can perform any logic that is required of our application.

Event capture

We've already demonstrated a couple of methods of watching for user interaction with the tree, but there are many events available as hooks for your custom code. Earlier, we discussed the use of the `checked` configuration option on a `TreeNode`. When the node checkbox is toggled, the `checkchange` event is fired. This could be useful for visually highlighting the check status:

```
tree.on('checkchange', function(node, checked) {
    node.eachChild(function(currentNode) {
        currentNode.ui.toggleCheck();
    });
}
```

We're propagating the check down through the children of the `TreeNode`. We could also highlight the nodes in question to clearly show that their check status has changed, or perform some other logic, such as adding information about the newly-checked nodes to an informational display elsewhere on the page.

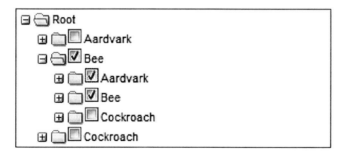

A more common use of the `TreePanel` events is to verify changes or persist them to a server-side store. For example, a tree of categorized products may have some logical restrictions—certain bargain categories may specify the maximum price of a product. We could use the `beforeappend` event to check for this:

```
tree.on('beforeappend', function(tree, parent, node) {
    return node.attributes.price < parent.attributes.maximumPrice;
});
```

This example demonstrates a pattern that you have seen throughout Ext JS—returning `false` from an event handler will cancel the action. In this case, if the price of the node being added is greater than the `maximumPrice` assigned to its parent, the function will return `false`, and the node will not be added.

Remembering state

In many applications, `TreePanels` are used as navigation aids, showing a hierarchical structure, with its nodes being HTML links to node detail pages. In this scenario, if a user wishes to view multiple node detail pages, one after the other, the default behavior of the `TreePanel` can lead to frustration. This is because the tree doesn't save its state between page refreshes, so any expanded node will be rendered as collapsed when the user navigates back to the page. If the user needs to drill down to the branch they are interested in every time they navigate back to the tree, they are quickly going to lose patience with the interface.

StateManager

Now that we have a good grasp of the way we can manipulate the `TreePanel`, working out how we can save and restore its state should be fairly straightforward. Essentially, what we need to do is record each expansion of a `TreeNode`, and when the page reloads, "playback" those expansions. We can use `Ext.state.Manager` with a `CookieProvider` to store our expansion. We can initialize this with:

```
Ext.state.Manager.setProvider(new Ext.state.CookieProvider());
```

This is standard fare for setting up a state provider. We now need to establish exactly what we're going to store, and the logical choice would be the path of the last expanded node. This means that we can simply expand out that path and present the user with the last part of the hierarchy they were interested in. Here's a naive implementation of that idea:

```
tree.on('expandnode', function (node){ Ext.state.Manager.
set("treestate", node.getPath());
});
```

In this code, we simply handle the `TreePanel`'s `expandnode` event to record the path, using `TreeNode.getPath`, of any node that is expanded. Because we overwrite that value on each expansion, the `treestate` should hold the path of the last node that was expanded. We can then check for that value when the page is loaded:

```
var treeState = Ext.state.Manager.get("treestate");
if (treeState)
    tree.expandPath(treeState);
```

If `treestate` has previously been recorded, we use that to expand the tree out to the last-expanded node.

Caveats

As mentioned, this is a naive implementation. It doesn't handle cases where the user expands and, then collapses a node, and then navigates away and back. In such cases, the collapse of the node wouldn't be saved. So when we restore the state, the user will see it expanded again. By handling the `collapsenode` event, we could take this issue into account. We also have a problem with the expansion of multiple nodes. If more than one branch is expanded our code will only expand the one the user clicked most recently. Storing an array of expanded nodes is one approach that could address this shortcoming.

Summary

Getting a feature-rich tree interface such as `Ext.tree.TreePanel` up and running in eleven lines of code is pretty impressive, and we've shown that it is possible. Over and above that, this chapter has demonstrated that the `TreePanel`'s strength is not simply in its ease of use, but in the way we can use its wealth of configuration options to deliver application-specific functionality.

The use of asynchronous loading is an important feature of the `TreePanel`, because it provides a way of consuming large amounts of dynamic data in a scalable fashion. It's also handled transparently by `Ext.tree`, which means that the implementation is as beneficial for the developer as it is for the end user.

Despite all of their power, the `Ext.tree` classes still manage to feel pretty lightweight in use. It's easy to tame that power by using the configuration options, the methods, and the events that the `TreePanel` and `TreeNode` provide, but it's not just about these classes. `TreeSorter` and `TreeNodeUI` are key parts of the puzzle, adding functionality and allowing customization for a standardized look and feel.

Because the `Ext.TreePanel` extends the `Panel`, which in turn extends `BoxComponent`, we get all of the strong component and layout support that comes from a fully-fledged Ext JS component. `BoxComponent` support will be particularly interesting as we move forward, because it means that trees can easily be included in various configurations within an `Ext.Window`. Which just happens to be our next topic.

Windows and Dialogs

9

In the olden days of the web, users of traditional backend systems would spend their time crunching data in list and form-based interfaces. Pick an item from a list of customer orders, then navigate to a detail form, rinse, and repeat. The trouble is that we're talking about thousands of entries in a list, and lots of detail in the forms. The chances are that in our customer order example, we might even need sub-forms to show all of the information that is available, and each time we move to another screen we're refreshing the whole page and getting all of that data all over again.

That's fine; it's how the web works. But in a data processing scenario, where your users are going back and forth throughout the day, there's a real benefit in optimizing the speed at which screens appear and data is refreshed. The Ext JS grid plays a key part in this, as we've seen, by bringing AJAX-powered paging and sorting of GridViews into play, to replace the old-style static lists.

Now we're going to take a look at the other part of the puzzle—Ext JS Window and dialog support. These classes allow developers to present any kind of information to their users, without forcing the users to navigate to another screen. By popping up as an overlay on top of the current page, a window, or dialog can present detailed data in the form of grids, tree, images, and text. We can also use them in a simplified form to show informational alerts or to quickly capture user data.

Opening a dialog

In this chapter, we'll talk about the main `Ext.Window` class and the `Ext.MessageBox` subclass, both of which have extensive applications in our enhanced user interface. While the `Window` itself is designed to be a flexible, multipurpose component, the `MessageBox` is a more specialized solution. It is used in a similar way to standard JavaScript pop ups such as `alert` and `prompt`, albeit with many more behavioral and presentational options available for it.

Ext.Window is another fully-blown Ext.Container, giving it a wealth of underlying settings which will be familiar from the other parts of the Ext JS framework. It also hints at the types of interfaces that we can build in a Window, given that we can set the internal layout of a Container to a range of different options.

We're also going to cover some extra classes which help us to manipulate multiple Windows: Ext.WindowGroup and Ext.WindowManager. In advanced applications, we can use more than one window to present drill-down views of information, or we can allow the user to view more than one record at once in separate windows. Window groups assist with these applications, giving us the power to act upon many windows at once.

Despite the fact that dialogs build on Ext.Window, we're going to address dialogs first. That's because the dialogs abstract away many of the powerful options of Ext.Window, making it a cut-down version of the superclass.

Dialogs

As previously mentioned, dialogs can be likened to the prompt and alert functions that are available in most browser implementations of JavaScript. Although the appearance of those pop ups is controlled by the browser and operating system, and their behavior is limited to the most common cases, these restrictions don't apply to the Ext JS dialogs.

 Although the dialog class is actually Ext.MessageBox, Ext JS provides a shorthand version - Ext.Msg. This shorthand version can make your code a little more concise, but it's up to you which one you use, as they're both functionally equivalent.

Let's take a look at the ready-made pop ups that Ext JS makes available.

Off the shelf

We've talked about how Ext provides a replacement for the JavaScript alert, so let's have a look at that first:

```
Ext.Msg.alert('Hey!', 'Something happened.');
```

The first thing to notice is that `Msg.alert` takes two parameters, whereas the standard alert takes only one. The first allows you to specify a title for the alert dialog, and the second specifies the body text. The previous code results in a `messagebox` like this:

As you can see, it performs very much the same function as a standard alert but with that familiar Ext JS look and feel. We can also convey a little bit more information by using the title bar. Showing `Msg.alert` doesn't temporarily halt script execution in the same way that a normal alert will; be conscious of this when using the Ext version. Later, we'll look at ways to use callbacks to replicate that halt functionality should you need it.

You can only use a single `Ext.MessageBox` at a time. If you try to pop up two boxes at the same time, the first will be replaced by the second. So in some cases, you'll want to check for the presence of an existing dialog in case you inadvertently overwrite the message it is presenting.

Let's take a look at another replacement, the `Ext.Msg.prompt`. This allows the capture of a single line of text in the same way that the JavaScript prompt does. However, instead of simply returning a value, it gives you a few more options. Here's a comparison of doing the same thing with each method:

```
var data = prompt('Tell me something');

Ext.Msg.prompt('Hey!', 'Tell me something', function(btn, text){
    if (btn == 'ok'){
        var data = text;
    }
}, this, false, '');
```

Again, `Msg.prompt` allows you to pass a title as the first argument, and the body text is the second. The third argument is a callback function that will be called when a button—either **OK** or **Cancel**—is clicked in the prompt. The callback has two arguments: the button that was clicked and the text that was provided by the user; you can use these as demonstrated in the example code.

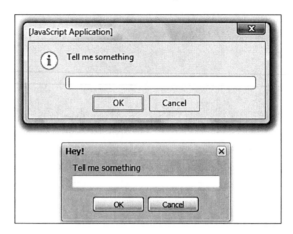

Note the other three options that come after the callback function. They are scope, multiline, and initial value, respectively. The multiline argument is interesting—accepting a boolean value, it allows a more flexible capture of text than the standard prompt.

Confirmation

Our final replacement `messagebox` is for the confirm pop up, which allows the user to choose between confirming an action or rejecting it. The code should be pretty familiar by now:

```
Ext.Msg.confirm('Hey!', 'Is this ok?', function(btn, text){
    if (btn == 'yes'){
        // go ahead and do more stuff
    } else {
        // abort, abort!
    }
});
```

Again we're using the title, body text, and callback arguments that we saw in the `Msg.prompt`, so there are no surprises here. An interesting difference between this and the standard confirm is that whereas the standard confirm gives the options **OK** and **Cancel**, the Ext JS one gives the user the choice of **Yes** and **No**. This is arguably a better default, particularly when you use a question in the body text of the confirm `messagebox`.

It's all progressing nicely

There's a fourth standard `messagebox` which is included with Ext JS one that isn't just a replacement for a basic JavaScript pop up. This is the progress dialog. `Ext.Msg.progress` isn't designed to be used independently like the other Ext messageboxes, and doesn't need user input. In fact, if you trigger it like this:

```
Ext.Msg.progress('Hey!', 'We\'re waiting...', 'progressing');
```

Then you're going to be waiting for a while, because you'll get a modal dialog which never progresses anywhere. The first two arguments are the title and body text as in the previous examples, while the third is the text that will appear in the progress bar.

So, if we don't want to be stuck with an eternal progress bar, how can we get things moving? The `Ext.Msg.updateProgress` method is provided just for this purpose. Here's an example which illustrates its use:

```
var count = 0;

var interval = window.setInterval(function() {
    count = count + 0.04;

    Ext.Msg.updateProgress(count);

    if(count >= 1) {
        window.clearInterval(interval);
        Ext.Msg.hide();
    }
}, 100);
```

This is a very contrived example, in which we're calling `updateProgress` every 100 milliseconds via a timer, and incrementing the progress using the count variable every time. The first argument to `updateProgress` is a value between zero and one, with zero representing start and one representing finish, the second allows you to update the progress bar text, and the third lets you change the body text. Updating the text can be handy if you'd like to provide additional feedback to the user, even if this is just to show a percentage representation—"x% complete"—of the current progress.

Back in our example code, note that you must also call `Ext.Msg.hide` in order to clear the progress dialog from the screen—`updateProgress` doesn't handle this for you, even if you set the current progress to a value of greater than one.

The four included messageboxes, alert—prompt, confirm, and progress—are the foundation of the Ext JS dialog support, but we can also weak their functionality to support some custom scenarios.

Roll your own

The four methods for creating messageboxes that we've just covered are essentially shortcuts to a fifth method: Ext.Msg.show. This method takes a configuration object as its single argument, and the configuration options within this object allow the creation of a messagebox that supports all of the features available via our shortcut methods. The simplest example of this method is:

```
Ext.Msg.show({
    msg: 'AWESOME.'
});
```

This is closer replication of the JavaScript alert than the standard Ext JS one—but it's not as functional. Something a little better would be:

```
Ext.Msg.show({
    title: 'Hey!',
    msg: 'Icons and Buttons! AWESOME.',
    icon: Ext.MessageBox.INFO,
    buttons: Ext.MessageBox.OK
});
```

Now we've got our title back as well as our button, but there's an icon as well.

The means of configuring buttons and icons is interesting: pass in one of the constants that Ext JS provides, and you'll get a pre-configured button or CSS class that shows an icon. Here's the list of the icon constants:

- Ext.Msg.ERROR
- Ext.Msg.INFO
- Ext.Msg.QUESTION
- Ext.Msg.WARNING

And the button constants:

- Ext.Msg.CANCEL
- Ext.Msg.OK

- `Ext.Msg.OKCANCEL`

- `Ext.Msg.YESNO`

- `Ext.Msg.YESNOCANCEL`

This variety of ready-made options provides you with a fair bit of flexibility when it comes to the appearance of your messageboxes, but we can go further. As mentioned, the icon constants are simply strings representing CSS class names. For example, `Ext.Msg.QUESTION` provides the `ext-mb-question` string. This ties in to the Ext JS stylesheets and provides the styles for a question icon. The logical conclusion is that we can provide our own strings in place of these constants, allowing full customization of the icon areas.

The button constants are a bit less flexible, and contain object literals specifying how the dialog buttons should be displayed. For example, `Ext.Msg.YESNOCANCEL` contains the following (represented in JavaScript Object Notation for easy reading):

```
{ cancel:true, yes: true, no:true }
```

This is specifying that all of the `yes`, `cancel`, and `no` buttons should be included. You can use this to selectively turn off particular buttons, but you can't change the order or add new buttons in this manner. This means that providing custom button definitions in this way is of limited use.

 In addition to accepting the `Ext.Msg` button constants, the `show` method options will also accept a standard Ext JS button configuration object.

However, we can tweak the dialog in other ways. It's possible to supply `Ext.Msg.show` with `width` and `height` options to restrict the dimensions of your pop up. This could be handy in a situation where you have a long message to display and would like to prevent it from stretching to one long line across the screen.

The `show` configuration object also allows us to use the `cls` option to specify a CSS class to apply to the container of the dialog. A developer could use this to target any child objects of the container by using custom CSS rules, potentially paving the way for multiple dialogs that have totally different appearances. Do you need to provide a bright-pink pop up for your users? This configuration option allows you to do this.

Behavior

So far, the configuration options for `Ext.Msg.show` have addressed appearance, but there are a few options that can also adjust behavior. If we use the `progress` property, then we can replicate the standard Ext JS progress dialog:

```
Ext.Msg.show({progress:true});
```

By using this in tandem with other options such as `title` and `msg`, you can create a custom progress dialog.

Similarly, the `prompt` and `multiline` options allow the creation of a custom input pop up:

```
Ext.Msg.show({prompt:true, multiline:true});
```

Here, we create a pop up that accepts multiple lines of input. But by omitting the `multiline` value or setting it to `false`, we can limit the pop up to a single line. Again, using the other configuration options for `Ext.Msg.show` allows us to expand this sample code into a fully-featured input dialog.

Another option that changes the default behavior of a pop up is `modal`. This option allows you to specify whether the user can interact with the items behind the pop up. When set to `true`, a semi-transparent overlay will prevent interaction.

As we have discussed earlier, the `Ext.Msg` pop ups don't block script execution in the same way as standard JavaScript pop ups. This means that we need to use a callback to trigger code after the dialog is dismissed. We can do this using `show`'s `fn` configuration option, which gets called with two arguments: the ID of the button that has been clicked, and the text entered into the text field in the dialog (where the dialog includes an input field). Obviously, for a simple alert prompt, you're not going to receive any text back, but this function does provide a consistent means of consuming callbacks across the whole range of dialogs that you can build using `Ext.Msg.show`.

We briefly touched on the fact that the `Ext.Msg` messageboxes are actually customized `Ext.Windows`. If you think we're able to tweak `Ext.Msg` a lot...wait till you see what `Ext.Window` can let us do.

Windows

Any computer user will be familiar with the concept of windows; an informational panel that appears on the screen to provide more data on the current user's actions. We can replicate this concept using the `Ext.Window` class, a powerful component that supports many advanced scenarios.

Starting examples

We can open a window using a very minimal amount of code:

```
var w = new Ext.Window({height:100, width: 200});
w.show();
```

Running this gives you an empty pop up window that in itself is…well, completely useless; but it does show off a few of the interesting default features of an Ext. Window. Straight out of the box, without any configuration, your window will be draggable, resizable, and will have a handy close icon in the upper right corner of the dialog box. It's still not a very impressive demonstration, however, because our window doesn't actually show anything.

The easiest way to populate a window is with plain old HTML. Here's an extended example that demonstrates this feature:

```
var w = new Ext.Window({
    height: 150, width: 200,
    title: 'A Window',
    html: '<h1>Oh</h1><p>HI THERE EVERYONE</p>'
});
w.show();
```

We've added two new configuration options here. First, a title option that allows you to set the text in the title bar of the window, and second, an html option that accepts a string of raw HTML that will be displayed in the window.

The use of this approach is immediately apparent—we can go back to basics and inject whatever HTML we require directly into the content area of the window. This allows us to tweak our window right down to the markup level, and provide lots of CSS hooks for styling. Even so, it's not the truly integrated experience that we've come to expect from Ext JS. However, another configuration option lets us take a more familiar approach.

Paneling potential

Remember that Window is a subclass of Panel, and Panel has all kinds of interesting tricks up its sleeve. The items configuration option accepts an array of configuration objects or component instances:

```
var w = new Ext.Window({
    items:[
        { xtype: 'textfield', fieldLabel: 'First Name'},
        new Ext.form.TextField({fieldLabel: 'Surname'})
    ]
});
w.show();
```

In the above example we have added two textfields, the first one using "lazy" xtype initialization, and the second one using standard object initialization. These two items will be added to the window's internal panel, but the manner in which they are displayed can be controlled based on the window's layout property.

Layout

Ext JS defines a number of layout models within the Ext.layout package, and each of these layouts is used with a panel to allow the components within it to be arranged in a specific manner. In our previous example, we showed how we can add a couple of textboxes to a Window, but we can also enhance the appearance of the window simply by using the appropriate layout. In this case, we need Ext.layout. FormLayout, which provides support for field labels and the general spacing and positioning you'd expect from an edit form:

```
var w = new Ext.Window({
    layout: 'form',
    items:[
        { xtype: 'textfield', fieldLabel: 'First Name'},
        new Ext.form.TextField({fieldLabel: 'Surname'})
    ]
});
w.show();
```

We use the layout configuration option to specify that we want to use a form layout, and immediately the difference in appearance becomes clear. In the next figure, the first dialog box does not use a layout, and the second one does.

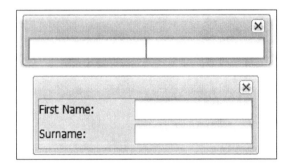

This is not a feature of Ext.Window; it comes straight from the Panel superclass. But the fact that Window supports this feature is extremely important for an application developer—especially when you consider how long it would take to create a rich form using our previous HTML injection technique. The other layouts within the Ext.layout package provide many more approaches to windows design, expanding the scenarios that a window can support.

Configuration

In addition to the various ways of filling the window's content area, we also have a great deal of flexibility when it comes to the appearance and behavior of each pop up. There are many configuration options provided by the Ext.Window's superclass hierarchy, which starts with Ext.Panel, while also having a wealth of options of its own.

When I'm cleaning windows

In our very first window example, I demonstrated how we get a number of great features for free—resizing, dragging, and a close button. Windows with strict layouts aren't really meant to be resized, so we can prevent this behavior with the configuration option resizable set to false. Dragging is often just a matter of preference, and in most cases there's little harm in leaving it enabled. That said, there are times when it's simply not necessary functionality, so I prefer to disable it by using the draggable option set to false.

```
var w = new Ext.Window({
    height:50,
    width: 100,
    closable: false,
    draggable: false,
    resizable: false
});
w.show();
```

When using a form window, it's often preferable to have text buttons explaining that different actions will, for example, either save a record, or cancel any changes that have been made, and in such cases, the **close** icon can be disabled by having the closable option set to false. There's a second option that gives a little bit more control over this behavior: closeAction can be set to either hide or close, with hide simply causing the window to vanish, but not destroying it, and close actually removing the window from the DOM. This is an important difference if you think you're going to be re-using the window later, as simply hiding and re-showing it is more efficient than re-creating the window every time.

The extras

With the default functionality under control, we can begin to review the ways we can further tweak and augment the features of the Ext.Window. We've already demonstrated the use of the height and width options that set the fixed dimensions of the window and crop any content that exceeds these dimensions dimensions.

We do have another option. The `autoHeight` and `autoWidth` config settings, which are both booleans, allow you to fill your window with components without having to to worry about ensuring that your `height` and `width` values are absolutely correct. This is a really useful tool during development, when it's unlikely that you know the exact dimensions of whatever you're creating; just set `autoHeight` and `autoWidth` to `true` and forget about it. Even better, these options can be used separately, so that you can set your `width`, but have the `height` automatically calculated. This is useful if you're putting dynamic content into a window, because you will need to make sure that it doesn't stretch the window off the sides of your screen.

Desktopping

The most pervasive example of a windowing system is the computer desktop, with multiple windows representing applications or elements of the filesystem. In such systems, users are allowed to hide windows for later use, or minimize them; they're also able to expand windows to fill the screen, or maximize it (also referred to as maximizing the window). These are familiar terms, and are of course supported by `Ext.Window` via the `maximizable` and `minimizable` boolean configuration options.

These features are disabled by default, but they are fully-featured and work in much the same way as their desktop equivalents. When set to `true`, new icons appear in the upper right of the window that are similar in appearance to the ones on the Windows operating system. `Maximizable` allows the window to be expanded to fill the whole of the browser viewport, as expected, but `minimizable` is a little trickier. Ext JS doesn't know where you want the window to vanish to—on the Windows operating system it would be the task bar, but for other operating systems it could be somewhere else. So you've got to provide the minimize functionality yourself. Ext only gives you the icon and a minimize event that must be handled in a manner appropriate to your application. Later in this chapter, we'll provide a brief example on how this can be achieved using the events available for the `Ext.Window` class.

Further options

Ext JS windows support another means of cutting down the real-estate of your window, and this is built right into the framework. The `collapsible` boolean adds another button to the upper right of the window and allows the user to shrink it down to cause only the title bar to be shown. A second click expands the window back to its original state.

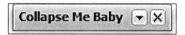

We can also use the `expandOnShow` configuration to specify that a hidden window will always be expanded to its full dimensions when it is shown. This is useful for windows that have been previously hidden and need to be brought back to the user's attention.

Framing our window

As well as the standard title bar and body content area, we also have the ability to add further content areas to a window. Some of these areas can be fully customized, and some are a little bit more restrictive, but together they provide yet another method for creating functional windows.

Every window has the built-in capability to add toolbars to the top and the bottom. These toolbars can include any valid toolbar items, be it buttons, menus, or text. In addition, we can use the `footer` element to contain some further buttons via the `buttons` configuration option.

Depending on your requirements, you may choose to use one or more of these content areas to provide tools to allow your users to manipulate and consume the information within the window. A typical example would be to create a window with a form layout, which then includes the **Save** and **Cancel** buttons within the footer. This reflects the typical style of a data entry form, and will be positioned automatically by Ext JS with little configuration being required.

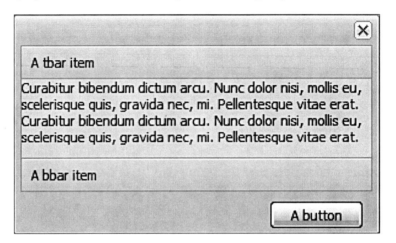

Manipulating

When our windows are on-screen, we have a range of methods that we can use to change their position, appearance, and behavior. In fact, we've already used one of these methods in our examples—show—which is used to display the window in the first place. Although we've always used show in its most simple form, it can take up to three arguments—all of which are optional.

```
myWin.show('animTarget', function() { alert('Now Showing'); }, this);
```

Firstly, we can specify an element, or the ID of an element, to form the starting point from which the window should animate when opening. This cosmetic effect can also be specified using the animateTarget configuration option. The second argument is a callback function, fired when the rendering of the window is complete, and the third argument is simply the scope for the callback. It turns out the show method isn't so basic after all!

The obvious companion to show is hide. Indeed, it takes the same arguments, and will cause the window to vanish from the screen for later use. If you're sure that you don't want to use the window later then it's probably better to use the close method, which will remove it from the DOM and destroy it.

The functionality delivered by the `close` and `hide` methods has already been demonstrated—it is provided by the window's close icon. There are a few more methods that allow programmatic control over items, that we've already covered, such as the `minimize` and `maximize` methods. This basic functionality is augmented by the `restore` method, which is used after `maximize` to return the window to its previous dimensions, and `toggleMaximize`, which is simply a shortcut to switch between `maximize` and `restore`. And in terms of setting the window back to its defaults we can also use the `center` method, which sets the window in the middle of the browser's viewport.

We can further manipulate the position of our windows: `alignTo` allows a developer to programmatically move a window to next to a specified element. This method has three parameters:

- The element to align to—as a string or full element
- The position to align with—as detailed in the `Element.alignTo` documentation, and briefly discussed in *Chapter 10—Effects*
- A positioning offset, specified as an `[x,y]` array

This method is useful when you have an application with a dynamic workspace—you need to ensure that your windows appear in the correct place in relation to other items being displayed. A useful compliment to this feature is the `anchorTo` method, which takes the same arguments and allows a window to remain anchored to another element, even when the browser window has been resized or scrolled.

While many of the `Ext.Window` methods simply give a developer access to existing functionality via their code, there are a few additional ones that provide for advanced scenarios or for features that would be laborious to code by hand.

Events

Pretty much all of the actions we've covered so far have their own events that serve as hooks for your custom code. `Minimize` is one which we've explicitly mentioned earlier, because you have to handle this event if you want the minimize icon to do anything. Ideally, you'd expect the window to be stored in some kind of 'taskbar'-style area for later retrieval.

```
var w = new Ext.Window({
    height: 50,
    width: 100,
    minimizable: true
});
w.on('minimize', doMin);
w.show();
```

In the above example, we're creating a new window, which we set as `minimizable`, and then add an event listener for the `minimize` event. We then show the window on the screen. Our `doMin` event handling function looks like this:

```
function doMin() {
    w.collapse(false);
    w.alignTo(document.body, 'bl-bl');
}
```

We simply tell our window to collapse down to the title bar (passing in a parameter of `false` simply indicates that we don't want to animate the collapse) and then use the `alignTo` method, which we've discussed previously. With the parameters we've chosen, the window's bottom left will be aligned to the bottom left of the document body—just like the first window in a taskbar would be.

Of course, with further windows, you'd end up with an overlapping stack in the bottom-left; not ideal for a real world application. However, it does show how the minimize event can be handled, and can be used as an alternative to the collapse method.

State handling

State handling with windows is a relatively simple process. Windows are fully integrated with the standard Ext JS state management facilities via the `stateful` configuration flag. Assuming that we want to track the position, minimize status, size and z-order of a window through page refreshes and user sessions, we can use code such as this:

```
var w = new Ext.Window({
    stateful: true,
    stateevents:['resize'] // track the resize event
});
```

We use the `stateevents` option to set an array of window events, which will cause the component to save its state. Unlike state handling with the `TreeNodes` in Chapter 8—*Ext JS Does Grow On Trees*, we don't need to hook into the `beforestatesave` event this time around. The window component will look after itself, and automatically set its configuration to reflect its previous state.

Window management

In a rich Internet application, it can be desirable to allow the user to have many windows open simultaneously, reviewing a variety of information without having to navigate to separate pages. Ext JS allows for this: you can create any number of non-modal windows and manipulate them as you see fit. However, we face a problem when using a multitude of windows—how do we manage them as a group? For example, the users may wish to clear their workspace by minimizing all open windows. We can achieve this functionality, and more, by using a **window group**.

Default window manager behavior

When you create an Ext.Window, it will automatically be assigned to a default Ext.WindowGroup which, by default, can always be referred to via the Ext.WindowMgr class. However, you can create as many additional WindowGroups as your application requires, assigning windows to them via the manager configuration option.

Why would your application require a method of grouping windows? Well, multiple windows are affected by z-order, in that they can be stacked on top of each other. We can use WindowMgr.bringToFront to bring a particular window to the top of the stack, perhaps if it has been updated with new information and we want to draw the user's attention to this. In some situations, this would be the same as using Ext.Window.toFront. However, the WindowMgr approach will respect the z-order grouping of individual WindowGroups, and so is a safer method when building a large application with many windowing options.

The grouping and z-ordering of windows is a confusing topic, so let's put these advanced features into a real-world context.

Multiple window example

We're going to build a very basic simulation of a customer service application. Our user will be the supervisor of a live chat system, where customers who are online can ask questions and get answers straight away. The supervisor will take some of these questions, but they also monitor the status of other agents who are dealing with customer sessions. We'll only be interested in the windowing aspect of this application, so it's going to be filled with a lot of dummy data to illustrate our point.

Here's a screenshot of the a simple application developed to support this:

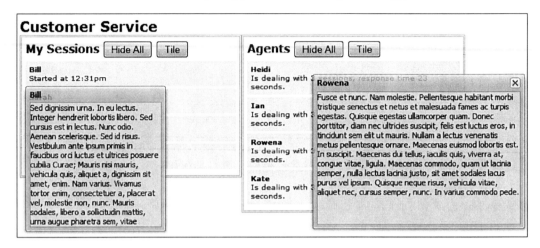

The lists have deliberately been left plain to avoid the need for extra JavaScript code—an application such as this could really benefit from grids or data views displaying the sessions and agents, but we really don't need them just to demonstrate our windowing code.

We're going to use a JavaScript object literal to structure our example. Here's the shell:

```
var customerService = {

    sessionsGroup : null,
    agentsGroup : null,

    init : function() {
    }
};
Ext.onReady(customerService.init, customerService);
```

We have a couple of local variables that will hold our window groups, and an empty `init` function that gets called, with the `customerService` object as its scope, from the `Ext.onReady` statement. Now that we've got our JavaScript skeleton, we need to take a look at the markup that is going to power our customer service app:

```
<div id="mySessions">
    <h2>My Sessions
        <button id="hideSessions">Hide All</button>
        <button id="tileSessions">Tile</button>
    </h2>
    <div id="s-p1">
```

```
            <h3>Bill</h3>
            <p>Started at 12:31pm</p>
            <div class="content"></div>
        </div>
    </div>
    <div id="agents">
        <h2>Agents
            <button id="hideAgents">Hide All</button>
            <button id="tileAgents">Tile</button>
        </h2>
        <div id="a-h1">
            <h3>Heidi</h3>
            <p>Is dealing with 3 sessions...</p>
            <div class="content"></div>
        </div>
    </div>
```

This is the HTML that will go straight into the body of our document. We've got two main containers—mySessions and agents—which then contain h2 tags with a few buttons, and some div tags. For example, within mySessions, we have the div #s-p1, containing an h3, a paragraph, and another div with the content class. The #s-p1 div is one of many that could appear within mySessions, with these divs being named as #s-xxx, with xxx being a unique identifier for that session.

Within agents, we have a similar structure with slightly different IDs—for example, the agent divs are named as #a-xxx. The various IDs in the HTML are extremely important for our JavaScript, as they'll be used to hook up event handlers, as we'll see in a moment. Let's take a look at our full init function (note that each code snippet will build on what came before).

```
init : function() {
    var s = Ext.select;
    var g = Ext.get;
    this.sessionsGroup = new Ext.WindowGroup();
    this.agentsGroup = new Ext.WindowGroup();

    s('#mySessions div').on('click', this.showSession, this);
    s('#agents div').on('click', this.showAgent, this);
}
```

The first two lines of this block of code are just shortcuts to clean up our code—we're storing references to the Ext functions in a variable with a smaller name. Nothing fancy. The next two lines see us creating two distinct window groups—one that will hold our session information window, and one for the agent information windows.

The next few lines make more sense given the HTML we discussed previously. We use our shortcut to `Ext.select` to add event listeners to all of the divs within #mySessions—handled by the `showSession` function—and within #agents—handled by `showAgent`. The third argument to the `on` function ensures that we maintain scope when the handlers are called. Let's take a look at the `showSession` function:

```
showSession : function(e){
    var target = e.getTarget('div', 5, true);
    var sessionId = target.dom.id + '-win';
    var win = this.sessionsGroup.get(sessionId);

    if(!win) {
        win = new Ext.Window({
            manager: this.sessionsGroup,
            id: sessionId,
            width: 200,
            height: 200,
            resizable: false,
            closable: false,
            title: target.down('h3').dom.innerHTML,
            html: target.down('.content').dom.innerHTML
        });
    }

    win.show();
    win.alignTo(target);
}
```

There's a lot happening here. The first line ensures that our target variable contains the session div that was clicked on, regardless of whether it was actually one of the session's child elements that was clicked. We then store a unique `sessionId` by taking the ID of the target session div and appending -win to it. Finally, we check if the session window group already has a reference to the window that we're about to create, by looking it up using the unique `sessionId`.

If the window doesn't exist then we need to create it. Most of the configuration options shown will be familiar from earlier in this chapter, but take note of our explicit assignment of the `sessionsGroup` as the managing group for this window. We're also using the `sessionId` as the ID for the window rather than relying on the automatically-generated ID that will be used by default. With the `title` and `html` options, we're using the `Ext.Element` DOM traversal facilities to assign the text of the session div's `h3` and `div.content` elements respectively.

We're now sure that the win variable holds a valid reference to a window, so we can go ahead and show the window. After we do so, we want to align it with the div that was clicked to show it, so the window's alignTo function is called. That's a whistle-stop tour of the showSession function. The showAgent function is almost identical, but refers to agentsGroup rather than sessionsGroup. Together these two functions make sure that our session and agent windows pop up successfully, so it's now time to take a look at how our WindowGroups can be used to manage them as a unit.

Customer service WindowGroups

We can add two lines to our init function that use window groups to perform a clearout of our customer service workspace:

```
g('hideSessions').on('click', this.sessionsGroup.hideAll);
g('hideAgents').on('click', this.agentsGroup.hideAll);
```

We can add event listeners to our hideSessions and hideAgents buttons that are directly handled by the hideAll functions of the sessionsGroup and agentsGroup. This short code snippet allows us to hide all of the agent or session windows with a click on the associated button. In a similar vein, we're going to add a couple more event listeners to our other buttons that will cause our windows to be tiled across the screen — organised into an easy overview:

```
g('tileAgents').on('click', this.tileAgents, this);
g('tileSessions').on('click', this.tileSessions, this);
```

This time the events are handled by tileAgents and tileSessions that look like this:

```
tileAgents : function(e) {
   this.sessionsGroup.hideAll();
   this.tile(this.agentsGroup);
},
tileSessions : function(e) {
   this.agentsGroup.hideAll();
   this.tile(this.sessionsGroup);
}
```

Again, we call the hideAll function to make sure that the other set of windows is cleared from the screen. When we've prepared the workspace, we can then pass the relevant window group to the tile function:

```
tile : function(group) {
   var previousWin = null;
   group.each(function(win) {
```

```
        if(previousWin) {
            if(win.getEl().getWidth() + previousWin.getEl().getRight() >
                Ext.getBody().getWidth()) {
                win.alignTo(document.body, 'tl-tl',
                            [0, previousWin.getEl().getHeight()]);
            } else {
                win.alignTo(previousWin.getEl(), 'tl-tr');
            }
        } else {
            win.alignTo(document.body, 'tl-tl');
        }

        previousWin = win;
    });
}
```

The key here is the `WindowGroup.each` function, which allows us to loop through every window assigned to the group and perform further actions and calculations. In this case, if it's our first iteration, then we align the window to `document.body`. For further iterations, the windows are aligned to the previous window in the loop, taking care to add a vertical offset if the window would have pushed off the rightmost side of the screen.

`hideAll` and `each` are useful ways of manipulating multiple windows. In this example, we've shown how two distinct groups of windows can be handled with very little coding overhead.

Summary

For me, the `Ext.Window` is one of the most fundamental aspects of a rich Ext JS application. Many of the other big components within the framework, such as the grid and tree, can display information in an easily-consumable and browsable manner, but the chances are that if you need to display or manipulate a record with a lot of information, need and do so without disrupting the user's workflow by navigating to a different page, you're going to want to use a window.

The great thing is that `Window` is flexible enough to slot straight into any application you may want to build with it. For ultimate power, simply fill it with custom HTML, or to create an integrated experience use Ext components. The fact is that the window subclasses panel provides you with the ability to construct complex pop ups by using the most suitable `Ext.layout` — be that of a form, or an accordion, or whatever — and have it look and feel the same as the rest of your application.

Although windows and dialogs will most likely have a place in your application, they should be used with care. There's a tendency to identify a requirement for displaying extra information and simply popping it up in the user's face; it could be that a less disruptive interface would be more suitable. Ultimately, `Window` and `Msg` sit alongside the other parts of Ext JS as tools that can be easily integrated into any application that requires them.

10
Effects

The easiest thing to do when writing a software application is to switch into programmer mode—to focus on the code, and not on the end user experience. The architecture of a system is extremely important, but if the user is not satisfied with their interactions with the system, then the project can only be seen as a failure.

Ext JS contributes to solving this issue by providing many slick components that react well to user input and maintain a consistent look and feel across the entire framework. "Feel" is a very fuzzy word when it comes to software design; the way a link acts when you hover over it or the way in which a window appears onscreen can be the difference between a pleasurable experience and a confusing one.

Many of Ext JS's components have transitional animations built in by default, allowing you to smoothly expand a `treenode` rather than suddenly pop it open, or to shrink down a window to a specified button that can be used to re-activate it later.

Features like this aren't just an added layer on top of the rest of the Ext framework; they're baked in at a low level to provide a consistent experience for both the developer and the end user.

It's elementary

The `Ext.Element` underlies many of the feature-rich widgets in Ext JS; indeed the `Ext.Component.getEl` method reflects the fact that widgets such as windows form fields and toolbars are supported by this fundamental building block.

`Ext.Element` mixes many methods from `Ext.Fx`, the class that is designed to provide slick transitions and animations for HTML elements and components alike. We're going to discuss the exciting possibilities that `Ext.Fx` provides, and also talk about the way in which it works together with `Ext.Element`.

Fancy features

As well as the building blocks of animation, we're going to examine various pieces of eye candy that you can find dotted around the Ext framework. There are a number of classes that provide added functionality to give your users feedback or assistance when they're using your application, and many components support these features straight out of the box. We can also use them in a standalone manner to create rich tooltips, mask items that are in the process of loading new data, or highlight individual parts of the screen to draw the user's attention to them.

It's ok to love

In truth, many of the functions we're going to cover in this chapter are superficial in nature. They add some whizz-bang transitions that are not strictly essential. There are two lines of defense for criticism. Firstly, a good developer understands that users are not machines—they're people—and a little bit of whizz-bang is good for everyone. Secondly, and perhaps more scientifically, it's much better to have a transition to signify a change than simply have something appear. A transition draws the eye and gives the user the opportunity to consume the visual cue that was presented.

A sudden change on screen results in a "what happened" response; a smooth transition provides a hint as to what's going on. As we tour the various features of Ext.Fx, bear in mind that they can be used for more than just eye-candy; they're great for adding value to your user experience.

Fxcellent functions

Ext.Fx is presented as a standalone class, architecturally independent of Ext. Element, but in reality it cannot be used on its own. Instead, it is automatically mixed into the methods and properties of the Ext.Element class, so that each action from Ext.Fx is available for each Ext.Element instance. The examples that follow will illustrate this point.

Methodical madness

As mentioned earlier, Ext.Fx has a range of methods that are called upon to perform the magic. Each of these methods is available for Ext.Element instances. So in the examples that follow, we're going to assume that you have a div element with an ID of "target" on your ready-to-go HTML page.

Fading

The term "fading" is used in `Ext.Fx` to refer to a change in opacity — from 100% opaque to 0%(fade out) and vice versa(fade in). In other words, we're making something disappear and reappear — but as this is the *Effects* chapter, the transition is animated. The two methods that perform these transitions are `Ext.Fx.fadeOut` and `Ext.Fx.fadeIn`, and both support simple zero-argument usage:

```
Ext.get('target').fadeOut();

window.setTimeout(function() {
    Ext.get('target').fadeIn();
}, 3000);
```

This usage will cause the target element to fade away slowly until it is completely invisible. The timeout happens three seconds later and causes the target to slowly re-appear, or fade in, until it is fully visible again.

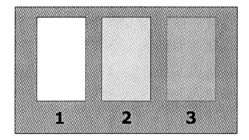

You can tweak the behavior of these methods using the `endOpacity` configuration option. In *theory*, this allows you to specify that the element will not fade out to complete invisibility, which can be useful if you simply want to indicate that an item is now less important. Alternatively, you can use it to dictate that an item will not return to total solidity:

```
Ext.get('target').fadeOut({endOpacity:0.25});

window.setTimeout(function() {
    Ext.get('target').fadeIn({endOpacity: 0.75});
}, 3000);
```

Note that I say "in theory"; actually, a limitation in Ext JS 2.2 means that the item in question will actually just vanish after reaching the `endOpacity`. I'd expect this to be fixed in the next release of the framework.

In the example just given, the initially-solid item is supposed to fade out to one quarter opacity before being restored after three seconds to only three quarters opacity.

In addition to the configuration options such as endOpacity that are specific to individual effects methods, there are also a number of common options shared by all Ext.Fx methods. These allow you to tweak the behavior of your effects even further. We'll discuss these later in this chapter.

Framing

Framing is reminiscent of a video game radar "ping". It radiates out from the point of origin, fading away with distance. A great use of this feature is to highlight a particular element on the screen—and the Ext.Fx.frame method also allows us to ensure that the user's attention is drawn by using multiple "pings". The simplest way of using it is without arguments:

```
Ext.get('target').frame();
```

This causes the target element to radiate a single light blue ping to draw attention to the element, which may be useful in some scenarios. However, to make sure that the user knows about a more important event, we could use something like this:

```
Ext.get('target').frame('ff0000', 3);
```

The first argument is the hexadecimal color of the framing effect, in this case, an angry red. The second argument specifies the number of times the ping is to be repeated. So here, we're using three red pulses to indicate that something pretty bad is about to happen.

These are the real strengths of the frame method: repetition, and the ability to use different colors to represent different situations and priorities.

Woooo: ghosting

Ghosts!-or rather ghosting—this is the term Ext JS gives to fading an element while it moves in a specified direction. This effect is used to give the impression that an element is transitioning from one area to another, for example the act of paging through a number of images could trigger ghosting when the **next** or **previous** link is selected. The default usage of ghost causes the element to drop down while fading out.

```
Ext.get('target').ghost();
```

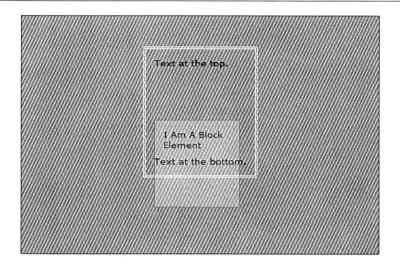

The default settings could be used to discard elements that are no longer needed—perhaps deletion events could be signified with a call to Ext.Fx.ghost. As mentioned previously, we can also cater for other situations by specifying different direction for the ghosting depending on the situation. The standard Ext.Fx anchor points, used in animation and alignment, can also be used with the ghost method:

```
Ext.get('target').ghost('tr');
```

Here, we indicate that the target will ghost out in the direction of its upper-right corner, but any anchor point is accepted. We'll talk more about anchoring later in the chapter. But it is this parameter that would allow us to replicate the paging functionality which was described earlier, that is, we can use left and right anchor points to move the ghost in the relevant directions.

Highlighting

If you're familiar with the term "Web 2.0", then you may also have heard of the "yellow fade technique". A quick web search will turn up numerous references to this JavaScript feature, which became popular when Web 2.0 was first becoming a buzzword. Typically used when an action has been completed and the user has been redirected to a new page, this effect causes a portion of the page—often an error message—to have its background highlighted in a different color. The highlight slowly fades away over a few seconds. Traditionally, the highlighted color has been a friendly yellow, but for error messages, we might favor something stronger. Having said that, yellow is the default for Ext.Fx.highlight:

> Looks like I'm highlighted in good ol' yellow...

This is triggered by the following basic code:

```
Ext.get('target').highlight();
```

Ext JS takes highlighting to the next level. While the standard usage affects the CSS background color of the target element, you can choose any CSS property, such as the color or border color. You can also specify the endColor of the highlight. In our second and more complex example, we can cause the text itself to start out white and end up green:

```
Ext.get('target').highlight('ffffff',{
    attr: 'color',
    endColor: '00ff00'
});
```

This is an extremely flexible method that can be used to highlight large portions of a page—perhaps a fieldset in a form, or just a block of text—perhaps in an online spellchecker. The point to be noted is that we can use it to respond and react to user input, and use its flexibility to indicate the state of our system in a noticeable manner.

Huffing and puffing

Ext.Fx's puff method tries to replicate the look of a puff of smoke slowly dissipating into the air. While some of the Ext.Fx effects are used to highlight areas, puff is used to transition an element off the screen. To do this, the element expands while becoming more transparent, eventually fading away completely. Puff doesn't have any special options of its own, so the default usage is pretty obvious:

```
Ext.get('target').puff();
```

Puff could be used with a quick transition to dismiss a window from the workspace, or a slower transition could illustrate the removal of an element, maybe an image from a gallery. However, there is one important point to note about this method: when used within the document flow, it will affect the position of the elements around it.

Although absolutely-positioned windows will not affect their surroundings, in our gallery example, it is possible that when you use puff, you'll get unexpected results as the expanding dimensions push your other images out of the way.

Developers who are aware of the potential side effects of using Ext.Fx.puff can add it to their toolkit, providing another interesting method of creating dynamic transitions in their applications.

Scaling the Ext JS heights

Scaling is one of the few Ext JS effects that has a specific use, rather than simply being an overlay on top of another action. It changes the dimensions of an element using a smooth transition, which has numerous applications. We can expand text areas to give more space for user input; we can replicate maximize and restore effects seen in the windowing applications; we can change the focus of a workspace by shrinking one portion and expanding another. The basic usage of `Ext.Fx.scale` looks like this:

```
Ext.get('target').scale(50, 150);
```

In this example, the target element will be smoothly-scaled to a width of 50 pixels and a height of 150 pixels. Both of these options also accept null values, which indicate that they should not be changed. This is useful if you want to restrict the scale to only horizontally or vertically.

 `Ext.Fx.scale` works only with those elements that have their display style set to block, to allow the width and height changes to take effect. Using it on inline elements won't trigger an error, but you will not see any change in the dimensions of the element, either.

Sliding into action

Within Ext JS, sliding refers to the transition of an element into or out of view. This is the same effect used in the `Ext.Fx.ghost` method, so we've seen it in action already. But in reality, there are two methods that fall under this heading — `:Ext.Fx.slideIn` and `Ext.Fx.slideOut`.

We can use these methods to either drop out an element that is no longer required, or introduce a new element onto the screen. An obvious application for this would be addition and deletion of records, where new items `slideIn` to the list and deleted items `slideOut`.

```
Ext.get('target').slideOut();

window.setTimeout(function() {
    Ext.get('target').slideIn();
}, 3000);
```

In the above example, we move the target out of view, and three seconds later bring it back in. By default, elements will `slideIn` and `slideOut` from their top edge, but the first argument to both functions allows you to use anchors to specify the direction of the movement:

```
Ext.get('target').slideOut('tr');
```

Here, we dictate that the target will `slideOut` to the top right. As with `Ext.Fx.puff`, you must be aware of the elements that surround the item you're sliding; text and other non-absolutely-positioned elements may be pushed around during the slide.

Switching from seen to unseen

The `switchOff` method is another means of removing an element from the screen. This one combines two actions: firstly a the element fades slightly to acknowledge the start of the effect, and then the element slowly collapses from the top and the bottom until it disappears. This two-stage effect means it can be used to draw the user's eye before the real vanishing act takes place. We can use `Ext.Fx.switchOff` in the following way:

```
Ext.get('target').switchOff();
```

As you can see, there are no unique arguments for this method, so it would seem that you're stuck with the default effect. But later we'll discuss the configuration options that are available for all of the `Ext.Fx` methods — the secret to complete control over your effects.

`SwitchOff` comes in pretty handy in situations where you'd like to cause an element to vanish without user interaction. For example, you might have some kind of monitoring screen on your website that displays the current visitors to your site, and tracks them as they move between pages. When their session expires, they will be removed from the list. Rather than simply transitioning off the screen you can highlight to the user that this is about to happen using `switchOff`: a quick flash to indicate that the action is about to occur, and then the actual collapse transition.

Shifting

The `Ext.Fx.shift` method may sound like a function in the same vein as `ghost` and `slideOut`, but in actual fact it's a little different. There's no default behavior associated with the method, so simply call it in this fashion:

```
Ext.get('target').shift();
```

This will have no effect. Instead, `shift` must be supplied with a literal containing one or more values from the following:

- `width`
- `height`
- `x`
- `y`

By setting one of these values and passing it to `shift`, we can cause the target element to move to the `x,y` coordinates and resize to the `width,height` dimensions — in the smooth manner which we've come to expect of `Ext.Fx`. Here's an example:

```
Ext.get('target').shift({
    x: 5,
    y: 300,
    width: 300,
    height: 200
});
```

In this example, our target element will move to a position of 5 pixels from the left and 300 from the top of the viewport, and will resize to 300x200 pixels. These changes happen simultaneously, with the element resizing as it moves.

Effectively, `shift` is a version of `Ext.Fx.scale` that adds the ability to reposition the element. This is a great mechanism for re-organizing a workspace — shifting panels of data from a place of prominence to a place more unobtrusive, and doing so in a smooth, dynamic manner.

And now, the interesting stuff

All of the methods that we've just covered have some broad similarities. But each of them has certain distinct differences which make them applicable as solutions for a range of very different problems. We're now going to discuss how an extra feature of `Ext.Fx` can tweak and tailor the effects we've already reviewed.

In many of the above examples, the functionality on offer is slightly limited. What's been glossed over until now is that each of the methods we've discussesd also accepts a standard configuration object that provides a host of common options to bring their full functionality to your fingertips.

The Fx is in

We've briefly touched upon the way in which anchoring options are used within `Ext.Fx`, for example, methods such as a ghost accepting a string representing the direction in which to move. Over the next few pages, we'll not only discuss this in detail, but we'll also go over the numerous configuration options that are common to all of the `Ext.Fx` methods.

Anchoring yourself with Ext

Specifying directions, anchors, alignment, and more is all based around a scheme of anchor positions. These are used by Ext JS's animation system to determine the direction of movement, and they have a pretty simple naming convention:

Anchor Position String	Description
tl	Top left corner
t	Center of the top edge
tr	Top right corner
l	Center of the left edge
r	Center of the right edge
bl	Bottom left corner
b	Center of the bottom edge
br	Bottom right corner

These options allow eight-way movement when using methods such as `Ext.Fx.ghost`. But the same concept is seen in methods such as `Ext.Element.alignTo` and `Ext.Element.anchorTo`, where two anchor points can be combined, and the "?" character can be used to dictate that the alignment will be constrained to the viewpoint.

In short, it pays to familiarize yourself with the Ext JS anchor positions, as you'll almost certainly use them in your application—either to move elements or to just bend them to suit your many needs. More than that, `Ext.Components` have underlying elements. So you'll most likely use these features when developing a solution with rich widgets.

Now, back to the topic at hand—taming the `Ext.Fx` class.

Options

As mentioned earlier, each of the `Ext.Fx` methods we've covered can take an optional configuration literal as its last parameter, which provides 11 settings for tweaking your effects. The simplest is probably `duration`, which specifies how long the effect should last. This is useful for ensuring that your transitions last long enough for your users to catch them. Although the default durations of each effect are usually pretty sensible, there are many use-cases for overriding this value. Here's an example of using duration, and indeed the configuration option argument in general:

```
Ext.get('target').switchOff({
    duration: 10
});
```

In this example, we pass a standard object literal to the switchOff method, and the duration property is set to 10, indicating that the switchOff should take place over ten seconds.

With the default behavior of some of the Ext.Fx methods, you end up with some sub-optimal transitions. For example, many of the effects that cause an element to vanish will actually just leave a big gap where the element used to be. This is because they complete the transition by setting the visibility of the element to hidden, rather than removing it from the DOM or from the document flow. We can rectify this using two more configuration options: remove and useDisplay.

The first, remove, signifies that we'd like to completely destroy the element when the transition has completed. The second, useDisplay, means that the element will be hidden using display:none rather than visibility:hidden, so that it will no longer affect the nodes around it. Using remove and useDisplay together is redundant. If the node is completely removed, it makes no difference how it's hidden. If you're planning on re-using or re-showing the element in question, then stick with useDisplay; otherwise you may as well be tidy (and avoid potential memory leaks) and use remove.

The configuration options also allow us to dictate what else happens when the effect has completed. We have two options that control the look of our element: afterCls and afterStyle, which allow a CSS class or raw CSS rules to be applied to the element at the end of our transition. This can be used to add a permanent change to the element in question, perhaps highlighting it as a newly-introduced item.

We have two more options that give us the power to perform further actions when the effect has completed: callback, which allows us to specify a function to be called at the end of the transition, and scope, which is the scope of the callback function. For example:

```
Ext.get('target').switchOff({
    callback: function() {
        alert('Effect complete!');
    }
});
```

The Ext.Fx class handles the queuing of effects automatically, so don't use this to trigger another effect. Instead, use it to trigger actions associated with the animation.

Easy does it

Our next configuration option is `easing`. In animation terminology, `easing` refers to the means by which the transition *eases* from a stop to movement and back to a stop again. By default, Ext JS effects will abruptly start and stop, but by using the `easing` option, we can specify how it will accelerate and decelerate at the start and end of the effect respectively.

 The easing effects supported by Ext JS vary depending on which adapter you're using. If you're using the Ext JS Base adapter, then you'll get the full works.

A basic example of this in action is the `easeBoth` value. This causes the animation to gradually speed up and then slow down in order to provide a smooth-looking transition:

```
Ext.get('target').scale(50, 150, {easing: 'easeBoth'});
```

Here, we're applying the easing option to the scale effect, and by using `easeBoth`, we can have a less jarring movement as it progresses. There are many more easing options:

- `easeNone`
- `easeIn`
- `easeOut`
- `easeBoth`
- `easeInStrong`
- `easeOutStrong`
- `easeBothStrong`
- `elasticIn`
- `elasticOut`
- `elasticBoth`
- `backIn`
- `backOut`
- `backBoth`
- `bounceIn`
- `bounceOut`
- `bounceBoth`

That's a list of the options supported by Ext JS Base. Ones like `bounceIn` provide a bit of a spring to the effect, which is perhaps more useful in a gaming application than in data entry, but the beauty of having such a wide choice is that you are likely to find something that fits your requirements.

The final few configuration options apply to the way your current effect interacts with other effects that may occur within its lifetime. For example, `block` will specify that no other effects are queued up while this one is running, which is useful in scenarios where triggering further changes could adversely affect your application's state. The `block` option tells all other effects to "bide your time" until things have calmed down.

```
Ext.get('target').shift({
    x: 5,
    y: 300,
    width: 300,
    height: 200,
    block: true
});
```

Here, we see an interesting usage of the `Ext.Fx.shift` method, in which the shift-specific configuration options are augmented by the common `Fx` ones.

We also have the `stopFx` and `concurrent` options. `stopFx` allows us to cancel all effects that get triggered after this one, while `concurrent` specifies whether subsequent effects will run in parallel with this one, or will be queued up until after this one has completed. By default, they'll queue up and run in sequence, but there are situations in which you will be able to apply multiple effects at a time, and we'll talk more about that in the next few sections.

Multiple effects

Most of the time, you'll use effects one at a time on different elements to achieve the look you're after, but in some circumstances, it can be useful to use multiple effects. There are a few different ways of handling this scenario, and in the next few sections, we're going to review these ways. We're also going to see how we can influence any running effects from our code.

Chaining

An easy way to set up a second effect to run after your first is completed, is to use method chaining. Because each of the main `Ext.Fx` methods returns the `Ext.Element` that was the target of the effect, you can then call further `Ext.Element` methods, including those provided by `Ext.Fx`:

```
Ext.get('target').slideIn().highlight();
```

As you can see from this example, we're calling `slideIn` followed by `highlight`, which indicates that `highlight` will be added to the effects queue to run after `slideIn` completes.

Queuing

Queuing is the default behavior for effects set up either by method chaining, or by multiple calls. The following code sample is functionally-identical to our previous example:

```
Ext.get('target').slideIn();
Ext.get('target').highlight();
```

In both cases, the `highlight` effect will be queued up behind `slideIn`. This negates the need for any complicated timing or callback-based set-ups to trigger effects that run sequentially.

Concurrency

Although queuing is the default, we also have the option of running effects in parallel by using the previously-discussed `concurrent` configuration option. This gives us the opportunity to combine effects—for example, we could `highlight` an element as it scales up:

```
Ext.get('target').scale(300, 200 ,{
    concurrent:true
}).highlight();
```

This provides a very powerful capacity for customization.

Blocking and Ext.Fx utility methods

There are a number of extra methods within the `Ext.Fx` class that aren't directly responsible for creating effects. Instead, they can be used to manage and monitor effects that are already in the queue. A great example of this is the `stopFx` method, which is as simple as it sounds—we can call it to cancel any animations that are currently running. It also clears the effects queue, and primes the element for user interaction or further manipulation.

Interestingly, `stopFx` returns the target `Ext.Element`, allowing the developer to chain up further methods. Perhaps you have set up a `slideIn` that is subsequently canceled and replaced with `slideOut`:

```
Ext.get('target').stopFx().slideOut();
```

Such code is useful if we need to interrupt an animation to give control back to the user — an ability that can be crucial in giving the user the responsiveness they require. However, in other circumstances you may want to prevent the user from interfering with the current state of the application, and if that's the case, we have the `hasFxBlock` method. Typically, this is used to make sure that the user can't queue up the same effect many times — we can prevent additional effect calls to the element if `hasFxBlock` returns true.

Elemental

As we've seen, the `Ext.Element` is the key to using `Ext.Fx`. It's important that, when rolling your own custom versions of Ext JS, you make sure that you include `Ext.Fx` if you want to be able to use its methods for `Ext.Element`. However, even when used stand-alone, `Ext.Element` has a number of methods all of its own that can provide some interesting possibilities for animation.

Making a move

There are many methods on `Ext.Element` that can be used to manipulate a target element, but some of them have a free extra. Pass in a `true` value as the last parameter, and the manipulation will be animated.

```
Ext.get('target').moveTo(300, 500, true);
```

In this case, the target element will move to a location 300 pixels from the left and 500 from the top of the viewport. But, because of this last parameter, it will not simply jump to that location, but will smoothly transition to the specified point.

In addition to simply passing in `true` as the third parameter, we can pass in a full configuration object instead. This uses the same animation options for `Ext.Fx` that we discussed earlier in the chapter.

 `Ext.Element` animations can be used at the same time as the ones from `Ext.Fx`, but they are not guaranteed to support the queuing features that are always available with the `Ext.Fx` methods.

There are many methods, such as `setOpacity` and `scroll`, that can be used in this fashion to provide the means for adding simple transitions. This is a good foundation, which `Ext.Fx` builds upon.

There's another piece of the animation puzzle that we're yet to touch upon: Ext.Element.animate. This is the generic means of applying animations to an element, and is a shortcut to the same underlying methods that are used by all of the Ext.Element methods that support animation.

Advanced applications of this method involve using the Ext.lib.anim entries that register all of the stock animation types available to Ext JS, and adding new registered animation handlers to support custom scenarios. In most cases, using the stock Ext.Element methods or the Ext.Fx methods will be sufficient, even for advanced cases.

Using Ext components

The animations which are available on Ext.Element are particularly interesting when you consider that many Ext.Components, such as the Window or FormPanel, have an underlying Element as their container. This means that you can apply these effects to full components as well as to standard elements, providing an added utility for these methods.

Bring out the flash

We've covered Ext.Fx and the other animation techniques that Ext JS offers in depth, now. But we've still got a few more features to cover when it comes to showing off with the framework. There are a number of Ext classes that provide a little extra sparkle to the top of the standard solutions. We've got LoadMask that allows you to mask off a portion of the screen while it's being refreshed, and QuickTip that offers a rich, configurable tooltip system.

These classes open up a new range of options when it comes to creating compelling user-experiences, and we're going to examine them in detail over the next few pages. A key feature of each is that they are reasonably simple to use, which is partly the reason why you'll want use them in many of your Ext JS applications.

You're maskin', I'm tellin'

The Ext.LoadMask class has a couple of different use cases. We can use it to simply display a message that keeps the user informed, or we can use it to prevent interaction with a component that is being refreshed.

Let's look at the first scenario-that is, using an `Ext.LoadMask` to simply overlay an element with a message.

```
var target = Ext.get('target');
var mask = new Ext.LoadMask(target);
mask.show();
```

In the above example, once we obtain an element using `Ext.get`, we pass it into the `Ext.LoadMask` constructor and call the `show` method on the `LoadMask` instance. There is also an optional second parameter for the `Ext.LoadMask` constructor: a configuration object with four properties:

Property Name	Description
msg	The loading message to be displayed in the center of the mask
msgCls	The CSS class to use for the loading message container
removeMask	Boolean; set to True to destroy the mask after the load is complete
store	Discussed later

When creating a load mask in this way, we can dismiss it by calling the `mask.hide` method. Although this masking approach is pretty straightforward, it's also a little verbose. So in some cases, it's better to use the shortcut method that `Ext.Element` provides:

```
Ext.get('target').mask('Loading...', 'x-mask-loading');
```

In this example, we're explicitly passing the message text and message CSS class as the first and second arguments respectively. This allows us to replicate the functionality provided by a basic `Ext.LoadMask` call, as shown in the first example, but they're both optional. When you're done with the mask, you can hide it by calling the `unmask` method of your `Ext.Element` instance. If you have stored a reference to the mask, you can call the `hide` method of that instance instead.

Data binding and other tales

Although it initially seems that the Ext.Element approach is better, there are actually a few compelling reasons for using the full LoadMask. The most interesting reason is that it can be tied to a specified Ext.data.Store instance, allowing you to automatically mask and unmask your element based on when the store is loading. This cuts down on your code when showing the mask, but it also negates the need to hook up an event listener for your load complete events. Let's take a look at how this feature can be used:

```
var slowStore = GetSlowStore();

var mask = new Ext.LoadMask(Ext.get('target'), {
    store:slowStore
});

slowStore.load();
```

We're not interested in how to create a store, so that's been hidden away in a function call. All we care is that our example store is going to take a couple of seconds to finish loading. We instantiate a new LoadMask with an element as the first constructor parameter, and a configuration literal as the second one. The store property accepts our slowStore as its value.

Now that everything's set up, we simply call the load method of the store. This will mask over our target element, and in a few seconds when it has finished loading, the mask will automatically be dismissed.

Considering components

As we've seen, there are a number of ways of manually masking elements, and you could use any of these approaches to the Ext.Elements that under-lie many Ext.Components. However, it's important to note that some components provide this functionality for you, cutting down on the code that you need to write in order to enable this feature in your applications. For example, the Ext.grid.GridPanel has a boolean loadMask configuration option, which not only masks the panel but also automatically ties in to the datasource that is feeding the GridPanel.

QuickTipping

It's often very useful to be able to supply further information for a button or form field, just in case your users are unclear as to its purpose. In many cases, it's impractical to put this information inline, next to the item in question, simply because it would make the interface highly cluttered. In this situation, tooltips are a great alternative to inline information, and with Ext JS these little pop-up snippets can contain any HTML that you'd like to show.

The `Ext.QuickTips` class is a singleton that provides a very easy method of creating rich tooltips. It allows you to put your `QuickTip` setup information directly into the markup of your page—a great method for reducing the configuration required. In many cases, having the description text within your main HTML makes the most sense. This approach is supported by the use of a number of extra attributes for any HTML element that you'd like to tie the `QuickTip` to, with `ext:qwidth`, `ext:qtitle` and `ext:qtip` being the most commonly-used:

```
<input type="text" ext:qtitle="Information" ext:qtip=
                "This field can contain text!" ext:qwidth="200" />
```

We need to activate the global `QuickTips` handler before this will start working:

```
Ext.QuickTips.init();
```

It's also worth mentioning that nonstandard attributes will cause After completing these two steps, you'll end up with the tooltip you see here:

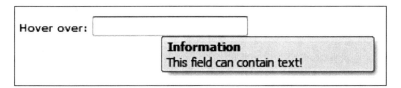

As well as using markup-based tooltips, we can also programmatically create more customizable ones with the `Ext.ToolTip` class. This provides a range of configuration options to change the behavior and appearance of the tooltips, and also allows you to pull tooltip data from an external source, by using the power of AJAX.

The simplest usage of this class is as follows:

```
new Ext.ToolTip({
    target: 'tipTarget',
    html: 'This is where our information goes!'
});
```

The constructor for `Ext.ToolTip` accepts a configuration literal as its only argument, and here we're using the mandatory `target` property to specify which element will trigger the tooltip; in this case it will be the one with the ID `tipTarget`. Note that we're using a string to refer to the ID, but in fact you can pass in an `Ext.Element` reference or a standard HTML node. We're then setting the `html` property to the text that we'd like to show in the tooltip. As the name of the property indicates, you can add any extra markup you like—even images.

`Ext.ToolTip` has a number of other interesting options, such as the ability to tweak the time it takes for the tooltip to appear and then vanish, by using the `showDelay` and `hideDelay` configuration properties. This can be useful if you need the tooltip to appear promptly when the user hovers over its associated element, or if you want to make sure that the information is on-screen long enough to be taken in.

We've also got the ability to set the title of the tooltip in the same way as we did with the markup-based solution, that is, by using the `title` option. In fact, many of the options, such as `title`, come from the fact that `Ext.ToolTip` is a subclass of `Ext.Panel`. This means that we can use features such as the `autoLoad` configuration option to grab content from a URL, or use the `closable` option, to force the user to dismiss the tooltip using a close widget.

`QuickTips` and `ToolTips` are great examples of Ext JS classes that aren't *essential* to an application, but that provide a layer of functionality that can take your solution from something ordinary to something highly usable.

Summary

There's a fine line between visual cues and annoying effects. Although we've reviewed many of the Ext JS features that allow you to gear your application towards either extreme, this chapter has only been about the tools—not how you should use them.

That said, we've also looked at a couple of examples that illustrate just how useful eye candy can be when helping out your users. By providing a little something extra when you're deleting a record or closing a data display, you can turn a potentially-confusing experience into one that is supported by gradual changes in visual state, rather than immediate shifts from one click to another.

The key is to ensure that those gradual changes aren't too gradual, that your animations aren't in-your-face, and that they aren't triggered every time the user presses a button. Software applications are about getting things done, and having portions of the page whizzing around the screen isn't likely to help with that.

Ext JS isn't just about these fancy effects, though. We've demonstrated a couple of classes that are utility tools with style. `ToolTips` and `LoadMasks` are genuinely useful in many scenarios, and could rarely be used in an "in your face" manner.

Using `ToolTips` can add a lot of value to a busy application, removing clutter by moving inline text into pop ups, and providing unified and attractive assistance to your users. Images, and even HTML links, can provide more information than could possibly be shown next to a form field.

The second of the classes we covered, LoadMask, can form a critical part of a system, ensuring not only that your users are prevented from interrupting a load operation, but also that the mask that appears is attractive, consistent, and can contain customized information that keeps the users informed.

In the next chapter, we're going to take a look at one of the most typical examples of Web 2.0 glitz: drag-and-drop. In a typical Ext JS manner, we're going to see how it's not only simple to use, but also powerful in its functionality.

11
Drag-and-Drop

In the world of software development, desktop applications are still number one. Although web sites and, latterly, web applications are developing rapidly using frameworks such as Ext JS, they are yet to reach the level of complexity that we see in our most extensive desktop programs.

Drag-and-drop, the subject matter of this chapter, is a good example of this. Moving items across the screen using the mouse on a standard computer desktop is all-pervasive; it is available for a great many actions and it is available in virtually every application, even if this is in a limited form.

Part of the reason for this is that implementing drag-and-drop using JavaScript is pretty hard. Coming up with a consistent methodology for turning any element into a draggable widget that can then be placed on another element, and have it work in every browser, and have it support scrolling, and take into account iframes is, to say the least, problematic.

At the start of the Web 2.0 revolution, we started to see some more consistent implementations of drag-and-drop appearing—ones that fulfilled many of the criteria we've just outlined. But even then, the Web didn't start using it in such a free and easy manner as the desktop, perhaps because of the poor use cases that were used as demonstrations for this new functionality. After all, does anyone really want to work with a drag-and-drop shopping cart system?

Drop what you're doing

The implementation of drag-and-drop that Ext JS provides succeeds on many levels. It is cross-browser and easy to use, but more importantly, it is used in multiple widgets within the framework, such as the `GridPanel` and `TreePanel`, making it easy to implement in useful real-world applications.

In addition, the Ext.dd package contains a number of classes that allow you to create simple drag-and-drop features with ease — shopping carts included. There is sufficient granularity to support more advanced scenarios as well, providing you with a means of creating custom drag-and-drop solutions that are fully integrated into your Ext application.

In this chapter, we'll review the Ext.dd package and ways in which it can extend your toolkit, but we'll also be looking at how to extend the drag-and-drop functionality provided by the various Ext components.

Life's a drag

There are clearly two parts to creating a working drag-and-drop feature — the dragging, and the dropping. As these are two separate operations, we'll handle them separately for our simple use case.

Sourcing a solution

The first part we need to look at is the drag action. Ext will enable this using the Ext.dd.DragSource, which actually makes the whole thing a breeze. Assume that you've got a <div> element on your page with an ID, dragMe:

```
new Ext.dd.DragSource("dragMe");
```

That's all you need to get up and running!

Try running this code and grab hold of your element. You can now drag it around the page, but there's a little bit more to it than that. Ext JS provides a few extra features by default which will be demonstrated by this code.

Approximating

When you begin dragging the element, you'll see that you don't actually drag the full element as you would in some drag-and-drop implementations that you might have seen. Instead, Ext JS automatically provides a proxy — a lightweight representation of whatever element you're dragging. This facility is provided by Ext in the form of the Ext.dd.StatusProxy class.

If you're using an element with a little bit of text in, you'll see that Ext uses that as the contents of the status proxy, but that's as far as it goes in trying to replicate your element when creating a visualization of the drag action. The dimensions of your element will be discarded, and the proxy will try and fit the content in as best it can. But if you've got a lot of data inside your element you may find that the status proxy is somewhat out of shape.

What's the advantage of having a status proxy, rather than just using the element itself? Well, one thing that you'll also see from our demonstration code is that Ext provides a little **no-entry** icon as you move the proxy around. That changes to a green tick when you move the proxy over a valid drop point, as we'll see shortly. But the great thing is that using a proxy will give you this indicator for free.

Another advantage of using the status proxy instead of the full element is that it's much more workable, both in terms of processing power and in terms of the actual stuff you're going to be dragging across the screen; moving a 10 column, 200 row table isn't going to be smooth and isn't going to look good either. A status proxy makes for a neat solution to these kinds of problems, and has some bonus features too—as we'll see later.

Snap!

Another built-in feature of an `Ext.dd.DragSource` is the action that occurs when you drop the element in a place that isn't a valid drop target—that is, when the proxy's red **no entry** sign is showing. It immediately "snaps" back to where it came from, highlighting the original element in light-blue to notify the user that it has returned to its original position.

Drop me off

Now that we've managed to drag something around, we can move to the second part of the plan—dropping. The idea is that we have a `drop target`—an element that triggers that green tick in the proxy to signify that you can drop the proxy into it.

In order to do this, we make use of the `Ext.dd.DropTarget` class, in pretty much the same way as we used `DragTarget`:

```
new Ext.dd.DropTarget("dropHere");
```

The DropTarget constructor accepts a mixed element object—in this case, the ID of an element on our page—and defines that element as a valid target for any drop operations. Running these two examples together will illustrate the changing status of the drag proxy icon—from red to green, when it's hovering over a drop target.

But wait: Nothing's happening!

The tricky thing about this kind of basic drag-and-drop is that nothing really happens when you perform the drop action. In fact, the dragged element just snaps back to its source just as it would if you'd dropped it when the proxy icon was red.

The trick lies in providing a function that overrides the DropTarget.notifyDrop method. By default, this method has no implementation and simply returns false, causing the dragged element to snap back to its source. By writing a little bit of custom code, we can make the drop action complete in whichever way we see fit.

 Why is this step necessary? Surely Ext JS should know that we want to drag that over to there? There are so many variations of drag-and-drop that it's impossible for Ext to understand what you're trying to do. Instead, it makes it trivial to add your own actions to drag-and-drop operations.

We're going to take a look at some sample code that hooks into this facet of the drag-and-drop support by creating a simple example that causes the dragged element to be inserted within the drop target. This is probably the behavior that you expected to see with the default setup. Although it won't be that useful within itself, it should help fill in some of the gaps.

Assuming that we have the same code as in our previous few examples, with a DragSource and a DropTarget, we now need to add an implementation of notifyDrop to the DropTarget:

```
new Ext.dd.DragSource('drag');
new Ext.dd.DropTarget('drop', {
    notifyDrop: function() { return true; }
});
```

This simple addition, which overrides the default implementation of notifyDrop, returns true and signifies that we do not wish the drag target to snap back to its original position. This is enough to partially fulfill our expectations of what our drag-and-drop code should have done in the first place. The drag source can be released over the drop target without snapping back to its original position. However, we do need to do a little more work to actually make the element move into the target, and we'll look at how to do this, shortly.

Interacting the fool

While the previous examples are interesting in the abstract sense — they give us an idea of how the Ext JS drag-and-drop system works — they aren't going to be setting your newest development alight. For that, we need to consider how multiple drag targets and drop targets can interact, and how we can set up more complicated systems for dragging around items of data.

Zones of control

We've seen how to hook up a single draggable item, but often, you'll want to have a number of elements ready to be moved around the screen. The solution here is to use `Ext.dd.DragZone` and `Ext.dd.DropZone` to enable the movement of multiple nodes. We're going to replicate a simple to-do list application, which will allow the user to move items from one list to another. However, this functionality will be seriously limited, allowing us to focus only on the relevant topics. First, we need to set up some basic HTML:

```
<h1>Today</h1>
<ul id="today">
    <li>Shopping</li>
    <li>Haircut</li>
</ul>

<h1>Tomorrow</h1>
<ul id="tmrw">
    <li>Wash car</li>
</ul>
```

We've got two lists, one with an `id` of `today` and one with an `id` of `tmrw`. Our user will be able to move items between the two lists to simulate reorganization of their next few day's tasks. Our first snippet of JavaScript will use the `Ext.dd.DragZone` to set these lists as containers of draggable items. Remember that your JS code needs to go inside an `Ext.onReady` call.

```
new Ext.dd.DragZone('today');
new Ext.dd.DragZone('tmrw');
```

This looks pretty straightforward, but there is one sticking point. Testing the code at this point will highlight the fact that it doesn't actually enable any functionality — nothing happens. Alongwith setting up the `DragZone`, we need to explicitly say which child nodes within those `DragZones` are going to be draggable.

Why the extra step? In complex applications, we may have many nested child nodes. So automatically setting all of them up as draggable could cause performance problems and unexpected behavior. Instead, we could do so manually, avoiding these potential issues.

In order to make our list items draggable, we need to register them with the `Ext.dd.Registry`:

```
var drags = document.getElementsByTagName('li');
for(var i =0; i< drags.length; i++){
    Ext.dd.Registry.register(drags[i]);
}
```

This is a pretty naïve implementation, simply registering all of the `<li>` elements on the page, but it should give you an idea of what is required. If you test the code now, you'll see that all of the items can be dragged around as you'd expect. So we need to move on to providing a place to drop them:

```
var cfg = { onNodeDrop: drop }
new Ext.dd.DropZone('tmrw', cfg);
new Ext.dd.DropZone('today', cfg);
```

We create a `cfg` object, which holds configuration data common to both of our `Ext.dd.DropZone` instances. The `onNodeDrop` method of `DropZone` is called by `DropZone.notifyDrop` automatically when it realizes that you've dropped a registered node. In this case, we're pointing to a function called `drop` that will override the existing, empty, implementation of `onNodeDrop`. The new implementation looks like this:

```
// dropNodeData-drop node data object
// source-drag zone which contained the dragged element
// event-the drag drop event
// dragNodeData-drag source data object
// this-destination drop zone
function drop(dropNodeData, source, event, dragNodeData) {

var dragged = source.dragData.ddel;
    var sourceContainer = source.el.dom;
    var destinationContainer = this.getEl();

    sourceContainer.removeChild(dragged);
    destinationContainer.appendChild(dragged);

    return true;
}
```

We use the arguments passed to this function to get hold of three elements: the item that is being dragged, the list that it came from, and the list it's being dragged to. With this information, we can remove the item from the source list and then append it to the destination list. We then return a value of `true` to prevent the item's proxy from snapping back to its point of origin.

Changing our lists

With this sample code, we've demonstrated the use of Ext JS drag-and-drop functionality in a practical manner. It's a very simple application, of course, but it's good. We can see how the powerful aspects of the `Ext.dd` package can be applied in a straightforward manner.

Later, we'll see how many aspects of the Ext JS framework support drag-and-drop with very little configuration, and how a knowledge of how the underlying classes work is essential if such support is to be shaped to your requirements.

Registering an interest

We've already discussed how the child nodes of a `DragZone` must be registered in the `Ext.dd.Registry` before they can be dragged around. This extra step can be a little painful, and we'll see ways around this later, but for now, let's concentrate on the advantages you get when a node is added to the `Ext.dd.Registry`.

In our previous examples, we used the `Ext.dd.Registry.register` method with a single parameter: the element to be registered. However, `register` also takes a second, optional parameter that allows you to add an extra metadata object to the item being dragged around. This metadata can be leveraged in any way you see fit for your application, but a possible use would be to pass "compatibility" information to the drop event. Imagine you are producing an application that lets you assemble a "virtual outfit" by dragging-and-dropping items of clothing. We could use metadata to make sure that only items of clothing from the "summer" range can be combined, by including range information as part of the drag data. There are many different applications for the metadata facility, but because it's just an arbitrary object, it really is up to you to decide how it can be used.

Although there is overhead associated with the use of `Ext.dd.Registry`, we've shown that it also has important benefits which, depending on the needs of your application, could outweigh the hassle of writing extra registration code.

Extreme drag-and-drop

One of the great things about drag-and-drop in Ext JS is that you can use it with many of the supplied Ext Components without having to delve into the guts of how they work. We're going to examine the use of drag-and-drop to create a master-detail layout with an `Ext.DataView` and an `Ext.FormPanel`. This way, we can demonstrate the integration of drag-and-drop with commonly-used components. Much of what we're going to cover will be familiar to you from our previous example, but the application of that knowledge will be slightly different.

We're going to be working with some very simple HTML:

```
<div id="people"></div>
<div id="detail"></div>
```

The `people` <div> will contain our `DataView`, listing a group of people pulled from a store. The `detail` <div> will contain the form that we can drag items onto.

DataView dragging

The first step is to create our `Ext.DataView`, and enable the dragging of its nodes. The code to initialize the view looks like this:

```
var personView = new Ext.DataView({
    tpl: '<tpl for=".">' +
            '<div class="person">' +
                '<h1>{name}</h1>' +
                '<div><img src="img/{image}" alt="{name}" /></div>' +
```

```
            '</div>' +
          '</tpl>',
      itemSelector: 'div.person',
      store: personStore
  });
  personView.render('people');
```

You'll notice that the implementation of the `personStore` isn't shown, but it needs to have an ID, name, image, city, and country items within its records in order to support what we're going to do. Note that within our template, we're showing a header containing the `name` of the person and an `image` representing them.

Based on our experience with list items, we can set up a `DragZone` for the `DataView` container, and register the `<div>` elements with a class, `person`, using the `Ext.dd.Registry`. If you try this approach, you'll see why it's not the right one for this particular application—it simply doesn't work! The `person` nodes can't be dragged around as you'd expect.

The reason for this lies with the `Ext.dd.Registry`. As the children of a `DragZone` need to be registered with the `Ext.dd.Registry`, before they can be dragged around, we would need to ensure that every possible child—in our case the `<h1>` and `<img>` tags—is registered. This is clearly not a very practical solution, and so we must take a different approach.

Dealing with drag data

We need to deal with this issue on a slightly higher level. Rather than dealing with each individual child node, we will look at overriding the default behavior of `Ext.dd.DragZone` in order to achieve our goal.

The `getDragData` method of the `DragZone` class is called whenever a `mousedown` occurs within the `DragZone` container. This means that we can use it to listen for the start of a drag event no matter which child node is clicked. In our circumstances, we'll examine the target of the `mousedown` event and navigate up through the DOM until we find the `person` node that represents the item we really want to use in our drag operation. So the code for setting up our `DragZone` would look like this:

```
  new Ext.dd.DragZone(personView.getEl(), {
     getDragData : function(e) {
        var container = e.getTarget('div.person', 5, true);

        return {
           ddel : container
        }
     }
  });
```

As mentioned earlier, we get the `person` container node from the `mousedown` event, and we use it to populate the `ddel` property of the object that is returned from `getDragData`. Earlier in the chapter, when dealing with dropping a node onto a `DropZone`, we looked at the `dragData.ddel` property to find the node that was being dropped. This is the same data, but from the other point of view — this is how it gets populated.

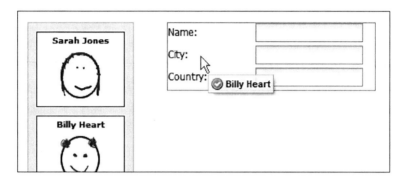

Now we've got our `DataView` working as we expected, but there are a couple of interesting additions that we can make at this point. Let's examine those now.

Proxies and metadata

When we specified the `ddel` property in `getDragData`, we were essentially populating the proxy that was going to follow the mouse pointer as we dragged our node around. This is a useful consideration. Consider the following code:

```
return {
    ddel : container.down('h1').dom
}
```

Now, instead of our proxy appearing as the full node, it'll only appear as the `h1` tag within our node. When we've talked about proxies before, we've mentioned that dragging a cut-down version of the full item can be a very useful approach, and this is how it can be achieved when using `DragZones`.

We also have the option of passing extra data into the drag by using other properties of `dragData`. In fact, any information that we add to the object will be available when the item is dropped. Here's what we're going to do in our example code:

```
return {
    ddel : container.down('h1').dom,
    record : personView.getRecord(container.dom)
}
```

We can actually pass the record associated with the item that was clicked as a data item in our drag operation. This is going to come in very handy when we come to populate our `FormPanel`.

Dropping in the details

This is the other side of the coin—handling the drop action that is triggered when we release a dragged node from our `DataView`. The concepts behind this will be familiar from our previous examples. We need to create a `DropTarget` from the `FormPanel` and then override its `notifyDrop` method to dictate what will happen when the drop action occurs.

Let's take a look at the code for our `FormPanel`:

```
var detailForm = new Ext.form.FormPanel({
    width: 250,
    height: 80,
    defaultType: 'textfield',
    items: [
        { fieldLabel: 'Name', name:'name' },
        { fieldLabel: 'City', name:'city' },
        { fieldLabel: 'Country', name:'country' }
    ]
});
```

This is all pretty standard stuff, but note that the names of the form fields match up with the names of the fields in our data record that was used to populate the drag node. We can now set up the `DropTarget`:

```
new Ext.dd.DropTarget(detailForm.body.dom, {
    notifyDrop  : function(source, e, data){

        var record = source.dragData.record;
        detailForm.getForm().loadRecord(record);

        return true;
    }
});
```

Note that we can grab the full record straight from the `dragData` on the drag source, and load it into the form. That's the strength of being able to put any data we like into `dragData`, and here it shows how we can populate the form with a minimum amount of code.

Drag-drop groups

We started off our tour of Ext.dd by looking at how individual nodes could be moved around the screen and placed in designated containers. From there, we described the methods used to enable dragging for many nodes at once, and how these could be dropped within containers with child nodes.

When you're dealing with lots of draggable elements, there's a third facility that can be used to make sure that your nodes behave in the way you'd expect: drag-drop groups. DragSource, DragZone, DropTarget, and DropZone accept the configuration option ddGroup that in turn accepts a string identifier indicating which group you'd like to assign your instance to.

But what does this configuration option actually do, in practical terms, and what new features does it provide for your applications? Well, strictly speaking, it means that a drag-drop class instance will only be able to interact with other drag-drop instances in the same group, but that's a rather dry way of explaining it. Let's look at a real-world use case.

Nursing our drag-drop to health

Imagine that you have a screen in your application with four separate containers, each of which is specified as both DragZone and DropZone. Without drag-drop groups, the default behavior here would be that the user could drag from any one of these defined areas to any of the other three.

In many cases, you're likely to want to limit these kinds of interactions. Let's say that containers one and two represent today and tomorrow's appointments for a doctor, and containers three and four are appointments for a nurse. Appointments for the doctor can't be transferred to the nurse, and ones for the nurse can't be given to the doctor. So the application needs to implement this restriction.

We could do this very easily by specifying a ddGroup of "doctor" for containers one and two, and ddGroup of "nurse" for containers three and four. This would mean that an attempt to drag a nurse appointment into a doctor container would fail, as the nurse drag-drop objects are not allowed to interact with items outside their own drag-and-drop groups.

This kind of advanced functionality becomes essential when you're writing applications that make extensive use of drag-and-drop. We don't need to write code to check whether the drop target is correct, as drag-drop groups take care of this for us.

It's all in the details

We've had a good overview of the main classes within the Ext.dd package now. So it's time to start looking at some of the interesting configuration options, properties, methods, and events that allow us to tweak the behavior of the drag-and-drop classes.

Configuration

The "big four" of Ext.dd—DragSource, DragZone, DropTarget, and DropZone—are notable within the Ext JS framework for being important classes that don't really offer much in the way of configuration options. That's because, despite being important, they're all relatively simple to set up: designate a linked node and away you go. That said, we've already covered one option that all of these classes support—ddGroup—and there are a couple more common options available.

The dropAllowed and dropNotAllowed options are both strings that dictate the CSS classes to be passed to the drag source when the respective conditions are true. For example, if the item is hovering over an invalid drop target, then the class specified by dropNotAllowed will be used.

DropTarget and DropZone have the overClass option in common. This allows you to change the CSS class applied to the drop target element when a drag source moves over it. This is blank by default, and so is a useful method of augmenting the graphical cue provided by the status proxy.

It's all under control

The drag-and-drop support within Ext JS is structured a little differently to the rest of the framework. Typically, to add in your own behavior, you will handle events that a class fires off, as we've seen when discussing the TreePanel and other components. With Ext.dd, there are very few events to handle. Instead, a number of abstract methods are provided for the developer to override.

 Ext JS describes these methods as "abstract methods", a concept rarely seen in Javascript as it is not strictly supported. Here, the term simply refers to an empty implementation that needs to be replaced by the developer in order to achieve the desired functionality.

We've already seen how the `notifyDrop` and `onNodeDrop` methods for `DropZone` need to be overridden to complete the drop process, but there are plenty of other abstract methods that we can hook in to. In fact, even for the drop action, there are a number of similar-sounding methods available for use in certain situations:

- `notifyDrop`
- `onContainerDrop`
- `onNodeDrop`

On the face of it, all of these could apply to the same scenario: handling the action performed when an item is dropped on a target. The trick is that the first three are actually related. On `DropZone`, `notifyDrop` isn't actually abstract; instead, it simply establishes whether `onNodeDrop` or `onContainerDrop` will be called. It's these two methods that need to be overridden if you want to perform a drop action.

Managing our movement

The `Ext.dd` package includes a `DragDropMgr` class, which is generally intended for use as an internal helper for the framework itself. However, there are a few interesting points to note about the class. Let's briefly review the way that this manager can fit into your own applications.

Global properties

As `DragDropMgr` is used to track all of the drag-and-drop manipulations that occur, we can use it to globally change the way those manipulations are handled. For example, the `clickPixelThresh` property can be changed to set the minimum number of pixels that the mouse needs to move before a drag is initiated. This can be useful in situations where your drag targets also accept a click event—you may wish to increase this value to prevent accidental drags.

Similarly, the `clickTimeThresh`, normally set to 1000 milliseconds or 1 second, dictates the delay time between clicking an element and starting the drag. This could be decreased to make the start of the process seem more responsive, or increased if it's interfering with other actions.

We can also fine-tune the way in which the drop action is handled. By default, the drag-and-drop mode is set to `POINT`, where the position of the mouse pointer is used to determine whether the object being dragged is within the drop target. We can change this behavior to `INTERSECT` mode:

```
Ext.dd.DragDropMgr.mode = Ext.dd.DragDropMgr.INTERSECT;
```

This means that the edges of the drag source and drop target are used to establish interaction. If the two items overlap them, then the drop target is considered valid. This can be handy if the items you wish to drag are going to be large as it could be easier for the user to simply make the edges touch rather than move the mouse pointer directly over the target.

These properties are only likely to be used in edge-cases, but would come in handy as part of our toolkit.

Scroll management

One very slick part of the drag-and-drop puzzle that can be handled automatically is scrolling a container while trying to drag an item into an off-screen region. The Ext.dd.ScrollManager means that you can either drag items off bounds from the document body, or cause an element with scrollbars to shift as you drag the elements within it. Setting this facility up is pretty simple:

```
Ext.dd.ScrollManager.register('myContainer');
```

With this code, we've set up the myContainer element to be scroll-managed. Note that the scrolls occur in short bursts as you reach the edges of the container. We can tweak the behavior of the scroll as well, by setting the ddScrollConfig of the element to be registered.

```
var el = Ext.get('myContainer');
    el.ddScrollConfig = {};
Ext.dd.ScrollManager.register(el);
```

The ddScrollConfig consists of a configuration object containing a number of options. The bursts of scrolling are animated by default, and it can be disabled by setting animate to false, or can have its duration changed by setting animDuration to a value other than the default of 0.4 seconds:

```
el.ddScrollConfig = {
    animDuration: 0.2 // anim takes 0.2 seconds to complete
};
```

We can increase the frequency of scroll bursts by setting the frequency to a millisecond value, and change the amount of pixels by which to scroll by using the increment option. We can also control the width of the trigger area on both the horizontal and the vertical sides by using the vthresh and hthresh options, which are both specified as pixel numbers.

Although the `Ext.dd.ScrollManager` performs a simple purpose and does so with very little code, the utility of this class should not be underestimated. Setting up this functionality manually would be taxing, and it is such a crucial part of drag–and-drop that without `ScrollManager`, we'd be hand-coding it in every application we write. So while `Ext.dd.ScrollManager` is a fairly simple utility class, it's the one that makes many common drag-and-drop scenarios a great deal easier to develop.

Dragging within components

As we've seen previously, there are a couple of components that offer drag-and-drop support completely out of the box. It's important to remember that these features exist. Given our new drag-and-drop knowledge, we could implement them from scratch. Instead, we'll quickly review the main Ext components that have this facility baked in.

TreePanel

The default `Ext.TreePanel` not only enables drag-and-drop via the provided configuration option, but exposes a number of events, such as `beforenodedrop`, that allow us to hook our own functionality into the component.

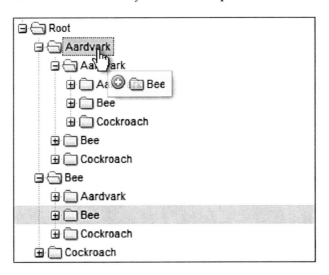

By using AJAX requests, we can persist the results of our drag-and-drop actions to the server for retrieval later. If you're using multiple `TreePanels`, you can even drag-and-drop between them, and restrict the direction of movement using the `enableDrag` and `enableDrop` configuration options.

GridPanel

The `Ext.grid.GridPanel` also provides drag-and-drop support out of the box with the use of the `enableDragDrop` configuration option. Setting this to `true` will allow you to begin dragging rows out of your grid. But you would still need to provide a custom `DropTarget` for the row destination. This could even be another `GridPanel`, but it means that you'll have to leverage the knowledge you gained earlier in this chapter to really put grid drag-and-drop to good use.

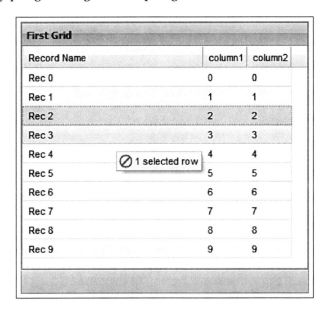

The custom `Ext.grid.DragZone` is also provided to facilitate these actions, giving you a shortcut to both the data being dragged and the grid that holds it. This class means that there's a bit less heavy lifting required when you want to drag rows within your application.

Using it in the real world

There are many cases where drag-and-drop is actually a barrier for the user-such as when adding an action that takes longer to complete than the more standard approach. Why drag-and-drop something when clicking it could be just as effective? The visual cue of the drag-and-drop status proxy may look great in a screenshot, but in a real-world situation there may be a more logical approach.

That said, the visual element of drag-and-drop is still its most important feature. There is no better way of organizing a list or a tree of information than by pulling it around the screen using the mouse. When completing tasks like these, a graphical representation of what's going on will not only help your users to get the job done more quickly, but, when backed by Ext JS, could also turn out to be the least development-intensive approach as well.

Ext.dd is a package that doesn't supply any widgets of its own. Instead it supports other segments of the framework and works as a behind-the-scenes facilitator of exciting end user functionality. As such, it can be a little difficult to come to grips with it, especially as it provides a variety of approaches to solve similar issues.

In this chapter, we've covered all of the major pieces of the Ext JS drag-and-drop puzzle. So, when you do come up with a problem that can be tackled using drag-and-drop, you can use DragZones, DropTargets, and StatusProxies to achieve the look and feel that your application requires.

Summary

It feels as if our knowledge of drag-and-drop on the Web has come pretty far from our understanding in the earlier chapters. We started off by discussing some of the typical demonstrations of drag-and-drop, which were developed to show off the Web 2.0 functionality. Some of those demonstrations suffered from a lack of real utility, but they were undeniably compelling. We showed how to create a few 'fancy but pointless' effects of our own to get a grasp of the underlying concepts of the Ext.dd package, and then quickly expanded our knowledge to harness the drag-and-drop classes that allow our applications to take advantage of this feature.

The wide range of in-built support that Ext provides is only part of the story, albeit a very important part. The TreePanel, for example, certainly wouldn't be as impressive a component were it not for its ability to rearrange nodes within a hierarchy using simple drag-and-drop. But the other part of our tale is just as interesting—the ways in which we can customize that built-in functionality and then replace, extend, and implement our own solutions which would enable the next level of desktop-like interactivity.

12
It's All about the Data

Ext JS is an extremely powerful, cross-browser library, providing any developer with a beautiful, consistent set of tools for laying out browser-based applications. But there's a lot more here than just pretty boxes and grids. As the title says, *it's all about the data*! An application without data is really nothing more than an interactive static page, and our users are going to want to manipulate real information. One of the wonders of web applications is that they've taken computing full circle, back to the days of the client/server application model. Ext JS's AJAXified objects provide us with the means to work with real-time data straight from the server, and in this chapter we'll cover the many different ways you can retrieve from and post data to your Ext JS based applications.

Understanding data formats

We have dozens of component objects available to us within Ext JS, and most of them can take dynamic data from the server. It's all in knowing what kind of data a component can take, and what formats are acceptable.

Basic remote panel data

You've probably noticed that many components are basically just a box. Tab Panels, Accordion Panels, and the content area of a window are all just large boxes (a `<div>` element), or panels. Each of these unique objects has its own methods and properties, yet each of them extends the `Ext.Panel` object.

Applying dynamic data to a basic panel is super simple, because it takes the simplest of formats: straight text or HTML. Our first example will load a simple HTML page into a panel. First, we'll need the rendering page:

Example 1: `ch12ex1.html`

```
...      <div id="mainContent">
           <div id="chap12_ex01"></div>
         </div>
...
```

Here, we have shown what will go inside the `<body>` tag of our example HTML page. Next, we'll need a server-side template to call for content:

Example 1: `chapter_12\example1ajax.html`

```
<b>William Sheakespeare:</b> <i>Poet Lauraette</i><br />
```

The last thing we'll need is the actual script to create our example `Panel`:

Example 1: `scripts\chapter12_01.js`

```
Ext.onReady(function(){
  var example1 = new Ext.Panel({
    applyTo:'chap12_ex01',
    title:'Chapter 12: Example 1',
    width:250,
    height:250,
    frame:true,
    autoLoad:{
      url:'example1ajax.html'
    }
  });
});
```

Calling the `ch12ex1.html` template in the browser will run this basic script. Let's look over the code to see what we're doing:

1. We wait until the DOM is rendered (`Ext.onReady()` function).
2. We create new `Ext.Panel` object, rendered to the `chap12_ex01` element (a div on the rendered page).
3. We load in the contents of the external URL `example1ajax.html`.

It is very simple to pull in an HTML template as content for a panel item. But we would really like dynamic data. Let's build on this example, and pull in data from an application server. We can use the same `autoLoad` attribute to call an application server processing page to return data.

Author's note:

Ext JS is a client-side scripting library and, as such, you can use any server-side programming language that you feel comfortable with. You may have noticed that some earlier examples in this book are coded in PHP. Examples within this chapter require the Adobe ColdFusion server to process the dynamic data, and require you to download and install the free Developer's Edition to run the examples. We're using ColdFusion, at this point, to illustrate two different points:

1) That any server-side processor can feed data to Ext JS.

2) That not every application server, or remote application, will return data in a standard format. Our examples of Custom Data Readers, later in this chapterwill iterate this point further.

The free Adobe ColdFusion Developer's Edition server is available at http://www.adobe.com. Review the sample README.txt file for more detailed instructions on accessing the example files for this chapter.

For Example 2, we'll change our <div> id to chap12_ex02, and use the chapter12_02.js file to load the data using a different approach, which now reads as follows:

Example 2: scripts\chapter12_02.js

```
var example2 = new Ext.Panel({
  applyTo:'chap12_ex02',
  title:'Chapter 12: Example 2',
  width:250,
  height:250,
  frame:true,
  autoLoad:{
    url:'Chapter12Example.cfc',
    params:{
      method:'example1',
      returnFormat:'plain',
      id:1289
    }
  }
});
```

You'll notice that the URL is now calling an Adobe ColdFusion Component(CFC), passing in some parameters to get its results. We have a very basic CFC, which runs a small query based on the passed parameters to generate the content that is passed back through the AJAX call.

Example 2: `chapter_12\Chapter12Example.cfc`

```
<cfcomponent output="false">
  <cffunction name="example2" access="remote" output="false"
                                    returntype="string">
    <cfargument name="id" type="numeric" required="true" />
    <cfset var output = "" />
    <cfset var q = "" />
    <cftry>
      <cfquery name="q" datasource="chapter12">
        SELECT  firstName,
            lastName,
            occupation
        FROM  People
        WHERE  ID = <cfqueryparam cfsqltype="cf_sql_integer"
                            value="#ARGUMENTS.id#" />
      </cfquery>
      <cfcatch type="database">
        <!--- Place Error Handling Here --->
      </cfcatch>
    </cftry>
    <cfif IsDefined("q.recordcount") and q.recordcount>
      <cfsavecontent variable="output"><cfoutput>
        #q.firstName# #q.lastName#: #q.occupation#<br />
      </cfoutput></cfsavecontent>
    </cfif>
    <cfreturn output />
  </cffunction>
</cfcomponent>
```

As the purpose of this book isn't to teach you a server-side language, let's break this down in the simplest way. The CFC takes an argument of ID, which is passed into a query of the People table. If a record is returned from the query, a basic string is returned in a predetermined format: FirstName LastName: Occupation. The AJAX call (autoLoad) is passing several parameters: the method to run within the CFC, the format type to return (plain text, in this case), and the method arguments (in this case id).

Gotchas with HTML data

You must remember that you should call data only via AJAX from the domain of your site. Attempting to reference data from a site outside of your domain will error out at the browser level, as it's considered to be cross-site scripting. Cross-site scripting is a means of delivering malicious scripts to an unsuspecting user, generally from outside of the site which they're visiting. Most modern browsers now have built-in facilities to prevent this type of attack. Ext JS does provide facilities for bypassing this restriction, via the `Ext.data.ScriptTagProxy`, but this should only be used if you are confident of the security of the data you are requesting, and its effect on your application.

Other formats

Ext JS has the capability to consume external data in a variety of formats:

Format	Example
Plain Text	Eric Clapton is a consummate guitarist
HTML	`<b>Jimi Hendrix is considered, by some, to have been one of the finest blues guitarists that ever lived</b>`
JSON	```var theBeatles = {
'members': 4,
'band': [
{'id':1,'first_name':'John',
'last_name':'Lennon'},
{'id':2,'first_name':'Paul',
'last_name':'McCartney'},
{'id',3,'first_name':'George',
'last_name':'Harrison'},
{'id':4,'first_name':'Ringo',
'last_name':'Starr'}
]
};```
XML	```<band>
<members>4</members>
<member>
<firstname>Jimmy</firstname>
<lastname>Paige</lastname>
</member>
<member>
<firstname>Robert</firstname>
<lastname>Plant</lastname>
</member>
. . .```

Format	Example

JavaScript Array	```var PinkFloyd = [```
	 ``` ['1','David','Gilmour'],```
	 ``` ['2','Roger','Waters'],```
	 ``` ['3','Richard','Wright'],```
	 ``` ['4','Nick','Mason']```
	 ```]```

The format that you choose may be decided according to the Ext JS object you are using. Many developers like to use XML, as many databases (MS SQL, Oracle, MySQL, PostgreSQL, and DB2 to name a few)can return it natively, and many RESTful web services use it. Although this is a good thing, especially when working with varying external applications, XML can be very verbose at times. Data calls that return small sets of data can quickly clog up the bit stream because of the verbosity of the XML syntax. Another consideration with XML, is the browser engine. An XML data set that looks fine to Mozilla Firefox may be rejected by Internet Explorer, and Internet Explorer's XML parsing engine is slow, as well. JSON, or JavaScript Object Notation, data packages tend to be much smaller, taking up less bandwidth. If the object you're using can accept it, a simple array can be even smaller, although you will lose the descriptive nature that the JSON or XML syntaxes provide.

The data store object

Most Ext JS objects (and even panels, with some additional work) take data as **Records**, or **Nodes**. Records are typically stored within a data store object. Think of a Store as being similar to a spreadsheet, and each Record as being a row within the spreadsheet.

The *data* package contains many objects for interacting with data. You have several different Store types:

- JsonStore: Store object specifically for working with JSON data
- SimpleStore: Store object for working with arrays and XML data
- GroupingStore: Store object that holds 'grouped' datasets

Any Store will require some kind of Reader object to parse the inbound data, and again the data package has several:

- ArrayReader: For working with JavaScript arrays
- JsonReader: For working with JSON datasets
- XmlReader: For working with XML datasets

The `TreePanel` object doesn't use a traditional data Store, but has its own specialized store called a `TreeLoader`, which is passed into the configuration through the `loader` config option. The `TreeLoader` accepts simple arrays of definition objects, much like those expected by an `ArrayReader`. See the Ext JS API (`http://extjs.com/deploy/dev/docs/`) for more information.

Defining data

Store objects are easily configured, requiring the source of the data and a description of the expected records. Our applications know to expect data, but we have to tell them what the data is supposed to look like. Let's say, for instance, that our application manages media assets for our site. We would have a server-side object that queries a folder in our file system and returns information on the files that the folder contains. The data returned might look something like this:

```
{
    files: [
        {name: 'beatles.jpg', path:'/images/', size:46.5, lastmod:
                                                 '12/21/2001'},
        {name: 'led_zepplin.jpg', path:'/images/', size:43.2,
                        lastmod: '2001-12-21 00:00:00'},
        {name: 'the_doors.jpg', path: '/images/', size:24.6, lastmod:
                                          '2001-12-21 00:00:00'},
        {name: 'jimi_hendrix.jpg', path: '/images/', size:64.3,
                        lastmod: '2001-12-21 00:00:00'}
    ]
}
```

This is a small JSON dataset. Its root is `files` followed by an array of objects. Now we have to define this data for our application:

```
var recordObj = new Ext.data.Record.create([{
  name: 'Name',
  mapping: 'name'
},{
  name: 'FilePath',
  mapping: 'path'
},{
  name: 'FileSize',
  mapping: 'size',
  type: 'float'
```

```
    }, {
      name: 'LastModified',
      mapping: 'lastmod',
      type: 'date',
      dateFormat: 'm/d/Y'
    }]);
```

We've applied a name that each field will be referenced by within our application, mapping it to a variable within a dataset object. Many variables will automatically be typed, but you can force (cast) the 'type' of a variable for greater definition and easier manipulation.

The various variable types are:

- auto (the default, which implies no conversion)
- string
- int
- float
- boolean
- date

We've also applied special string formatting to our date object, to have our output the way we want.

> Dates are typically passed as strings, which usually have to be cast into Date objects for proper manipulation. By specifying a date type, Ext JS will handle the conversion using the dateFormat we define. The Ext JS documentation for the Date object provides an extensive format list, which we can use to define the hundreds of Date string permutations we may come across in our code.

More on mapping our data

In the previous example, we covered the definition of a simple JSON object. The same technique is used for XML objects, with the only difference being how to map a Record field to a specific node. That's where the mapping config option comes in. This option can take a DOM path to the node within the XML. Take the following example:

```
<band>
  <members>4</members>
  <member>
    <firstname>Jimmy</firstname>
```

```
      <lastname>Paige</lastname>
    </member>
    <member>
      <firstname>Robert</firstname>
      <lastname>Plant</lastname>
    </member>
    . . .
```

To create a mapping of the `first_name` node you would have the config look like this:

```
mapping:'member > first_name'
```

JavaScript arrays are easier, as they don't require mapping, other than defining each field in the same order it would be seen in the array:

```
var PinkFloyd = [
  ['1','David','Gilmour'],
  ['2','Roger','Waters'],
  ['3','Richard','Wright'],
  ['4','Nick','Mason']
]
```

Note here that we won't `create()` a Record object, but just use the `fields` config option of the Store.

```
fields:[
  {name:'id'},
  {name:'first_name'},
  {name:'last_name'}
]
```

Pulling data into the store

It is almost as easy to retrieve data from the server as it was to populate that Panel object earlier, and we can do so using a very similar syntax.

Example 3: `scripts\chapter12_03.js`

```
var recordObj = new Ext.data.Record.create([{
    name: 'NAME',
    mapping: 'name'
  },{
    name: 'DIRECTORY',
    mapping: 'path'
  },{
    name: 'SIZE',
    mapping: 'size',
```

```
        type: 'float'
    },{
        name: 'DATELASTMODIFIED',
        mapping: 'lastmod',
        type: 'date',
        dateFormat: 'm/d/Y'
    }]);
    var ourStore = new Ext.data.JsonStore({
        url:'Chapter12Example.cfc',
        baseParams:{
            method: 'getFileInfo',
            returnFormat:'JSON',
            startPath: '/images/'
        },
        root:'files',
        id:'name',
        fields: recordObj,
        listeners:{
            beforeload:{
            fn: function(store, options){
                if (options.startPath && (options.startPath.length > 0)){
                    store.baseParams.startPath = fieldVal;
                }
            },
                scope: this
        }
        }
    });
    ourStore.load();
```

This ties all of our pieces together to create our data Store object. First, we use the url config option to define the location from where we will get our data. Then, we set the initial set of parameters to pass on the load request. Finally, it may be that we want to conditionally pass different parameter values for each request. For this, we can define a special 'listener' to pass new information. In this case, whenever the load() method is called, if the startPath property is passed into the method as an argument, before the Store retrieves the data it will change the startPath base parameter to match the value passed in.

Where's the screenshot?

Ok, that's a valid question. A data Store, by itself, has no visible output in the browser display. This is why tools like Firefox with the Firebug plug-in, or the Aptana development IDE can be so important when doing JavaScript development. These tools can allow you to direct processing output to special windows, to monitor what's going on within your application.

Using a DataReader to map data

Some applications can natively return data in XML, or even JSON, but it might not always be in the format Ext JS is expecting. As an example, the JsonStore, with its built-in JsonReader, expects an incoming dataset in the following format:

```
{
   'rootName': [
     {
        'variableName1': 'First record',
        'variableName2': '0'
     },{
        'variableName1': 'Second record',
        'variableName2': '3.5'
     }
   ]
}
```

This (JSON) object has a `rootName` property, which is the name of the *root* of the dataset, containing an array of objects. Each of these objects has the same attributes. The attribute names are in quotes. Values are typically in quotes, with the exception of numbers which may or may not be in quotes.

So, if a server-side call returns data in this expected format, then the base JsonReader included within the JsonStore will automatically parse the received datasets to populate the Store object. But what happens if the server-side application uses a slightly different format? As an example, the Adobe ColdFusion 8 server can automatically return JSON datasets for remote requests, translating any of ColdFusion's native data types into JSON data. But ColdFusion's JSON formatting is typically different, especially when dealing with query data (which is what a dataset would usually be created from). Here's an example of a JSON dataset being returned from a ColdFusion query object:

```
{
   "COLUMNS":["NAME","SIZE","TYPE","DATELASTMODIFIED","ATTRIBUTES",
                                              "MODE","DIRECTORY"],
   "DATA":[
     ["IMG1.jpg",582360,"File","June, 13 2003
      23:50:08","","","H:\\wwwroot\\ExtBook\\images"],
     ["IMG2.JPG",1108490,"File","June, 13 2003
      23:50:52","","","H:\\wwwroot\\ExtBook\\images"],
     ["IMG3.JPG",1136108,"File","June, 13 2003
      23:51:02","","","H:\\wwwroot\\ExtBook\\images"],
     ["IMG4.JPG",1538506,"File","June, 13 2003
      23:51:12","","","H:\\wwwroot\\ExtBook\\images"]
   ]
}
```

All of the data we need is here, but the format can't be properly parsed by the base JsonReader. So what do we do now?

Using a custom DataReader

Ext JS's built-in classes provide outstanding ease of use 'out-of-the-box', but (as we can see) sometimes we need something a little special, possibly due to a different implementation for a specific application server (such as ColdFusion), or possibly due to an external application API (Flickr for example). We could probably implement something on the server-side to put our data in the necessary format, but this creates unnecessary overheads on our server-side platform. Why not just use the client to handle these minor transformations? This helps distribute the load in our applications, and makes more effective use of all of the resources that we have on hand.

Ext JS provides us with the facilities for creating custom DataReaders for mapping our data, as well as simple means (the `reader` config option) for defining these readers in our store.

In our current exercise, we're lucky in that we don't have to write our own DataReader. Because the Adobe ColdFusion server platform is so widely used, the Ext JS community has already produced a custom reader just for this task. A simple search of the Ext JS Forums (`http://extjs.com/forum/`) will help you find many custom readers for data in a variety of formats. Just take the time to verify (read) the code prior to use, because it is is being provided by a third party. By using the CFJsonReader, with a few minor modifications to our script we can easily read the JSON data format being returned by ColdFusion.

First, let's convert our Record object into a simple array, which will become a model of our records. Include a script tag in your calling template to include the `CFJsonReader.js` file, prior to the script tag for your custom script. Then we'll make the following adjustments to our custom script:

```
var recordModel = [
  {name:'file_name',mapping:'NAME'},
  {name:'file_size',mapping:'SIZE'},
  {name:'type',mapping:'TYPE'},
  {name:'lastmod',mapping:'DATELASTMODIFIED'},
  {name:'file_attributes',mapping:'ATTRIBUTES'},
  {name:'mode',mapping:'MODE'},
  {name:'directory',mapping:'DIRECTORY'}
];
```

Now, we'll define our new DataReader as a `CFJsonStore` object:

```
var ourReader = new Ext.data.CFJsonReader(recordModel,
                        {id: 'NAME', root: 'DATA'});
```

Next, we'll change our data Store from being a JsonStore to being the `base Store` object type, and apply our `reader` config option to `ourReader`:

```
var ourStore = new Ext.data.Store({
    ...
    reader: ourReader
```

We also remove the `fields`, `id`, and `root` properties from the store definition, as these are now all handled from within the reader's definition.

The last thing we'll do is apply another custom listener to our script, so that we can verify whether the dataset is properly loaded. Let's modify our `listeners` config option, so that we can attach a function to the Store's `load` event listener:

```
listeners:{
  beforeload:{
    fn: function(store, options){
      if (options.startPath && (options.startPath.length > 0)){
        store.baseParams.startPath = fieldVal;
      }
    },
    scope:this
  },
  load:{
    fn: function(store, records, options){
      console.log(records);
    },
    scope: this
  }
}
```

If you're using Internet Explorer for development, then this line of code will break, as the `console.log()` method isn't natively supported in that environment (you can include additional scripts to use the `console.log()` method in IE, like the one found at (url: http://www.moxleystratton.com/article/ie-console)). Firefox, with the Firebug plugin, however will now give you some output once the data has been retrieved, parsed, and loaded into the data Store, so that we can see that the data is now in our Store.

A word about events

Many Ext JS objects have events that are fired when certain actions are taken upon them, or when they reach a certain state. An event-driven application, unlike a procedural programming model, can listen for changes in the application, such as the receipt of data or the change of a Record's value. Ext JS provides an extensive API, giving us the ability to apply custom event listeners to key actions within the application. For more information, review the object' information within the Ext JS API: `http://extjs.com/deploy/dev/docs/`.

Our final script might now look like this:

```
var recordModel = [
  {name:'file_name',mapping:'NAME'},
  {name:'file_size',mapping:'SIZE'},
  {name:'type',mapping:'TYPE'},
  {name:'lastmod',mapping:'DATELASTMODIFIED'},
  {name:'file_attributes',mapping:'ATTRIBUTES'},
  {name:'mode',mapping:'MODE'},
  {name:'directory',mapping:'DIRECTORY'}
];
var ourReader = new Ext.data.CFJsonReader(recordModel,{id:'NAME',ro
ot:'DATA'});
var ourStore = new Ext.data.Store({
  url:'Chapter12Example.cfc',
  baseParams:{
    method: 'getFileInfoByPath',
    returnFormat: 'JSON',
    queryFormat: 'column',
    startPath: '/images/'
  },
  reader: ourReader,
  listeners:{
    beforeload:{
      fn: function(store, options){
        if (options.startPath && (options.startPath.length > 0)){
          store.baseParams.startPath = options.startPath;
        }
      },
      scope:this
    },
```

```
    load: {
        fn: function(store,records,options){
            console.log(records);
        }
    },
    scope:this
    }
});
ourStore.load();
```

This now wraps up our code pieces, defining what our data will look like, configuring our custom reader, and setting up our data Store to pull in our JSON data. The load listener will display the Records retrieved from the server that are now in our Store.

Getting what you want: Finding data

Now that we have data, we'll typically need to manipulate it. Once we've loaded our data Store with Records, the entire dataset remains resident in the browser cache, ready for manipulation or replacement. This data is persistent until we move away from the page or destroy the dataset or the data Store.

Ext JS provides many different options for dealing with our data, all of which are documented within the API. Here, we'll explore some of the most common things to do.

Finding data by field value

The first thing we might want to do is find a specific Record. Let's say we needed to know which Record from our previous examples contains the picture of Jimi Hendrix:

```
var jimiPicIndex = ourStore.find('NAME','Jimi',0,false,false);
```

This method would return the index of the first record that had `Jimi` as part of the value of the `NAME` field. It would start its search from the first record(0), as it is in JavaScript array notation), look for the string from the beginning of the field's value (using `true` here will search for the string in any location of the `NAME` field within any record), and perform a case-insensitive search.

Finding data by record index

Having the index is nice; at least we know which Record it is now. But we also need to retrieve the Record:

```
var ourImg = ourStore.getAt(jimiPicIndex);
```

The `getAt()` method of the `Store` object will get a Record at a specific index position within the Store.

Finding data by record ID

The best way to look for a unique record is by `ID`. If you already know the `ID` of your record, this process just becomes easier. We used the `NAME` field as our `ID`, so let's find the record for that same record:

```
var ourImg = ourStore.getById('jimi_hendrix.jpg');
```

So, now we can find a Record by partial value within a field, get a Record by its specific index, or retrieve a Record by its `ID` value.

Getting what you want: Filtering data

Sometimes, you only need a specific subset of data from your Store. Your Store contains a complete dataset (for caching and easy retrieval), but you need it filtered to a specific set of Records. As an example, the `cfdirectory` tag we used in our ColdFusion server-side call can return an entire directory listing, including all subdirectories. After retrieving the data, it may be that we only need the names of the files within the `startPath` that we posted. For this, we can filter our client-side cached dataset to get only the Records of type, `File`:

```
ourStore.filter('TYPE','File',false,false);
```

This filters our dataset using the `TYPE` field. The dataset will now only contain Records that have a `TYPE` field, with a value of `File` (matched from the beginning, and case-insensitive).

After working with our filtered dataset, there will come a time when we want our original dataset back. When we filtered the dataset, the other Records didn't go away. They're still sitting in cache, to the side, waiting to be recalled. Rather than query the server again, we can simply clear our filter:

```
ourStore.clearFilter();
```

Remote filtering: The why and the how

Client-side filtering is great, reducing our trips to the server. Sometimes, however, our record set is just too large to pull in at once. A great example of this is a paging grid. Many times we'll only be pulling in 25 Records at a time. The client-side filtering methods are fine if we only want to filter the resident dataset, but most of the time we'll want a filter applied to all of our data.

Sorting data on remote calls is pretty easy, as we can set the Store's `remoteSort` property to `true`. So, if our Store was attached to a grid object, clicking on a column heading to sort the display would automatically pass the value in its AJAX request.

Filtering data on remote requests is a bit harder. Basically, we would pass parameters through the Store's load event, and act on those arguments in our server-side method.

So, the first thing we'll need is some server-side code for handling our filtering and sorting. We'll return to our ColdFusion component to add a new method:

Example 3: `Chapter_12\Chapter12Example.cfc`

```
<!---
/  METHOD: getDirectoryContents
/
/  @param  startPath:string
/  @param  recurse:boolean (optional)
/  @param  fileFilter:string (optional)
/  @param  dirFilter:string (optional - File|Dir)
/  @param  sortField:string (optional -
  NAME|SIZE|TYPE|DATELASTMODIFIED|ATTRIBUTES|MODE|DIRECTORY)
/  @param  sortDirection:string (option - ASC|DESC
                              [defaults to ASC])
/  @return  retQ:query
--->
<cffunction name="getDirectoryContents" access="remote"
                  output="false" returntype="query">
  <cfargument name="startPath" required="true" type="string" />
  <cfargument name="recurse" required="false" type="boolean"
                                        default="false" />
  <cfargument name="sortDirection" required="false" type="string"
                                        default="ASC" />
  <!--- Set some function local variables --->
  <cfset var q = "" />
  <cfset var retQ = "" />
  <cfset var attrArgs = {} />
  <cfset var ourDir = ExpandPath(ARGUMENTS.startPath) />
  <!--- Create some lists of valid arguments --->
  <cfset var filterList = "File,Dir" />
  <cfset var sortDirList = "ASC,DESC" />
  <cfset var columnList =
  "NAME,SIZE,TYPE,DATELASTMODIFIED,ATTRIBUTES,MODE,DIRECTORY" />
  <cftry>
    <cfset attrArgs.recurse = ARGUMENTS.recurse />
    <!--- Verify the directory exists before continuing --->
    <cfif DirectoryExists(ourDir)>
```

```
      <cfset attrArgs.directory = ourDir />
    <cfelse>
      <cfthrow type="Custom" errorcode="Our_Custom_Error" message="The
directory you are trying to reach does not exist." />
    </cfif>
    <!--- Conditionally apply some optional filtering and sorting
     --->
    <cfif IsDefined("ARGUMENTS.fileFilter")>
      <cfset attrArgs.filter = ARGUMENTS.fileFilter />
    </cfif>
    <cfif IsDefined("ARGUMENTS.sortField")>
      <cfif ListFindNoCase(columnList,ARGUMENTS.sortField)>
        <cfset attrArgs.sort = ARGUMENTS.sortField & " " &
          ARGUMENTS.sortDirection />
      <cfelse>
        <cfthrow type="custom" errorcode="Our_Custom_Error"
         message="You have chosen an invalid sort field.
         Please use one of the following: " & columnList />
      </cfif>
    </cfif>
    <cfdirectory action="list" name="q"
      attributeCollection="#attrArgs#" />
    <!--- If there are files and/or folders,
     and you want to sort by TYPE --->
    <cfif q.recordcount and IsDefined("ARGUMENTS.dirFilter")>
      <cfif ListFindNoCase(filterList,ARGUMENTS.dirFilter)>
        <cfquery name="retQ" dbtype="query">
        SELECT  #columnList#
          FROM  q
          WHERE  TYPE = <cfqueryparam cfsqltype=" cf_sql_varchar"
                  value="#ARGUMENTS.dirFilter#" maxlength="4" />
        </cfquery>
      <cfelse>
        <cfthrow type="Custom" errorcode="Our_Custom_Error"
          message="You have passed an invalid dirFilter.
          The only accepted values are File and Dir." />
      </cfif>
    <cfelse>
      <cfset retQ = q />
      </cfif>
    <cfcatch type="any">
      <!--- Place Error Handler Here --->
    </cfcatch>
  </cftry>
  <cfreturn retQ />
</cffunction>
```

This might look complicated, but it really isn't! Again, our mission here isn't to learn ColdFusion, but it is important to have some understanding of what your server-side process is doing. What we have here is a method that takes some optional parameters related to sorting and filtering via an HTTP POST, statement. We use the same `cfdirectory` tag to query the file system for a list of files and folders. The difference here is that we now conditionally apply some additional attributes to the tag, so that we can filter on a specific file extension, or sort by a particular column of the query. We also have a Query-of-Query statement to query our returned `recordset` if we want to filter further by the record TYPE, which is a filtering mechanism not built into the `cfdirectory` tag. Lastly, there's also some custom error handling to ensure that valid arguments are being passed into the method.

We'll make a few modifications to our previous Store script as well. First, we'll need a few methods that can be called to remotely filter our `recordset`:

```
filterStoreByType = function (type){
  ourStore.load({dirFilter:type});
}

filterStoreByFileType = function (fileType){
  ourStore.load({fileFilter:fileType});
}

clearFilters = function (){
  ourStore.baseParams = new cloneConfig(initialBaseParams);
  ourStore.load();
}
```

We have methods here for filtering our Store by TYPE, for filtering by file extension, and for clearing the filters. The values passed into these methods are mapped to the proper remote method argument names. Our Store's `beforeload` listener automatically applies these arguments to the `baseParams` prior to making the AJAX call back to the server. The important thing to remember here is that each added parameter stays in `baseParams`, until the filters are cleared.

It's also important to note that the `load()` method can take four arguments: `params`, `callback` (a method to perform on load), `scope` (the scope with which to call the callback), and `add` (to add the load to the already-existing dataset). In the format used above, the object used as an argument for `the load()` method is assumed to be the `params` argument, because no others are passed. If you are using all of the arguments (or at least the first three), they would have to be within an object.

```
ourStore.load({{dirFilter:type},someMethodToCall,this,false});
```

The `clearFilter()` method does not work with remote filtering, so we need to have a way to recall our initial `baseParams` when we need to clear our filters, and get our original dataset back. For this, we first abstract our `baseParams` configuration:

```
var initialBaseParams = {
    method: 'getDirectoryContents',
    returnFormat: 'JSON',
    queryFormat: 'column',
    startPath: '/testdocs/'
};
```

We then need a way to clone the config in our actual Store configuration. If we passed the `initialBaseParams` into the `baseParams` config option directly, and then filtered our dataset, the filter would be added to the `initialBaseParams` variable, as the variable gets passed by reference. Because we want to be able to recall our actual beginning `baseParams`, we'll need to clone the `initialBaseParams` object. The clone gets set as the `baseParams` config option. Filters don't touch our original object, and we can recall them whenever we need to `clearFilter()`.

For this, we'll need a simple method of cloning a JavaScript object:

```
cloneConfig = function (config) {
    for (i in config) {
        if (typeof config[i] == 'object') {
            this[i] = new cloneConfig(config[i]);
        }
        else
            this[i] = config[i];
    }
}
```

We can then change our `baseParams` attribute in our Store configuration:

```
baseParams: new cloneConfig(initialBaseParams),
```

We used the same function within our `clearFilters()` method, to reset our `baseParams` to their initial configuration. Here is what our entire script looks like now:

Example 4: `chapter12_04.js`

```
cloneConfig = function (config) {
    for (i in config) {
        if (typeof config[i] == 'object') {
            this[i] = new cloneConfig(config[i]);
        }
```

```
            else
                this[i] = config[i];
        }
}

Ext.onReady(function(){
    var recordModel = [
        {name:'file_name',mapping:'NAME'},
        {name:'file_size',mapping:'SIZE'},
        {name:'type',mapping:'TYPE'},
        {name:'lastmod',mapping:'DATELASTMODIFIED'},
        {name:'file_attributes',mapping:'ATTRIBUTES'},
        {name:'mode',mapping:'MODE'},
        {name:'directory',mapping:'DIRECTORY'}
    ];

    var ourReader = new Ext.data.CFJsonReader({id:'NAME',root:'DATA'},
                                              recordModel);

    var initialBaseParams = {
        method: 'getDirectoryContents',
        returnFormat: 'JSON',
        queryFormat: 'column',
        startPath: '/testdocs/'
    };
    var ourStore = new Ext.data.Store({
        url:'Chapter12Example.cfc',
        baseParams: new cloneConfig(initialBaseParams),
        reader: ourReader,
        fields: recordModel,
        listeners:{
            beforeload:{
                fn: function(store, options){
                    for(var i in options){
                        if(options[i].length > 0){
                            store.baseParams[i] = options[i];
                        }
                    }
                },
                scope:this
            },
            load: {
                fn: function(store,records,options){
                    console.log(records);
                }
```

```
      },
      scope:this
    }
  });
  ourStore.load({recurse:true});
  filterStoreByType = function (type){
    ourStore.load({dirFilter:type});
  }
  filterStoreByFileType = function (fileType){
    ourStore.load({fileFilter:fileType});
  }
  clearFilters = function (){
    ourStore.baseParams = new cloneConfig(initialBaseParams);
    ourStore.load();
  }
});
```

To test our changes, we can put some links on our HTML page to call the methods that we've created for filtering data, which we can then monitor in Firebug.

Example 4: `ch12ex4.html`

```
<div id="chap12_ex04">
  <a onclick="filterStoreByType('File')"
  href="javascript:void(0)">Filter by 'File's</a><br />
  <a onclick="filterStoreByFileType('*.doc')"
  href="javascript:void(0)">Filter by '.doc File's</a><br />
  <a onclick="clearFilters()" href="javascript:void(0)">
                                    Clear Filters</a><br />
</div>
```

After the page has loaded, we see the console logging the initial recordset being loaded into the Store. Clicking our first link will remove all of the directory Records through filtering. Clicking our second link takes it a step further, and filters out any files other than those ending in `.doc`. The last link resets the filters to the original `baseParams` and reloads the initial recordset.

Dealing with Recordset changes

One of great things about Ext JS data Stores is change management. Our applications might attack changing Records in a variety of ways, from editable data `Grids` to simple `Forms`, but making changes really only means something when we act on it. We might only change our display, but we are more than likely to send changes back to the server.

One of the easiest things to do is to apply an update event listener to our Store object. We've applied two other listeners in the past: the beforeload and load listeners. Now, let's apply an update listener to our script.

```
listeners:{
  beforeload:{
    fn: function(store, options){
      for(var i in options){
        if(options[i].length > 0){
          store.baseParams[i] = options[i];
        }
      }
    },
    scope:this
  },
  load: {
    fn: function(store, records, options){
      console.log(records);
    },
    scope: this
  },
  update: {
    fn: function(store, record, operation){
      switch (operation){
      case Ext.record.EDIT:
        // Do something with the edited record
        break;
        case Ext.record.REJECT:
          // Do something with the rejected record
          break;
        case Ext.record.COMMIT:
        // Do something with the committed record
          break;
      }
    },
    scope:this
  }
}
```

When a Record is updated, the update event fires in the Store, passing several objects into the event. The first is the Store itself, which is good for reference. The second is the Record that's been updated. The last object is the state of the Record that was updated. Here, we have laid out a quick switch/case statement to trigger different actions according to the state of the Record. We can add code into the action block for the Ext.record.EDIT state to automatically send every edit to the server for immediate Record revision.

One other option that we can address is the `Ext.record.COMMIT` state. It is sometimes better to let the user affect many different changes, to many different records, and then send all the updates at once.

```
ourStore.commitChanges();
```

This will collect all of the edited Records, flag them by using `Ext.record.COMMIT`, and then the `update` event would fire and affect each Record. Our last operation `state` is perfect for processing this situation, for which we can add additional client-side validation, or AJAX validation, or whatever our process might call for.

The `Ext.record.REJECT` state is generally set directly by the data Store, whereby the Store rejects any changes made to the Record, and will revert the Record's field values back to their original (or last committed) state. This might occur if a value of the wrong data type is passed into a field.

Many objects take a Store

The beauty of the `Store` object is in its many uses. So many objects, within the Ext JS library, can consume a `Store` as part of their configuration, automatically mapping data in many cases.

Store in a ComboBox

For example, the `ComboBox` object can take a `Store`, or any of its subclasses, as a data provider for its values:

```
var combo = new Ext.form.ComboBox({
    store: states,
    displayField: 'state',
    valueField: 'abbreviation',
    typeAhead: true,
    mode: 'remote',
    triggerAction: 'all',
    emptyText: 'Select a state...',
    selectOnFocus: true,
    applyTo: 'stateCombo'
});
```

This `ComboBox` takes a `Store` object called `states`, and maps its **state** field to the display, while mapping the **abbreviation** field to its underlying selected value.

Store in a DataView

The DataView object is one of the most powerful objects within Ext. This object can take a Store object, let us apply a Template or XTemplate to each Record (which the DataView refers to as a Node), and have each item render within the DataView, contiguously, wrapping items as they run out of space. The DataView opens up some very interesting ways to visually produce contact lists, image galleries, and file system explorers, and opens up our applications to be able to exchange data among a variety of objects through custom drag-and-drop functionality.

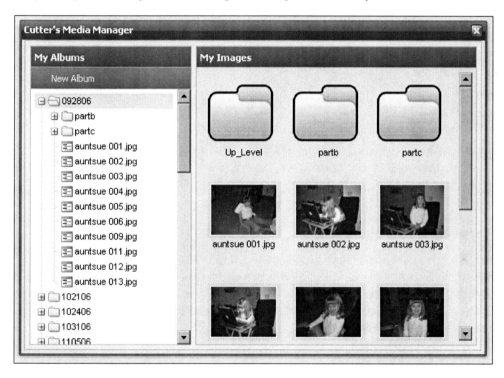

Stores in Grids

We've seen examples of applying a data Store to a Grid in a previous chapter (Chapter 5) of this book. There are several different types of Grids (Editor, Grouping, Property, and Basic Grids), but all of them take Store objects as input, and the applicable ColumnModel, to coordinate their data display.

The `Grid` objects and the `ComboBox` are probably the most prevalent uses of `Store` objects, with the `Grid` and the `DataView` being the two primary means of displaying multiple Records of data. The `Tree` object takes a special data source called a `TreeLoader`. The `TreeLoader` is actually part of the `Tree` package of classes, and does not extend the base `Store` object, although it operates in much the same way. Rather than `Record` objects, the `TreeLoader` takes an array of objects, which it then converts into `Nodes`. The structure to its incoming data is something like this:

```
var dataset = [{
   id: 1,
   text: 'Node 1',
   leaf:: false
},{
   id: 2,
   text: 'Node 2',
   leaf: true
}];
```

When a leaf is `true`, then it is an expandable item, which will query the server for further data when passing the node data. A `leaf:false` statement says that the `Node` has no children.

Summary

In this chapter, we've learned how to pull dynamic, server-side data into our applications. Ext JS's `Store` objects, with their versatility and mappable syntax, are easily-configured datasources for a lot of Ext JS objects. In this chapter, we've bound simple external data to a `Panel` object, gone over the various data formats that Ext JS can consume, and seen a basic overview of the `data Store` object and some of its more important subclasses.

Getting into the meat of things, we learned how to define our data using the Record object, after which we learned how to populate our Store with Records from a remote data source. We also learned about the purpose behind `DataReaders`, the different ones available to you, and how to configure a custom `DataReader`.

Pulling it all together, we got busy learning `Store` manipulation techniques such as finding Records by field values, indexes, or IDs. We also touched on filtering our Stores to get a working subset of data Records. We also talked about dealing with local data changes via the update event listener.

Finally, we covered some of the other Ext JS objects that use the `Store`, opening the doors to external data within multiple facets of our applications.

13

Code for Reuse: Extending Ext JS

In this chapter, we'll discuss how we can create our own custom components by extending the Ext JS library. We'll talk about how we can create our own namespaces, differentiating our custom components from others. We'll also discuss some other core object-oriented concepts (just enough to understand what we need here) and the concept of Event-Driven application architecture.

Object-oriented JavaScript

Over the last several years, we've seen a drastic shift with regards to client-side scripting in browser-based web applications. JavaScript has become the defacto standard in client-side scripting, with support for it built into every major browser available.

The issue has always been in each browser's implementation of the Document Object Model. Microsoft's Internet Explorer, having taken the majority share of the browser marketplace, helped to gather support for a modern Document Object Model, to which all other browsers had to adapt. However, after the release of Internet Explorer 6, Microsoft halted new development of their browser for several years, other than to provide security fixes. Added to this was Microsoft's play to try and create new standards. Rather than implement JavaScript, Internet Explorer actually implemented JScript, which ran JavaScript files, but had a slightly different implementation that never garnered momentum (other than in Internet Explorer), possibly because it did not adhere to the ECMAScript standard. This created several issues. The World Wide Web Consortium (W3C) had created a standard for the Document Object Model, which companies like Mozilla and Opera adhered to and furthered. Yet Internet Explorer (the dominant browser) was stagnant.

These events led to very hard times for client-side developers, as a great deal of time and effort went into creating client-side code that was cross-browser compliant. Netscape and Internet Explorer had been waging the browser war over several versions, slowly growing more divergent in their standards acceptance, with cross-browser development consistently becoming more of a challenge. The landscape had changed, in that a large degree of client-side development had become relegated to basic form validation and image rollovers, because few developers were interested in investing the time and effort necessary to write large, cross-browser compliant, client-side applications.

Enter Web 2.0. The buzzword of the day was AJAX, or Asynchronous JavaScript And XML. AJAX wasn't a new technology, but its use had been fairly minimal and obscure. Developers with a deep knowledge of JavaScript, looking to create greater and more dynamic web sites, had begun to implement the technology as a way of reinvigorating the client-side movement, creating richer and more interactive user experiences.

With this renewed interest in client-side scripted applications, but the same issues existing around cross-browser compatibility, several cross-browser JavaScript libraries (Dojo, Prototype, Yahoo UI, and so on) had begun life, in response to minimizing the previous woes involved in cross-browser, client-side development. The developers of these libraries, with their knowledge of JavaScript, had kept pace with the changes in this language as well. JavaScript had travelled well beyond the confines of a solely procedural scripting language, with full support for object-oriented development. In developing their libraries, these developers took full advantage of an object-oriented style of development that JavaScript's prototype-based model allowed, creating small objects of functionality that could build upon one another to provide extensive resources of re-usable code.

Author's note

In the coming pages, I will often use the words object and class interchangeably, because it seems a little easier to understand. Technically, JavaScript is a classless language, and our objects are built with JavaScript's prototype-based programming model.

Object-oriented programming with Ext JS

Ext JS is a perfect example of this shift. The Ext JS library is an extremely extensive collection of packages of classes of re-usable code: small pieces of functionality that can be taken on their own, or combined to create some truly fantastic client-side magic. An additional part of its beauty is the ability to extend the library further, creating our own custom components as extensions of those already there. This gives us the ability to create our own re-usable pieces of code. We can write our own objects, as extensions of the library. This means that we don't have to write all of our functionality on our own, as much of this work has already been done for us. We expand upon the foundation, providing our own custom functionality.

Inheritance

To gain a full understanding of what we need to do, we have to understand one of the key concepts of object-oriented programming—*inheritance*.

As we write our own components, these components will usually *inherit* some other component of Ext JS, extending that component's functionality by providing our own properties and overriding the component's existing methods. We are creating new classes from an existing Ext JS class to determine whether the method that has been called is that of our new class, the method of the extended (parent) class, or a combination of the two.

Break it down and make it simple

Confused yet? It's a lot to take in. Let's break this down into a basic example that may clarify a few things. Say we are writing a Customer Resource Management application for a company. This company has salespeople, who have clients (and client contacts), and the company also has vendors that they utilize, who also have contacts. Here we've identified three similar objects within our application. if we take these objects down to the base level, we notice that each one of these objects is a Person (the Clients and Vendors would more clearly be Companies):

* Salesperson
* Client Contact
* Vendor Contact

Each one of these Person objects will share some basic attributes and methods, because each person has a name, an email address, a phone number, and an address. We'll create a quick class diagram to visually represent the Person object:

Author's note

Class diagrams, and UML diagramming in general, are a great way to visually represent different programming constructs. A full explanation is outside the purview of this text, but I highly recommend that you become familiar with them. Our diagrams here show the class name, the attributes, and methods of the class.

Person
name:string
emailAddress:string
phoneNumber:string
address:Address
setName(name:string):void
getName():string
setEmailAddress(emailAddress:string):void
getEmailAddress():string
setPhoneNumber(phoneNumber:string):void
getPhoneNumber():string
setAddress(address:Address):void
getAddress():Address

Note that the Person object has four attributes: name, emailAddress, phoneNumber, and address. Also note that the address attribute is, in itself, another object. We've included some simple methods for the object as well, to get and set our attributes.

Each one of these objects also has its own object-specific properties such as a salesPersonID, a clientContactID, or a vendorContactID.

SalesPerson (extends Person)
salesPersonID:int
setSalesPersonID(salesPersonID:int):void
getSalesPersonID():int

Note that in our diagram of the SalesPerson object, you do not see any of the Person-specific properties and methods. Because SalesPerson extends (*inherits*) the Person object, all of the properties and methods of the Person object become a part of the SalesPerson object as well. We can now create a SalesPerson.

```
var sp = new SalesPerson();
```

This creates a new instance of the `SalesPerson` object, with all of the attributes and methods of the `SalesPerson` object, including those of the parent `Person` object, by extension.

Sounds cool, but what does it mean?

By default, the `SalesPerson` object, being an extension of `Person`, allows you to set that `SalesPerson`'s name as:

```
SalesPerson.setName('Zig Ziggler')
```

You don't have to reference the methods, or the attributes, by calling on the object's (`SalesPerson`) parent object (`Person`) directly because, through *inheritance*, `SalesPerson` is a `Person`.

Now, what was this overriding stuff?

Through inheritance, all of the methods and attributes of a parent object become the child's as well. However, there will be times when you may want the child object's method to be different from that of its parent. Case in point: let's say our `Person` object had its own `validate()` method, which has validated all of the attributes and returned its own error array, but your `SalesPerson` object has some additional attributes to validate as well. By defining a `validate()` method within the `SalesPerson` object, you are overriding the `validate()` method of its **Person** parent object.

```
validate: function() {
   // Some validation code here
}
```

But, in this case, you would want total attribute validation; both the internal object-specific properties, as well as those of the parent object. So here, you would also need to call the `validate()` method of the parent object:

```
validate: function() {
   var errorArr = ourObjects.salesperson.superclass.validate.
call(this);
   // The salesperson specific validate stuff, appending the errorArr
   return errorArr;
}
```

These are the basic pieces of OO that we need to understand so that we can begin to create our own custom classes with Ext JS. Well, almost…

Understanding packages, classes, and namespaces

There are a few final pieces that of the object-oriented puzzle we need, in order to keep a solid grasp of our goals. We've talked about how Ext JS is a large collection of objects extending other objects, but it's also important to understand a few other pieces of basic OO terminology, and how they help in keeping things organized.

Packages

A **package** is a collection of `classes` that share something in common. For instance, the `Ext.data` package is a collection of classes for dealing with data, such as the different types of data Stores, Readers, and Records. The `Ext.grid` package is a collection of classes for the various grid objects, including all of the different grid types and selection models. Likewise, the `Ext.form` package contains classes for building forms, to include all of the classes of the different field types.

Classes

A **class** is what we call a specific JavaScript object, defining that object's attributes and methods. Going back to our previous examples, `Person` and `SalesPerson` would both be written as class objects, and both would probably be part of the same package.

Namespaces

Classes are a part of packages, and packages generally have their own namespace. **Namespaces** are containers of logically grouped packages and class objects. As an example, the Ext JS library falls into the `Ext` namespace. Forms within Ext JS fall into the `Ext.forms` namespace, where `forms` is a package of the various classes used to make up forms. It's a hierarchal relationship, using dot notation to separate the namespace from the package from the class. Variables from one namespace must be passed into another namespace, so applying a namespace helps to encapsulate information within itself. `Ext.grid`, `Ext.form`, and `Ext.data` are all custom namespaces.

What's next?

Now that we have our terminology down, and a basic understanding of these core object-oriented concepts, we can finally get down to applying them within the context of creating Ext JS custom components.

Ok, what do we extend?

Typically, we'll be writing an application and will see ourselves writing the same basic piece over and over again. Or, we may be lucky enough to identify it early enough that we can just choose the best piece and move forward right away. It usually comes down to deciding which Ext JS component is the best one to extend.

Let's revisit our previous scenario, a Customer Resource Management system. We know that we have several `Person` objects within our application. From a display perspective, we will probably need something to display a person's contact details.

There are several different components for the display of information, and we must choose the right one. A grid object would work, but a tabular display across so many different values might clutter our application, and in this scenario, we probably only need to see the details of one person at a time. A `PropertyGrid` is a little different from a standard grid, but we're just going to output a name and an address. We really don't need the user to see the field names so much as the data itself. We can pretty much eliminate the DataView as well, for the same reasons as rejecting the grid. We really need only one record at a time.

This brings us to a form or a Panel. Forms imply editing of information, so for a display-only application you really come back to a Panel. Panel objects are extremely versatile objects, being the core of many other objects within Ext JS. The body of a Window object is a Panel. The different pieces of an Accordian are Panel objects. The bodies of the tabs in a TabPanel are Panel objects. Creating a custom component that extends the Panel object opens the doors to a variety of different display areas within an Ext JS application.

Creating a custom namespace

We want to create our custom components within their own custom namespace for encapsulation, quick reference, and to help us organize our code. It may be that our packages or class may be named the same as other packages and classes already within Ext JS. A custom namespace prevents conflicts from occurring between classes of the same name, as long as each is defined within its own separate namespace. A common naming convention for user-defined objects is to use the `Ext.ux` namespace.

```
Ext.namespace('Ext.ux');
```

Because we're going to be creating a collection of display Panels for our CRM application, we'll really set our namespace apart from the rest.

```
Ext.namespace('CRM.panels');
```

We need to place this line at the top of each class definition template.

Our first custom class

First, let's take a look at a fairly simple script that takes a single record of information and lays it out in a Panel on the screen.

Example 1: `ch13ex1.js`

```
var userData = [

    {ID:1,FIRSTNAME:'John',LASTNAME:'Lennon',EMAIL:'john@beatles.com',
PASSWORD:'apple1',ADDRESSTYPE:'Home (Mailing)',STREET1:'117 Abbey Road
',STREET2:'',STREET3:'',CITY:'New York',STATE:'NY',ZIP:'12345',PHONETY
PE:'Cell',PHONE:'123-456-7890'},
    {ID:2,FIRSTNAME:'Paul',LASTNAME:'McCartney',
EMAIL:'paul@beatles.com',PASSWORD:'linda',ADDRESSTYPE:'Work
(Mailing)',STREET1:'108 Penny Lane',STREET2:'',STREET3:'',
CITY:'Los Angeles',STATE:'CA',ZIP:'67890',PHONETYPE:'Home',
PHONE:'456-789-0123'},
    {ID:3,FIRSTNAME:'George',LASTNAME:'Harrison',
EMAIL:'george@beatles.com',PASSWORD:'timebandit',
ADDRESSTYPE:'Home (Shipping)',STREET1:'302 Space
Way',STREET2:'',STREET3:'',CITY:'Billings',STATE:'MT',
ZIP:'98765',PHONETYPE:'Office',PHONE:'890-123-4567'},
    {ID:4,FIRSTNAME:'Ringo',LASTNAME:'Starr',
EMAIL:'bignose@beatles.com',PASSWORD:'barbie',
ADDRESSTYPE:'Home (Mailing)',STREET1:'789 Zildizhan Pl',
STREET2:'',STREET3:'',CITY:'Malibu',
STATE:'CA',ZIP:'43210',PHONETYPE:'Home',PHONE:'567-890-1234'}
    ];

    var userDetail = new Ext.Panel({
      applyTo: 'chap13_ex01',
      width: 350,
      height: 250,
      title: 'Chapter 13 Example 1',
      data: userData[0],
      tpl: new Ext.XTemplate([
        '<img src="/resources/images/s.gif" width="21" height="16"
                    /><b>{FIRSTNAME} {LASTNAME}</b><br />',
          '<img src="/resources/images/icons/silk/database_edit.gif"
width="16" height="16" id="emailEdit_{ID}" class="iconLnk" align="Edit
Email Address" border="0" />{EMAIL}<br />',
```

```
      '<img src="/resources/images/icons/silk/database_edit.gif"
width="16" height="16" id="phoneEdit_{ID}" class="iconLnk" align="Edit
Phone" border="0" />{PHONE} ({PHONETYPE})<br />',
      '<b>{ADDRESSTYPE} Address</b><br />',
      '<img src="/resources/images/icons/silk/database_edit.gif"
width="16" height="16" id="addrEdit_{ID}" class="iconLnk" align="Edit
Address" border="0" />{STREET1}<br />',
      '<tpl if="STREET2.length &gt; 0">',
      '<img src="/resources/images/s.gif" width="21" height="16"
/>{STREET2}<br />',
      '</tpl>',
      '<tpl if="STREET3.length &gt; 0">',
       '<img src="/resources/images/s.gif" width="21" height="16"
                                        />{STREET3}<br />',
      '</tpl>',
      '<img src="/resources/images/s.gif" width="21" height="16"
                                    />{CITY}, {STATE} {ZIP}'
    ]),
    listeners:{
      render:{
        fn: function(el){
          this.tpl.overwrite(this.body,this.data);
        }
      }
    }
  });
```

What we have here is a simple array of data objects, and a Panel definition. We're passing a single data item into the Panel's configuration, defining an XTemplate for the record's display, and applying a listener which will apply the data to the XTemplate when the Panel is rendered.

Turning this into a reusable component is very easy, as the majority of our code will just be moved into our custom class definition. First, we'll create a new class template, `ContactDetails.js`, and define its initial class declaration as extending the `Ext.Panel` class. Ext JS actually provides custom methods for extending components.

Example 2: `ContactDetails.js`

```
Ext.namespace('CRM.panels');

CRM.panels.ContactDetails = Ext.extend(Ext.Panel,{
   // The panel definition goes here
});
```

Our next step is to begin defining the custom properties and methods of our component. We begin with the default properties that are specific to our component. Some of these properties may be overridden in our object configuration, but these defaults allow us to only pass in what we might need to change for our individual application.

```
width: 350,
height: 250,
data: {
   ID: 0,
   FIRSTNAME: '',
   LASTNAME: '',
   EMAIL: '',
   ADDRESSTYPE: 'Home (mailing)',
   STREET1: '',
   STREET2: '',
   STREET3: '',
   CITY: '',
   STATE: '',
   ZIP: '',
   PHONETYPE: 'Home',
   PHONE: ''
},
tpl: new Ext.XTemplate([
   '<img src="/resources/images/s.gif" width="21" height="16"
                     /><b>{FIRSTNAME} {LASTNAME}</b><br />',
   '<img src="/resources/images/icons/silk/database_edit.gif"
width="16" height="16" id="emailEdit_{ID}" class="iconLnk" align="Edit
Email Address" border="0" />{EMAIL}<br />',
   '<img src="/resources/images/icons/silk/database_edit.gif"
width="16" height="16" id="phoneEdit_{ID}" class="iconLnk" align="Edit
Phone" border="0" />{PHONE} ({PHONETYPE})<br />',
```

```
    '<b>{ADDRESSTYPE} Address</b><br />',
    '<img src="/resources/images/icons/silk/database_edit.gif"
width="16" height="16" id="addrEdit_{ID}" class="iconLnk" align="Edit
Address" border="0" />{STREET1}<br />',
    '<tpl if="STREET2.length &gt; 0">',
        '<img src="/resources/images/s.gif" width="21" height="16"
                                    />{STREET2}<br />',
    '</tpl>',
    '<tpl if="STREET3.length &gt; 0">',
        '<img src="/resources/images/s.gif" width="21" height="16"
                                    />{STREET3}<br />',
    '</tpl>',
    '<img src="/resources/images/s.gif" width="21" height="16"
                                    />{CITY}, {STATE} {ZIP}'
]),
```

Pit stop!

Does anything look familiar here? Yes, it should, especially after looking at the 'records' within `userData`. A class is an object, just like each 'record' in the `userData` array is an object. At its most base level, an object is a collection of name/value pairs. The only true difference is that a class will also have functions as the `value` of an attribute name of the object, and the object can be referenced by its class (the name of the class). Each of these name/value pairs forms the constructor of the `ContactDetails` class.

Overriding methods

Continuing to build our first custom class, we get into overriding methods. As we have previously mentioned, we can override a method of our parent class by defining a method of the same name in the child class. A key component of the Panel class is the `initComponent()` method, which (as the name suggests) initializes the Panel component. Most methods will never need to be overridden, but sometimes, we'll need to override a specific method to add to, or change, the default behavior of a component.

```
initComponent: function(){
    CRM.panels.ContactDetails.superclass.initComponent.call(this);
        if (typeof this.tpl === 'string') {
        this.tpl = new Ext.XTemplate(this.tpl);
    }
},
```

[
> **Author's note**
>
> Ext JS uses `superclass` as the programmatic reference to the object's parent class object, as `CRM.panels.ContactDetails` is a subclass of it's parent (superclass) `Ext.Panel`.
]

With our component, we needed a way to apply a new `XTemplate` to our component, should one be passed into our `ContactDetails` class. Because a developer can pass in the template configuration via the `tpl` argument, instead of an actual `XTemplate` object, it is important to validate that input and adjust accordingly. Our first action is to call the `initComponent()` method of our parent Panel class, and then adjust the value of the `tpl` argument as needed.

Understanding the order of events

In our previous example (Example 1), we used the `render` event to apply our `XTemplate` to our Panel object. In our custom component, we take the same tack, by writing an overriding method for the `onRender()` method.

```
onRender: function(ct, position) {
  CRM.panels.ContactDetails.superclass.onRender.call
                              (this, ct, position);
  if (this.data) {
    this.update(this.data);
  }
},
```

Here, we've called the `onRender()` method of our parent Panel (super) class. After that, we verify that we have a value for our `data` attribute, before calling the custom `update()` method of our component.

```
update: function(data) {
  this.data = data;
  this.tpl.overwrite(this.body, this.data);
}
```

The `update()` method takes an argument of data (a `record` object from our array), applies that argument to the component's `data` attribute, and then applies the component's `XTemplate` to the 'body' of the component. This is a custom method of the component, not an overridden method of the parent Panel class. What's important to our discussion is the need for this method.

When can we do what?

Our XTemplate does not get immediately applied to our component, as it isn't able to overwrite the Panel body until the Panel body has actually been rendered. This is what we mean by 'order of events', and can initially be very confusing, until you put a little thought into it. For instance, say we had dynamically tried to apply a custom ID argument as part of our constructor:

```
id: 'ContactDetails_' + this.data.ID,
```

This would have broken our component. Why? Because this.data is also an item within our constructor, and doesn't actually exist until the component is instantiated into memory. The same thing would have happened, if we had tried to apply our XTemplate within the initComponent() method:

```
initComponent: function(){
    CRM.panels.ContactDetails.superclass.initComponent.call(this);
    this.tpl.overwrite(this.body, this.data);
},
```

This would have failed when initComponent() begins the process of creating the component. The component, at this stage, still isn't part of the browser's Document Object Model, so there isn't any 'body' for the XTemplate to be applied to yet. Getting a handle on the 'order of events' is one of the biggest challenges in learning Ext JS, if you don't know about it, and the order of events may be different with different Ext JS classes as well.

What is an event-driven application?

Now we get down to the real juice. One huge barrier to cross, when transitioning from a procedural programming style into object-oriented development, is understanding the **event-driven** application model. Not all OO programs are event-driven, but the paradigm is definitely shifting in that direction, and Ext JS is no exception. Basically, the flow of an application is determined by sensing some change of state or user interaction, called an *event*. When the event occurs, the application *broadcasts* that the event has taken place. Another piece of the application (a *listener*, also known as an *observer*) is listening for the event broadcast. When it sees that the event has been broadcast, it then performs some other action.

Our ContactDetails class is no different. As an extension of the Panel class, it automatically contains all of the events and event listeners that are a part of the Panel class. An event, render, was previously defined. The process of building the display of the Panel fires off a 'broadcast' of the render event.

```
this.fireEvent('render');
```

The `Ext.Panel` object has already defined an event listener for the `render` event. Once the `render` event has been handled, it calls the `onRender()` method.

```
this.addListener('render',this.onRender,this,
        {ct:this.ct,position:this.position});
```

An event has been reached, which is then broadcast. An event listener is listening for that broadcast. Upon hearing the broadcast, it executes additional pre-configured actions that have been defined for that event. Understanding this process plays a key part in how we develop event-driven applications, and our own applications with Ext JS.

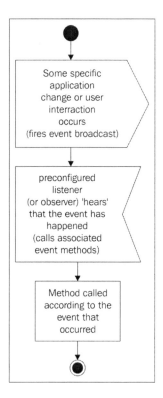

Creating our own custom events

We may just as easily apply our own custom events within our Ext JS applications. We can either register new events, that an end developer can then add listeners to, or we can add our own listeners to kick off other methods within our custom component.

By way of example, let's create a new `update` event within our custom component. We'll adjust our `initComponent()` method to register our new event:

```
initComponent: function(){
  CRM.panels.ContactDetails.superclass.initComponent.call(this);
  if (typeof this.tpl === 'string') {
    this.tpl = new Ext.XTemplate(this.tpl);
  }
  this.addEvents('update');
},
```

This new code is all it takes to register our new event. We'll also go ahead and register a new, internal, **event listener**, which we'll use to call a new method that we'll write in a moment:

```
initComponent: function(){
  CRM.panels.ContactDetails.superclass.initComponent.call(this);
  if (typeof this.tpl === 'string') {
    this.tpl = new Ext.XTemplate(this.tpl);
  }
  this.addEvents('update');
  this.addListener({
    update:{
      fn: this.onUpdate,
      scope: this
    }
  });
},
```

What this states is that whenever the update event is broadcast, our application will turn around and call the `onUpdate()` method of our `ContactDetails` component.

```
onUpdate: function(data){
  console.log('in onUpdate');
}
```

The `onUpdate()` method, in this case, only outputs a short message to the debugging console, which you can see if you are debugging your application in Firefox with the Firebug plugin (*console* is not supported in Internet Explorer). The final step is having the update event broadcast. We already have an `update()` method, so it would make sense for us to broadcast the *update* once it's completed:

```
update: function(data) {
  this.data = data;
  this.tpl.overwrite(this.body, this.data);
  this.fireEvent('update', this.data);
},
```

Here we broadcast our update event by calling the Ext JS's `fireEvent()` method, and passing along our data as the argument to any method listening for the update event. We can have any number of event listeners configured for a particular event, either internal to the component, or externally within a script referencing our custom component.

Our first custom component: Complete

Here's the final component we've been constructing. At this point in time, we don't really need the custom update event. We'll leave it in, as it may be useful later, and we'll just remove the `onUpdate()` method for now.

Example 2: `ContactDetails.js`

```
Ext.namespace('CRM.panels');

CRM.panels.ContactDetails = Ext.extend(Ext.Panel,{
   width: 350,
   height: 250,
   data: {
      ID: 0,
      FIRSTNAME: '',
      LASTNAME: '',
      EMAIL: '',
      ADDRESSTYPE: 'Home (mailing)',
      STREET1: '',
      STREET2: '',
      STREET3: '',
      CITY: '',
      STATE: '',
      ZIP: '',
      PHONETYPE: 'Home',
      PHONE: ''
   },
   tpl: new Ext.XTemplate([
      '<img src="/resources/images/s.gif" width="21" height="16"
                        /><b>{FIRSTNAME} {LASTNAME}</b><br />',
      '<img src="/resources/images/icons/silk/database_edit.gif"
width="16" height="16" id="emailEdit_{ID}" class="iconLnk" align="Edit
Email Address" border="0" />{EMAIL}<br />',
      '<img src="/resources/images/icons/silk/database_edit.gif"
width="16" height="16" id="phoneEdit_{ID}" class="iconLnk" align="Edit
Phone" border="0" />{PHONE} ({PHONETYPE})<br />',
      '<b>{ADDRESSTYPE} Address</b><br />',
```

```
      '<img src="/resources/images/icons/silk/database_edit.gif"
width="16" height="16" id="addrEdit_{ID}" class="iconLnk" align="Edit
Address" border="0" />{STREET1}<br />',
    '<tpl if="STREET2.length &gt; 0">',
      '<img src="/resources/images/s.gif" width="21" height="16"
                                            />{STREET2}<br />',
    '</tpl>',
    '<tpl if="STREET3.length &gt; 0">',
      '<img src="/resources/images/s.gif" width="21" height="16"
                                            />{STREET3}<br />',
    '</tpl>',
    '<img src="/resources/images/s.gif" width="21" height="16"
/>{CITY}, {STATE} {ZIP}'
  ]),
  initComponent: function(){
    CRM.panels.ContactDetails.superclass.initComponent.call(this);
    if (typeof this.tpl === 'string') {
      this.tpl = new Ext.XTemplate(this.tpl);
    }
    this.addEvents('update');
  },

  onRender: function(ct, position) {
    CRM.panels.ContactDetails.superclass.onRender.call
                              (this, ct, position);
    if (this.data) {
      this.update(this.data);
    }
  },
  update: function(data) {
    this.data = data;
    this.tpl.overwrite(this.body, this.data);
    this.fireEvent('update', this.data);
  }
});
```

With our new custom component, we now have a new way of calling it into our applications as well.

Example 2: ch13ex2.js

```
    var userData = [
      {ID:1,FIRSTNAME:'John',LASTNAME:'Lennon',
EMAIL:'john@beatles.com',PASSWORD:'apple1',
ADDRESSTYPE:'Home (Mailing)',
STREET1:'117 Abbey Road',STREET2:'',STREET3:'',
```

```
CITY:'New York',STATE:'NY',ZIP:'12345',PHONETYPE:'Cell',
PHONE:'123-456-7890'},

{ID:2,FIRSTNAME:'Paul',LASTNAME:'McCartney',
EMAIL:'paul@beatles.com',PASSWORD:'linda',
ADDRESSTYPE:'Work (Mailing)',
STREET1:'108 Penny Lane',STREET2:'',
STREET3:'',CITY:'Los Angeles',STATE:'CA',ZIP:'67890',
PHONETYPE:'Home',PHONE:'456-789-0123'},

{ID:3,FIRSTNAME:'George',LASTNAME:'Harrison',
EMAIL:'george@beatles.com',PASSWORD:'timebandit',
ADDRESSTYPE:'Home (Shipping)',STREET1:'302 Space Way',STREET2:'',STREE
T3:'',CITY:'Billings',STATE:'MT',ZIP:'98765',
PHONETYPE:'Office',PHONE:'890-123-4567'},

{ID:4,FIRSTNAME:'Ringo',LASTNAME:'Starr',
EMAIL:'bignose@beatles.com',PASSWORD:'barbie',
ADDRESSTYPE:'Home (Mailing)',STREET1:'789 Zildizhan Pl',
STREET2:'',STREET3:'',CITY:'Malibu',STATE:'CA',ZIP:'43210',PHONETYPE:'
Home',PHONE:'567-890-1234'}
];

var userDetail = new CRM.panels.ContactDetails({
  applyTo: 'chap13_ex01',
  title: 'Chapter 13 Example 1',
  data: userData[0]
});

updateContact = function(event,el,data){
 userDetail.update(data.data);
}

xt.get('actionLink').on('click',updateContact,this,
                                {data:userData[1]});
```

We've taken an anchor element, with an `id` of `actionLink`, from our calling page, and given it an `onclick` event that updates the data of our `ContactDetails` object, `userDetail`. Clicking on the **Update Data** link on the page changes the contact details from `John` over to `Paul`.

What's next? Breaking it down

Ok, we've now created our first custom component. That was fairly painless. But, looking back at what we've done, it looks as if we've pushed ourselves into a small corner again. As it stands, every aspect of our application that requires contact information would have to display the name, email address, phone number, and address of our contact, every time. What happens if we required only the address? Or just the name, or email, or the phone number?

Well, this is where we refactor, creating even more custom components. For our purposes, we'll quickly break this down into two components: one for `UserDetail`, and one for `AddressDetail`.

Example 3: `UserDetail.js`

```
Ext.namespace('CRM.panels');

CRM.panels.UserDetail = Ext.extend(Ext.Panel,{
  width: 350,
  height: 125,
  data: {
    ID: 0,
    FIRSTNAME: '',
    LASTNAME: '',
    EMAIL: '',
    ADDRESSTYPE: 'Home (mailing)',
    STREET1: '',
    STREET2: '',
    STREET3: '',
    CITY: '',
    STATE: '',
    ZIP: '',
    PHONETYPE: 'Home',
```

```
        PHONE: ''
    },
    split: false,
    tpl: new Ext.Template([
        '<img src="/resources/images/s.gif" width="21" height="16"
                            /><b>{FIRSTNAME} {LASTNAME}</b><br />',
        '<img src="/resources/images/icons/silk/database_edit.gif"
width="16" height="16" id="emailEdit_{ID}" class="iconLnk" align="Edit
Email Address" border="0" />{EMAIL}<br />',
        '<img src="/resources/images/icons/silk/database_edit.gif"
width="16" height="16" id="phoneEdit_{ID}" class="iconLnk" align="Edit
Phone" border="0" />{PHONE} ({PHONETYPE})<br />'
    ]),
    initComponent: function(){
     CRM.panels.UserDetail.superclass.initComponent.call(this);
     if (typeof this.tpl === 'string') {
       this.tpl = new Ext.XTemplate(this.tpl);
     }
    },
    onRender: function(ct, position) {
     CRM.panels.UserDetail.superclass.onRender.call
                            (this, ct, position);
     if (this.data) {
       this.update(this.data);
     }
    },
    update: function(data) {
      this.data = data;
      this.tpl.overwrite(this.body, this.data);
    }
});

Ext.reg('userdetail',CRM.panels.UserDetail);
```

Example 3: AddressDetail.js

```
Ext.namespace('CRM.panels');

CRM.panels.AddressDetail = Ext.extend(Ext.Panel,{
  width:350,
  height:125,
  data: {
    ID: 0,
    FIRSTNAME: '',
    LASTNAME: '',
```

```
      EMAIL: '',
      ADDRESSTYPE: 'Home (mailing)',
      STREET1: '',
      STREET2: '',
      STREET3: '',
      CITY: '',
      STATE: '',
      ZIP: '',
      PHONETYPE: 'Home',
      PHONE: ''
    },
    split: false,
    tpl: new Ext.XTemplate([
      '<b>{ADDRESSTYPE} Address</b><br />',
      '<img src="/resources/images/icons/silk/database_edit.gif"
width="16" height="16" id="addrEdit_{ID}" class="iconLnk" align="Edit
Address" border="0" />{STREET1}<br />',
      '<tpl if="STREET2.length &gt; 0">',
        '<img src="/resources/images/s.gif" width="21" height="16"
                                    />{STREET2}<br />',
      '</tpl>',
      '<tpl if="STREET3.length &gt; 0">',
        '<img src="/resources/images/s.gif" width="21" height="16"
                                    />{STREET3}<br />',
      '</tpl>',
      '<img src="/resources/images/s.gif" width="21" height="16"
                                  />{CITY}, {STATE} {ZIP}'
    ]),
    initComponent: function(){
      CRM.panels.AddressDetail.superclass.initComponent.call(this);
      if (typeof this.tpl === 'string') {
        this.tpl = new Ext.XTemplate(this.tpl);
      }
    },
    onRender: function(ct, position) {
      CRM.panels.UserDetail.superclass.onRender.call
                              (this, ct, position);
      if (this.data) {
        this.update(this.data);
      }
    },
    update: function(data) {
      this.data = data;
      this.tpl.overwrite(this.body, this.data);
    }
});
Ext.reg('addrdetail',CRM.panels.AddressDetail);
```

By breaking these into two separate components, we can now use either piece in any area of our application, independently.

Example 3: `ch13ex3.js`

```
var userData = [

{ID:1,FIRSTNAME:'John',LASTNAME:'Lennon',EMAIL:'john@beatles.com'
,PASSWORD:'apple1',ADDRESSTYPE:'Home (Mailing)',STREET1:'117 Abbey Roa
d',STREET2:'',STREET3:'',CITY:'New York',
STATE:'NY',ZIP:'12345',PHONETYPE:'Cell',PHONE:'123-456-7890'},

{ID:2,FIRSTNAME:'Paul',LASTNAME:'McCartney',
EMAIL:'paul@beatles.com',PASSWORD:'linda',
ADDRESSTYPE:'Work (Mailing)',STREET1:'108 Penny Lane',STREET2:'',STREE
T3:'',CITY:'Los Angeles',STATE:'CA',
ZIP:'67890',PHONETYPE:'Home',PHONE:'456-789-0123'},

{ID:3,FIRSTNAME:'George',LASTNAME:'Harrison',
EMAIL:'george@beatles.com',PASSWORD:'timebandit',
ADDRESSTYPE:'Home (Shipping)',STREET1:'302 Space Way',
STREET2:'',STREET3:'',CITY:'Billings',STATE:'MT',ZIP:'98765',
PHONETYPE:'Office',PHONE:'890-123-4567'},

{ID:4,FIRSTNAME:'Ringo',LASTNAME:'Starr',
EMAIL:'bignose@beatles.com',PASSWORD:'barbie',
ADDRESSTYPE:'Home (Mailing)',STREET1:'789 Zildizhan Pl',
STREET2:'',STREET3:'',CITY:'Malibu',STATE:'CA',ZIP:'43210',
PHONETYPE:'Home',PHONE:'567-890-1234'}
];

var userDetail = new CRM.panels.UserDetail({
  applyTo: 'chap13_ex03a',
  title: 'User Detail',
  data: userData[0]
});

var addrDetail = new CRM.panels.AddressDetail({
  applyTo: 'chap13_ex03b',
  title: 'Address Detail',
  data: userData[0]
})

updateContact = function(event,el,data){
  userDetail.update(data.data);
  addrDetail.update(data.data);
}

  Ext.get('actionLink').on('click',updateContact,this,
                                  {data:userData[1]});
```

Best Practice

Ok, looking at our two custom components, it's fairly obvious that they are essentially the same object with different XTemplates applied, and it would probably be best for them to have their own parent class of overloaded, template-applying methods, and just be repositories of the XTemplate defaults and our xtypes. But, for our examples, we're going to try and keep it simple for now.

Using xtype: The benefits of lazy instantiation

In our previous example, a new line was added to the bottom of each class file:

```
Ext.reg('userdetail',CRM.panels.UserDetail);
```

What we've done here is register our new custom component as an xtype. Well, what does that mean exactly? An xtype is a component container element, registered with the Ext JS library, for lazy object instantiation. What this means is that we can use the xtype as a quick object identifier, when laying out our applications, and that these types of objects are only loaded into browser memory when they are actually used. This can greatly improve the overall performance of our application, especially when a view may contain many objects. We'll use xtype wherever possible while writing object configuration, so that objects that might not immediately be displayed won't take up valuable memory resources. Next, we'll look at this in practice.

Using our custom components within other objects

Now that we've created our custom components, we can add them to any other container object within Ext JS. We can now use our xtype to refer to the component type, for lazy instantiation, and we can get all of the benefits of modular design. Let's apply our two new components with a border layout, for side-by-side viewing.

Example 4: ch14ex4.js

```
var ContactDetail = new Ext.Panel({
  title: 'Contact Details',
  applyTo: 'chap13_ex04',
  width: 400,
  height: 125,
  layout: 'border',
```

```
    frame: true,
    items:[{
        region: 'west',
        xtype: 'userdetail',
        width: 200,
        data: userData[0]
    },{
        region: 'center',
        xtype: 'addrdetail',
        width: 200,
        data: userData[0]
    }]
});
```

We have identified the West and center regions of our `BorderLayout` as belonging to the `UserDetail` and `AddressDetail` class types respectively. If this layout were part of a window object, these two classes wouldn't even be loaded into memory until the window was shown, helping to reduce browser memory usage.

Summary

Extending the various classes of the Ext JS library is one way to place ourselves on a fast track to Rapid Application Development, by allowing us to easily create modular, re-usable components. Within this chapter, we've discovered some of the most powerful aspects of the Ext JS library.

We had a brief overview of object-oriented development with JavaScript, and then covered how object-oriented program design applies to the Ext JS library. We spent a little time covering some of the basics of object-oriented programming such as inheritance, method overriding, and some basic terminology.

We then began applying some of these concepts within Ext JS such as defining custom namespaces, creating custom components, and overriding methods of our object's parent (super) class.

We followed up by giving a small explanation of event-driven application architecture, and applied that by writing a custom event and listener for our custom component.

Finally, we covered xtypes and the importance of lazy instantiation on application performance, and then modified our code to use xtypes for our new custom components to add them into other Ext JS object containers.

14

The Power of Ext JS: What Else Can You Do?

Throughout this book, we've gone over some of the core components of Ext JS: Windows and Dialogs, Grids, Trees, Data Stores, and more. This is some of the flashiest, coolest, and most consistent stuff on the Web today, for taking a drab old HTML display and giving it the sizzle and pop such a dynamic development platform deserves. But we've still only scratched the surface of what's available within the complete Ext JS library.

So much to work with

The Ext JS site (`http://www.extjs.com`) provides a wealth of information for those learning to develop with Ext JS. A quick view of the **Samples and Demos** area of this site will show us quite a bit of what we've covered in this book, but a thorough examination of the source code will show us some things that we may not immediately have known were available. These are the pieces that aren't necessarily apparent, such as a panel or a grid, but these little things ultimately hold it all together and truly allow us to create robust applications.

Form widgets

What's a widget? Well, a widget is a tiny piece or component of functionality, say (for instance) a slider or a progress bar. Most applications are made up of forms, so it's no accident that Ext JS includes some form widgets that we can't get with straight HTML. TextFields and Checkboxes and Radio buttons are standard fare, but Ext JS sweetens the pot by going to the next level, providing us with components that we're used to seeing in most desktop applications.

DateField

The **DateField** is a perfect example. Handling dates within most HTML forms can be a chore, but Ext JS provides a very basic component for handling dates:

Example 1: `ch14ex1.js`

```
Ext.onReady(function(){
  var formPanel = new Ext.form.FormPanel({
    title:'DateField Example',
    applyTo:'chap14_ex01',
    layout:'form',
    labelAlign:'top',
    width:210,
    autoHeight:true,
    frame:true,
    items:[{
    xtype:'datefield',
      fieldLabel:'Date of Birth',
      name:'dob',
      width:190,
      allowBlank:false
    }]
  });
});
```

What we have here is a basic `FormPanel` layout, that puts our `DateField` into proper context and allow for certain necessary attributes (like putting our label above the field). Within the layout we have a single `DateField` component. On initial load, it looks like a basic `TextField`, with the exception of the **trigger** to the right. Clicking the trigger shows the beauty of Ext JS's consistent component "look-and-feel", displaying an attractive calendar layout for the selection of a date. You can select a day, move from month-to-month, or even click on the month itself to choose a different month and year.

Apart from its rich display, the **DateField** also provides a rich set of attributes for specialized customization, including the ability to determine different accepted date formats, and the ability to disable entire blocks of days. The component will also automatically validate manually-entered data.

TimeField

Dealing with time can be more difficult than dealing with dates, but Ext JS, again, provides a component to assist us. The **TimeField** is, ultimately, a basic ComboBox that will automatically show a set of time, in increments that we want, for quick selection:

Example 2: ch14ex2.js

```
Ext.onReady(function(){
  var formPanel = new Ext.form.FormPanel({
    title:'DateField Example',
    applyTo:'chap14_ex02',
    layout:'form',
    labelAlign:'top',
    width:210,
    autoHeight:true,
    frame:true,
    items:[{
      xtype:'timefield',
      fieldLabel:'Time',
      minValue: '9:00 AM',
        maxValue: '6:00 PM',
        increment: 30
    }]
  });
});
```

As in our last example, this simple `FormLayout` contains one item, in this case the `TimeField`. Click on the **trigger**, and we get our options, defined by our code as times between 9 AM and 6 PM in increments of 30 minutes. Other configuration options allow you to define multiple accepted time formats, and also implement custom validation. Basic validation is provided by default.

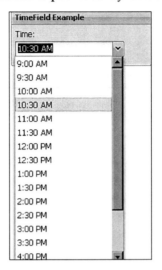

NumberField

The **NumberField** doesn't *look* very special—it's just a basic 'text' field. What makes it special is how it allows us to 'dummy-proof' our Ext JS applications. Client-side data validation is essential for ensuring data integrity prior to sending values to the server, allowing us to prevent errors from our remote procedure calls. Components such as this one simplify that process for us. The NumberField provides automatic keystroke filtering and validation to allow the entry of only numeric data, allowing us to specify whether it can take negative numbers or float values, and even specify how many decimal places are accepted.

CheckboxGroups and RadioGroups

Ext JS 2.2 brought two new form controls: the `CheckboxGroup` and the `RadioGroup`. These controls allow us to 'group' sets of checkbox or radio buttons, providing them with custom formatting and special, group-level validation capabilities. For example, say we have a form with two checkboxes for the users to select their gender. By placing these within a `CheckboxGroup`, we can apply our validation to the *group* so that at least one option is selected when the form is submitted. We can apply many more complex validation rules as well, depending upon the scenario. See the Ext JS API for more details.

HtmlEditor

Ext JS includes a nice, limited, WYSIWYG HtmlEditor, to drop right into your forms:

Example 3: chapter14_03.js

```
Ext.onReady(function(){
  var formPanel = new Ext.form.FormPanel({
    title:'HtmlEditor Example',
    applyTo:'chap14_ex03',
    layout:'form',
    labelAlign:'top',
    width:600,
    autoHeight:true,
    frame:true,
    items:[{
      xtype:'htmleditor',
      id:'bio',
      fieldLabel:'Blog Entry',
      height:200,
      anchor:'98%'
    }]
  });
});
```

Here we dropped the HtmlEditor into our FormLayout for a quick demonstration. The HtmlEditor is applied to a basic text area, in much the same way as other WYSIWYG editors, say FCKEditor or TinyMCE. We have the ability to enable or disable the various menu buttons related to formatting, as well as call various methods (like those to get or set the text of the editor, its position, and so on), or apply event listeners, just like the other components of Ext JS.

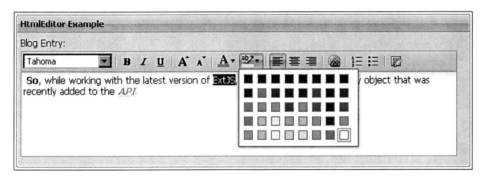

We get the same, consistent Ext JS look and feel, while giving our users the ability to format their own content directly from within our applications. In this image, note that the HtmlEditor uses Ext JS's built in **ColorPalette** component for selecting colors.

Data formatting

We all know that we don't always receive data in the format in which we want it to be displayed. Ext JS provides many different components specifically for address such issues. First among these is the `Format` object in the `Ext.util` package, which gives us a wide variety of functions for everything from creating the US currency format for a number to methods for stripping scripts and HTML from strings. The Ext JS library also extends several native JavaScript objects and provides us with additional methods for manipulating them. Specifically, the `String`, `Number`, and `Date` objects have all been extended. You can now strip off unnecessary whitespace, constrain numbers to a minimum and maximum value, and even create `Date` objects from a variety of format options.

Basic string formatting

The `String` object has been extended to provide several formatting options, including the `format()` method. This simple method allows you to return a formatted string of text, with the first parameter being the string to return, and all other parameters (as many as you like) being *bound* to pieces of the string, using a basic form of binding expression, whereby curly braces surround a variable reference. Typical binding expressions, used by Ext JS, would contain a dot-notated variable reference surrounded by curly braces (that is, `{this.firstName}`), but this instance will bind values to the arguments that will follow using their array order:

Example 4: `chapter14_04.js`

```
Ext.onReady(function(){
  var cls = "Band";
  var member = {
    firstName: 'Eric',
    lastName: 'Clapton',
    position: 'Lead Guitarist'
  };

  var pnl = new Ext.Panel({
    applyTo: 'chap14_ex04',
    width: 200,
    height: 100,
    bodyStyle: 'padding:5px',
    title: 'Band Member',
    html: String.format('<div class=\'{0}\'>{2}, {1}: {3}</div>',
            cls, member.firstName, member.lastName, member.position)
  });
});
```

This small block of code displays a simple `Panel` element, which calls the formatting function to build the HTML of the `Panel`. The `format()` method's arguments are applied to different parts of the string that we are building.

Band Member
Clapton, Eric: Lead Guitarist

Formatting dates

The `Date` object has also been extended to provide additional formatting and parsing capabilities. The API provides a complete listing of the date part identifiers that can be used when parsing a string into a `Date` object, or when outputting a `Date` object in the desired format:

Example 5: `chapter14_05.js`

```
Ext.onReady(function(){
  var cls = "Band";
  var member = {
    firstName: 'Eric',
    lastName: 'Clapton',
    position: 'Lead Guitarist',
    birthDate: new Date('03/30/1945')
  };

  var pnl = new Ext.Panel({
    applyTo: 'chap14_ex05',
    width: 200,
    height: 100,
    bodyStyle: 'padding:5px',
    title: 'Band Member',
    html: String.format('<div class=\'{0}\'>{2}, {1}: {3}<br />DOB:
{4}</div>', cls, member.firstName, member.lastName, member.position,
member.birthDate.format('F j, Y'))
  });
});
```

We've extended our previous example to add Eric's birthday. We've created a new `Date` object, as part of the `Member` object, and then used the `format()` method of the `Date` object to format our date for display.

Band Member
Clapton, Eric: Lead Guitarist DOB: March 30, 1945

Other formatting

The `Ext.util` package provides many different classes and methods for formatting various types of data, including many for working with `strings`, `dates`, and `numbers`. A good example is the `usMoney()` method:

```
var annualSalary = 123456.345;
Ext.util.Format.usMoney(annualSalary);
```

This will return a pre-formatted US currency string of `$123,456.35`. This can come in very handy when working with e-commerce applications. This is only one of the many methods within the classes of the `Ext.util` package.

Author's note

Currently, as far as working with currency is concerned there is only a `usMoney()` method in the `Format` class. But, with Ext JS's extensible architecture, it would be possible to create methods for formatting other foreign currencies. A quick search of the Ext JS forums will pull up several posts on creating formatting methods for other currency types.

Another common function is the ability to strip HTML from a `string`. Say we have a simple comment form on our page, and want to ensure that the user doesn't include any HTML in the input, so that our data isn't polluted before going to the server. Ext JS includes a simple method for stripping out HTML from any string:

```
var firstName = '<b>jimi</b>';
var adj = Ext.util.Format.stripTags(firstName);
```

We may also want to make sure that a particular input, say a name, is capitalized before we pass it back to the server:

```
var adj2 = Ext.util.Format.capitalize(adj);
```

We may also want to apply a default value to a variable in case one does not exist already:

```
var adj3 = Ext.util.Format.defaultValue(favoriteBlog,
                                        'Cutter\'s Crossing');
```

These are just a few of the many formatting methods that are available within the Ext JS library. A thorough review of the API will provide you with a full understanding of everything that is available.

Managing application state

Core to any application (especially an event-driven application) is maintaining and controlling 'state'. This can encompass many different things, from keeping user preferences on grid sorting, to managing multiple Windows or layout areas on the screen, and even being able to use the **Back** button in the browser and have it change your application without reloading the wrong page. Luckily, Ext JS provides several `Manager` objects for handling many of these exact scenarios.

Basic 'state'

The `Ext.state.Manager` class is automatically checked, and utilized, by every state-aware component within Ext JS. With one simple line of code we can set this manager in place, and with little or no additional work, our application's view state is automatically registered.

To put this in perspective, suppose that we have a rather large application, spanning many different HTML documents. Ext JS plays a part in the application, because we've implemented a data grid for displaying users. While we work on our grid, it may be necessary to change the sort order from the default **LastName** column to an unlikely column, say the **UserName** column. Now let's say we had to go into an inventory editor for a moment. If we use the `Manager`, when we return to the user editor our grid will automatically come up sorted again by **Username**, as that was the last state change that we made:

```
Ext.state.Manager.setProvider(new Ext.state.CookieProvider());
```

This line creates our `state Manager`, setting the provider to a `CookieProvider`. What this means is that the application state is saved to a value within a cookie on the client machine, which in turn is read to re-enable the state upon returning to a state-aware component.

Side Note

The `CookieProvider` also provides a simple API for the general management of client-side cookies for our sites, and can be used as a standalone class for referencing and manipulating cookie objects.

How do I get that window?

Many Ext JS applications will be confined to a single HTML page, and might commonly come down to a collection of Ext JS `Window` objects on the screen. But what happens if a user is in one window, and we want to show them another window that is already open, without closing the one they've been working on? By default, all Ext JS windows are created, and registered, within the global `WindowGroup`. We can easily control the state of these windows by using the `WindowMgr` class. This manager class allows us to grab any window of a `WindowGroup`, and bring it to the front, send it to the back, or even hide all of the windows in the group.

Using the back button in Ext JS applications

One common problem among **Rich Internet Applications** is handling the **Back** button of the browser. Say we have a large Ext JS based application with Tabs, Grids, and Accordions. A user, navigating our application by using these components, might hit their **Back** button to go back to their last action, or screen, or panel. This is expected behavior in most Internet applications, because most Internet applications go from one HTML page to another.

But most Rich Internet Applications, like those built with Ext JS, are usually a collection of different states within the same HTML page, and the **Back** button would typically take a user out of our application and back to the last viewed HTML page. Thankfully, Ext JS 2.2 (the latest library update, as of this writing) introduced the `History` class, giving us the ability to control how the browser history is used, and how the browser's **Back** button would be handled within our applications.

Manage this

There are several other Manager classes within Ext JS. The `StoreMgr` provides easy access to our various data Store objects. The `ComponentMgr` allows us to quickly retrieve specific components to act upon. The `EventMgr` allows us to control events within Ext JS objects. A good review of the Ext JS API will give us more information on these Manager objects and their many uses.

Accessing the DOM

Custom library adapters allow for the use of Ext JS with other libraries, say JQuery or Prototype. But Ext JS provides its own internal libraries for DOM manipulation as well.

Finding DOM elements

The first task when manipulating the **DOM(Document Object Model)** is to find what we're looking for. The DomQuery class provides us with several methods for this purpose, including returning entire groups of DOM nodes that meet specific criteria, or selecting a single node by its selector. We can even start the search from a specific node in the page. There are several different selector types that can be used when searching for a specific element:

- base Element Selectors
- Attribute Selectors
- Pseudo Classes
- CSS Value Selectors

What's more, we can chain together a series of selectors to find the exact element we're searching for:

```
var myEl = Ext.DomQuery.selectNode
            ('a.iconLnk[@href*="cutterscrossing"]:first');
```

This will return the first anchor element with a class name of iconLnk that contains 'cutterscrossing' within its href attribute:

- a: Is an anchor element
- .selectNode: Is a class of selectNode
- [@href *= "cutterscrossing"]: Is an href attribute containing 'cutterscrossing' somewhere within its value
- :first: Is only the first element matching the criteria

Manipulating the DOM

The DomHelper class allows us to manipulate the DOM of the rendered page on the fly. Whether we want to add a new element below a collection of others, remove a specific element, or even overwrite the body content of an element, the DomHelper class contains the methods that can accomplish the task:

```
Ext.DomHelper.insertAfter(ourGrid, newForm);
```

This line will place the newForm object directly after ourGrid in the current page's DOM. You could just as easily use insertBefore() to place the form before the grid. You could even use insertHtml() to insert a block of HTML into the DOM with a particular relation to a specific DOM element. A thorough review of the API will give you a complete view of the power of the DomHelper class.

Working with styles

The DomHelper class also provides a simple method for setting the style of an individual element, through the use of the applyStyles() method. But sometimes we may need to change the style sheet of our entire document. For this, Ext JS has the Ext.util.CSS class, which allows us to create a new stylesheet that will automatically be appended to the Head of our document, remove entire stylesheets, or swap one stylesheet for another. We can even act upon their entire set of rules:

```
Ext.util.CSS.swapStyleSheet('defaultDisplay','print.css');
```

This little script will swap out the current stylesheet, which is identified by the link tag's id attribute, and replace it with the print.css stylesheet.

Ext JS for the desktop: Adobe AIR

One of the great things about being a web application developer is that we have the opportunity to write truly cross-platform applications. The traditional model for this has always been writing browser-based applications that work primarily under a client/server paradigm, with the browser as the client and a web application server as the server.

But desktop applications have a lot of their own benefits, including access to their own local file systems (something you cannot do with web-based applications, because of security concerns). The biggest issue with building desktop applications is writing them for all of Windows, Unix/Linux, and the Mac. None of these systems share common display libraries or file access systems, so writing a cross-platform application would require writing separate versions of the code to accommodate each system. There are languages that provide cross-platform virtual machines, which give this kind of access to the system resources, but they require learning languages that may be of outside the average web developer's toolbox.

Adobe came up with an interesting idea. How could they let people develop cross-platform applications using web-based technologies such as HTML, JavaScript, AJAX, and Flash?

With their purchase of Macromedia, Adobe gained the rights to the Flash player and the Flash application platform. The Flash player is distributed on 97% of the user desktops as a plug-in for every major browser. They also gained access to a new technology called Flex, which is a framework and compiler that allows developers (rather than designers) to script Flash based applications.

But, part of what they truly gained was an understanding of how to create a cross-platform application delivery engine. So, they built upon their new-found knowledge, and set out to create the **Adobe Integrated Runtime**, better known as **AIR**. AIR is a desktop engine for rendering content written in HTML, JavaScript, and/or Flash (and more), which allows local access to the client system's resources, regardless of the operating system. Built upon the open source **WebKit** platform, which is the same platform used by **Apple** in their **Safari** web browser, AIR has access to the local file system and storage, while maintaining Internet awareness, thereby creating a bridge between offline process and online content. AIR even provides access to local databases created with SQLLite. SQLLite is a server-less library for delivering databases, with its own transactional SQL database, engine that can be directly embedded into an application.

Adobe and Ext JS already have a great relationship, because Adobe contracted Ext JS so that it could use the Ext JS component library as the foundation of the AJAX-based components generated by ColdFusion Markup Language, which is processed on Adobe's popular ColdFusion application server. And Considering the cross-platform nature of AIR, it was befitting that some of the first HTML/JavaScript sample applications were written in another cross-platform library, Ext JS. The **tasks** sample application is included with the Ext JS download, and is an excellent primer on how to write HTML and JavaScript applications for AIR.

Ext JS 2.1 was released on the same day that Adobe AIR was officially released, and included an entire package of components dedicated to developing Ext JS-based AIR applications. The classes of the `Ext.air` package interact with AIR's own classes for interacting with the runtime and the desktop. Aptana, a popular JavaScript editor and Eclipse plugin, added support for creating AIR applications directly as projects from within its IDE (Aptana already supported Ext JS development), with simple wizards to help get you started, as well as for packaging completed AIR applications.

To make life easier, the base Ext JS class provides an `isAir` Boolean property that can be used to conditionally run applications concurrently on the web and within an AIR application, utilizing the same codebase. The `Ext.air` package includes special packages for managing application state, including the `NativeWindowGroup` and `FileProvider` classes (AIR's answer to the `WindowGroup` and `CookieProvider` classes). There are even classes for controlling sound and system menus.

More information:

For more information on developing Adobe AIR applications, visit the AIR and AJAX Developer Center (`http://www.adobe.com/devnet/air/ajax/`). For details look at AIR/Ext JS integration, study the 'tasks' sample application, included in the complete Ext JS download. There's also the *Ext.air for Adobe AIR* topic within the Ext JS Forums.

Ext JS community extensions

Chapter 13 of this book discussed how developers can write their own custom extensions to Ext JS. Being an open source project, the Ext JS community is very active in contributing new components to extend existing functionality, and sometimes these components even go on to become a part of the framework.

Many custom extensions are found directly in the forums area of the Ext JS website, as posts from members who have come up with solutions to a problem they had identified. There is, however, a section of the **Learning Center** area of the site that is dedicated to showcasing custom extensions. Here are a few fan favorites:

DatePickerPlus

Building on the `DateField` class, the **DatePickerPlus** provides multi-calendar displays, allowing a user to select a range of dates. There are multiple configuration options available, and the level of control available to the developer is very comprehensive.

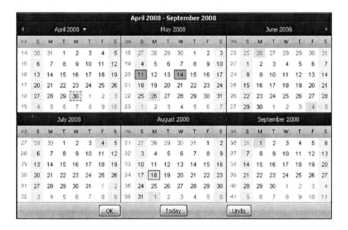

PowerWizard

The `PowerWizard` class allows us to create powerful, multi-step 'wizard-like' processes, with field (and multi-field) validation and decision trees, as well as data persistence between frames.

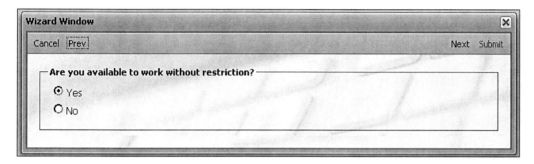

TinyMCE

Yes, for those times when the HtmlEditor just isn't enough, someone wrote a custom extension to wrap the TinyMCE WYSIWYG editor into the Ext JS applications.

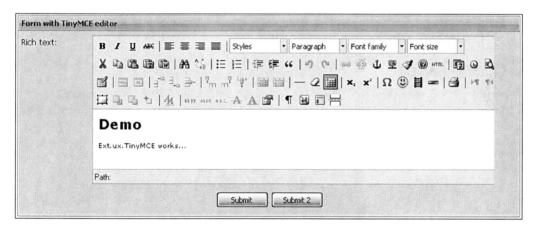

SwfUploadPanel

How many times would it have been nice to be able to upload more than one file at a time through our web application interface? Someone converted the popular SwfUpload project into a custom Ext JS component, allowing multi-file uploads from within our application.

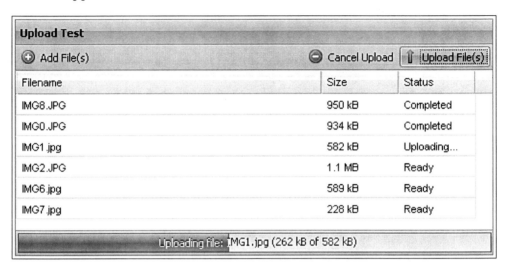

ColorPicker

The built-in `ColorPalette` component can seem rather limiting, only showing a few of the colors available for web display. For this reason, there is the `ColorPicker` giving the user the option of selecting any color they wish.

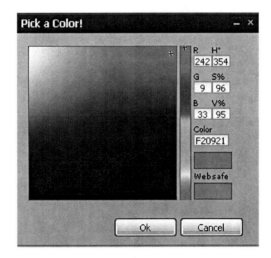

These are just a few of the outstanding community contributions to the library. There are many more available through the **Community Extensions** section of the **Learning Center** area of the Ext JS website, as well as throughout the **Forums** (Checkout the *Ext: User Extensions and Plugins* topic for more).

Additional resources

Knowing where to find good information is the biggest trick to learning anything new. Although this book is a good resource, there is a wealth of information available on the Internet, especially on the Ext JS site (`http://www.extjs.com`).

Samples and demos

The **Samples and Demos** area of the Ext JS site (`http://extjs.com/deploy/dev/examples/samples.html`) will likely be the first real exposure that anyone has to the power of the Ext JS library. These small samples are broken down into various categories, providing us with solid examples of how to use many of the components of Ext JS. With easily-accessible source code, we can see exactly what it takes to write this type of functionality for our own applications.

Ext JS API

The Ext JS interactive API (`http://extjs.com/deploy/dev/docs/`) is an outstanding resource, giving us access to the underlying properties, methods, and events that are available within each class of Ext JS. Peppered throughout are additional code samples to illustrate their use. The Ext JS team even provides a desktop AIR version of this API browser, so that we can have it available offline.

Side note:

The Ext JS team also supports the older 1.1 framework, which is what runs the underlying AJAX components of the **Adobe ColdFusion 8** server. The samples and demos for the 1.1 framework are actually included in the 1.1 API browser (`http://extjs.com/deploy/ext-1.1.1/docs/`), which is available through the **Learning Center** area of the website (`http://extjs.com/learn/`).

Ext JS forums

The Forums for Ext JS (`http://extjs.com/forum/`) show what an active community there is, developing the Ext JS library. With over 40,000 threads and more than 200,000 posts, this is the place to ask questions. Topics range from the very easy to the ultra-advanced, and members of the core Ext JS development team are frequent contributors.

Step-by-step tutorials

Step-by-Step Tutorials(`http://extjs.com/learn/Tutorials`) can be found within the **Learning Center**, with content ranging from simple component usage to advanced project development. Some of these tutorials come directly from the Ext JS development team, but many are contributed by members of the Ext JS community.

Community manual

One can also find the **Ext JS Community Manual** within the **Learning Center**. This wiki-style development manual is maintained by the Ext JS community itself, and contains topics relating to most of the aspects of Ext JS development.

Spket IDE

We can find resources for Ext JS all over the Internet. One good example is from Spket Studios (`http://www.spket.com/`), makers of the Spket IDE. This free IDE comes as a plug-in for the **Eclipse** development platform. With a few simple steps, Spket can provide complete code introspection for our Ext JS classes and extensions, as well as in-depth code assistance. It even has a built-in theme builder to automatically create new skins for your components.

Aptana Studio

Aptana Studio is quickly becoming a major contender in the web-based IDE market. Even the free version provides code introspection and assistance with multiple JavaScript libraries, built-in wizards for creating Adobe AIR applications, built-in debugging tools, and much more.

Google

Yes, Google (or any other search engine) is a fantastic resource, because there are thousands of articles, tutorials, and blog posts available. A quick search on "Ext JS" brings up over a million possible matches, and that's growing every day.

Summary

In this chapter we've discussed some of the lesser known pieces of the Ext JS library. We briefly covered some of the form components not found in traditional HTML, such as the `DateField` and the `HtmlEditor`. We also learned about the various classes available for formatting data for the desired output, as well as those classes needed for managing application state and manipulating the Document Object Model. We also briefly talked about creating Ext JS desktop applications with Adobe AIR.

Finally, we also talked about the various resources that are out there for continuing to learn about Ext JS development. We talked about the community extensions, the brilliant samples, and API browser, as well as the forums, tutorials, and the community manual. We even touched on some IDE's for doing Ext JS development.

Where do we go from here?

It is our hope that, with this brief introduction to the Ext JS JavaScript component library and framework, we've given our readers a good foundation upon which some truly amazing things can be built some truly amazing things. Ext JS provides such an immense wealth of user interactivity within web applications, possibly to a degree never achieved before. With its deep, consistent, and rich component set, its full-featured and intuitive API, and its constant development and growth, Ext JS has the potential to truly springboard web (and even desktop) applications beyond the traditional paradigms, by providing users with an experience well beyond the web applications of the past.

Our imagination is the only limit to what we can hope to have in the future.

Charles F. Kettering

US electrical engineer and inventor (1876 - 1958)

Index

X

Packt Open Source Project Royalties

When we sell a book written on an Open Source project, we pay a royalty directly to that project. Therefore by purchasing Learning Ext JS, Packt will have given some of the money received to the Ext JS project.

In the long term, we see ourselves and you—customers and readers of our books—as part of the Open Source ecosystem, providing sustainable revenue for the projects we publish on. Our aim at Packt is to establish publishing royalties as an essential part of the service and support a business model that sustains Open Source.

If you're working with an Open Source project that you would like us to publish on, and subsequently pay royalties to, please get in touch with us.

Writing for Packt

We welcome all inquiries from people who are interested in authoring. Book proposals should be sent to author@packtpub.com. If your book idea is still at an early stage and you would like to discuss it first before writing a formal book proposal, contact us; one of our commissioning editors will get in touch with you.

We're not just looking for published authors; if you have strong technical skills but no writing experience, our experienced editors can help you develop a writing career, or simply get some additional reward for your expertise.

About Packt Publishing

Packt, pronounced 'packed', published its first book "Mastering phpMyAdmin for Effective MySQL Management" in April 2004 and subsequently continued to specialize in publishing highly focused books on specific technologies and solutions.

Our books and publications share the experiences of your fellow IT professionals in adapting and customizing today's systems, applications, and frameworks. Our solution-based books give you the knowledge and power to customize the software and technologies you're using to get the job done. Packt books are more specific and less general than the IT books you have seen in the past. Our unique business model allows us to bring you more focused information, giving you more of what you need to know, and less of what you don't.

Packt is a modern, yet unique publishing company, which focuses on producing quality, cutting-edge books for communities of developers, administrators, and newbies alike. For more information, please visit our website: www.PacktPub.com.

PUBLISHING

Learning Dojo

ISBN: 978-1-847192-68-4   Paperback: 230 pages

A practical, comprehensive tutorial to building beautiful, scalable interactive interfaces for your Web 2.0 applications with Dijits

1. Learn real-world Dojo programming with detailed examples and analysis of source code

2. Comprehensive guide to available Dojo widgets (dijits) and how to use them

3. Extend Dojo by creating your own dijits

Learning jQuery

ISBN: 978-1-847192-50-9   Paperback: 380 pages

Better Interaction Design and Web Development with Simple JavaScript Techniques

1. Create better, cross-platform JavaScript code

2. Learn detailed solutions to specific client-side problems

3. For web designers who want to create interactive elements for their designs

4. For developers who want to create the best user interface for their web applications.

Please check **www.PacktPub.com** for information on our titles

Building Responsive Web Applications
AJAX and PHP

Cristian Darie   Filip Chereches-Tosa
Bogdan Brinzarea   Mihai Bucica   PACKT

AJAX and PHP

ISBN: 190-4-811-82-5   Paperback: 275 pages

Enhance the user experience of your PHP website using AJAX with this practical tutorial featuring detailed case studies

1. Build a solid foundation for your next generation of web applications

2. Use better JavaScript code to enable powerful web features

3. Leverage the power of PHP and MySQL to create powerful back-end functionality and make it work in harmony with the smart AJAX client

---

**Learning the Yahoo!
User Interface Library**

Get started and get to grips with the YUI JavaScript development library!

Dan Wellman   PACKT

Learning the Yahoo! User Interface library

ISBN: 978-1-847192-32-5   Paperback: 380 pages

Develop your next generation web applications with the YUI JavaScript development library.

1. Improve your coding and productivity with the YUI Library

2. Gain a thorough understanding of the YUI tools

3. Learn from detailed examples for common tasks

Please check **www.PacktPub.com** for information on our titles

Breinigsville, PA USA
09 November 2010
249001BV00003B/7/P

9 781847 195142